ICARO MODERNO
244

To my father
who pinned little wings
on my shoulders

GIAN PIERO MILANETTI

SOVIET AIRWOMEN
OF THE GREAT PATRIOTIC WAR
A PICTORIAL HISTORY

IBN EDITORE

Copyright © IBN Istituto Bibliografico Napoleone 2013
Via dei Marsi, 57 - 00185 Roma (Italy)
phone: + 39 06 4469828 - Fax + 39 06 4452275
e-mail: info@ibneditore.it

www.ibneditore.it

ISBN (10) 88-7565-146-9
ISBN (13) 9788875651466

4   3   2   1   *2013   2014   2015   2016*

Cover & page design: Diego Pirro
Printed: Atena.net (Italy)

INDEX

ACKNOWLEDGEMENTS

This book in English about the Soviet airwomen of the Great Patriotic War (1941-45) would not have been possible without the widespread interest and assistance of the following persons who, over the past years, gave their time and expertise, creating a final legacy to the women and men of the air: Galina Brok-Beltsova, veteran of the *125 GvBAP*; Inna Kalaceva-Kalinosvskaya, veteran of the *586 IAP*; Anatoly Plyac, historian and son of Hero of the Soviet Union Raisa Aronova; Valentin Rusakov, son of pilot Tamara Rusakova (missing in the North Sea after the war); Valentina Vashchenko, director of the Museum of the War and Glory in Krasnyi Luch, Ukraine; Alexandra Ivanovna, director of Lidya Litvyak Museum in Dmitryevka, Ukraine; Marina Tyumentseva, translator and precious assistant; Lyudmilla Datsyuk; Vladimir Pluteshko; Leonardo Paleari and Anna Sabatini.

Greatest thanks to Christer Bergström (who helped me to orientate through the complex *Luftwaffe Planquadrat Koordinaten* system) and to Thijs Hellings, famed aircraft archeologist, who provided me with rare photographs. The help of the Russian aviation association *Aviatrisa* which supported me during my research, is also acknowledged.

AUTHOR'S BIOGRAPHY

A graduate in history and literature from University "La Sapienza" of Rome, Gian Piero Milanetti has taught creative writing, history, geography, and Italian in Rome public schools. He has won the coveted literary prize for "Penna Alata" (*Winged Pen*) and wrote the novel "Ménami, Mamma." Milanetti is the author of the unique aviation history book "Le Streghe della Notte" (*The Night Witches*), about the female aviatrixes of the Soviet Union. This work inspired *Voyager* documentary "Le Streghe della Notte" which was broadcast by Italian Public Television Channel Rai 2. He has travelled extensively in Russia and Ukraine, visiting the battlefields and interviewing the surviving airwomen to get their stories. He has uncovered much new information and exploded myths surrounding the Soviet Union's most famous female ace Lydia Litvyak. A tireless journalist for over two decades, this author has written hundreds of articles for Italian newspapers "Il Messaggero", "Il Tempo", "Il Gazzettino di Venezia" and "Il Giornale."

Gian Piero Milanetti has done an excellent job researching and writing about a subject that is still little known to Western readers: the contributions of Soviet airwomen in World War II. Milanetti's book is important to understanding the history of women in conflict. The story of these wartime pilots, the first women in the world to fly in combat, is inspiring. The reader will not soon forget the thrilling tale of these young warriors who fought valiantly for their country in the skies above Europe.

Amy Goodpaster Strebe

author of Flying for Her Country:
The American and Soviet Women Military Pilots of World War II

Gian Piero Milanetti is a rare forensic historian who has cut through long cherished myths and Soviet propaganda to bring out the truth. He lets the surviving participants tell their tales, recounting one of the most exciting chapters in combat aviation history. The author covers their personal battles from both sides to the point where he has even identified their opponents by name! His deep knowledge of the Soviet airwomen makes this book an absolute must!

Christer Bergström

author of "Black Cross - Red Star Air War over the Eastern Front" series

FOREWARD

"Soviet Airwomen of the Great Patriotic War" is the best book ever written on the story of the Soviet "Night Witches" and their daylight counterparts!

Unlike many historians who have never visited the battlefields nor interviewed the veterans involved, Gian Piero Milanetti has! He has travelled many times to Russia and Ukraine, met the surviving female combatants and their families, and has conducted researches for years. Gian has become the most eminent European researcher of the subject. And all on his modest teacher's salary. That's dedication!

Milanetti's work pays magnificent tribute to the women combat aviators and groundcrew, who worked as a team to bomb the invading Germans in their rickety biplanes at night. Very little was known about them in the West. Women and teenagers can read, enjoy, and derive inspiration from Milanetti's masterpiece. When it came to defending the Motherland, Soviet women were even tougher than men. I wish I could have written this book!

Henry Sakaida
Los Angeles, California
December 17, 2012

We, the Soviet airwomen, veterans of the Great Patriotic War, sincerely and from the depths of our hearts, express our gratitude to the titanic and hard-working efforts of the author Gian Piero Milanetti. He has now written and published a book in English about the heroic Soviet airwomen who fought air battles in the threatening skies of that long ago war. It was the most bloody and destructive period of the century. We hope that this book will remind Western readers of the sacrifice of the hundreds of thousands of Soviet women who voluntarily abandoned their homes and families, embraced arms, or climbed into their war planes. Our Motherland was endangered and many of us stood up to defend her even at the cost of our lives.

This book is a gift of immense value to us, aviatrixes, veterans of the Great Patriotic War.

Galina Brok-Beltsova

SOVIET AIRWOMEN
OF THE GREAT PATRIOTIC WAR

Before the War

Sophiya Vladimirovna Osipova (left), future mechanic of aircraft in the *586 IAP* (female fighter regiment), with two colleagues in Factory 22's Aeroclub, 1935.

Soviet Voroshilov sharpshooters. After the Bolshevik Revolution and the subsequent Russian Civil War, women were allowed to serve in the military. In 1917, Mariya Bonchareva, a peasant woman who had received permission by the *tsar* to enlist in the Imperial Infantry, formed a "Women's Battalion of Death" (300 female soldiers) that went into battle. They successfully attacked the Revolution's enemy troops before being pushed back with heavy losses. Actually, according to Marxist political doctrine, women and men were considered equal in rights and duties. According to the "Universal Military Service Laws of 1925 and 1939," only men were subject to regular conscription. Women were formally allowed to enroll as volunteers, and not only as nurses or doctors. Still, many women were discouraged from serving in the military. In the picture, extreme left, Olga Kulikova, future political commissar of the female fighter regiment, 1927.

Soviet pilots (left to right) Georgy Baydukov, Valery Chkalov, and Alexander Belyakov. They flew a record flight (9,734 km/6.044 miles), lasting 56 hours, from Russia through the North Pole to Udd Island (renamed Chkalov Island by Stalin in commemoration of the record breaking event) near the Isle of Sakhalin. In the 1930s, the Soviet leaders placed an increasing importance on the development of aviation. Air transport was regarded as essential in such a big country, with few railways and badly maintained roads. Moreover, setting new world aviation records had an immense propaganda value for the Communist regime. The flights of the record-breaking pilots were meant as the proof that the Soviet Union had the technology and the human resources to win the industrial and economic competition with the major Western nations. So the Soviet aviators rose to the highest status of heroes, along with deceased political leaders, Polar explorers, and record-breaking workers like miner Alexey Grigoryevich Stakhanov.

Stalin congratulates Valery Pavlovich Chkalov (Валерий Павлович Чкалов), the Soviet Union's most famous pilot, after one of his record flights. Chkalov (born on 2 February 1904) was a Russian test pilot. He was the first person to fly from Moscow to the United States via a polar route. Afterwards he wrote in an article that Stalin was "our father." Stalin was reportedly very interested in aviation. He involved himself by listening carefully to aviators' proposals and to aviation planners, tracing the flight routes, suggesting who would fly, and giving the final permission. The hero-pilot, according to historians, was the representation of Stalin's conception of the Man in the New Communist Society, "a master of nature" and an eternally youthful... individual hero". Chkalov, declared Hero of the Soviet Union, died on 15 December 1938, while testing a fighter prototype without the approval of the aircraft designer, the famous Nikolai Nikolaevich Polikarpov.

The *Tupolev TB-3* (Тяжёлый Бомбардировщик, *Tyazholy Bombardirovschik*, Heavy Bomber). It was a heavy bomber aircraft which was deployed by the Soviet Air Force in the 1930s and during the Great Patriotic War. It was the world's first cantilever wing four-engine heavy bomber. Specially modified aircraft were used to transport personnel and equipment of the Soviet Artic expeditions right to the North Pole, in some cases landing on drifting ice fields. Some of the most skilled Soviet pilots (Mikhail Vodopyanov, Vasily Molokov, Anatoliy Alekseev, Ilya Mazuruk, and Mikhail Babushkin, among the others) participated in these historical flights. The *TB-3* was used as a record-breaking aircraft. Despite obsolescence and being officially withdrawn from service in 1939, the *TB-3* was used in combat in the early stages of the Great Patriotic War, suffering appalling losses at the hands of the *Luftwaffe* fighter aces. Subsequently the aircraft was relegated to night bombing operations and to paratrooper droppings.

Raisa Aronova, future "Night Witch" and Hero of the Soviet Union, with her mother. Aronova decided to become a pilot under the influence of two books: *Memoirs of a Pilot* by G.F. Baydukov (Chkalov's co-pilot during the record flight - 8,504 km/5.280 miles - from Moscow to the USA on 18-20 June 1937) and *Memoirs of a Navigator* by Marina Raskova, navigator during the flight of the *Rodina* (see pictures of Raskova). Aronova was born on 10 February 1920, in the city of Saratov, on the Volga River near Engels. Abandoned in 1936 by her father, a railroad worker, Aronova was raised by her mother, an illiterate woman, who worked as a washerwoman and subsequently as a painter in a railway car repair establishment. Aronova, while still in high school, attended a Voroshilov sharpshooter course and after enrolling at the Saratov Institute of Agricultural Mechanization, joined the local flying club of the paramilitary association *Osoaviakhym* (the Society for Cooperation in Defense and Aviation-Chemical Development), founded in 1927.

Marina Raskova, regarded as the Soviet "Amelia Earhart." Undoubtedly the most famous female aviator of 1930s in the Soviet Union, she had no early interest in aviation. Born in Moscow on 28 March 1912, she was the daughter of a teacher, Anna Spirodovna. Her father (later killed after being hit by a motorbike) taught her singing. Financial hardships and illness forced her to stop studying music and study chemistry (in School Nr. 32). She graduated in 1929 and became a laboratory technician in a dye factory. There she met Sergey Raskov, an engineer, and married him (she divorced in 1935). She was offered a job as a draftswoman in the N. Ye. Zhukovskiy Air Force Engineering Academy. So she became interested in aviation. She started to study engineering, physics, mathematics, radio theory, and navigation. In 1934, she became the first Soviet woman certified as an aircraft navigator and started to participate in air races.

Valentina Grizobudova. Born in Kharkov (today Kharkiv, Ukraine) on 31 January 1910, she was the daughter of a pioneer aircraft designer. At the age of 19, she graduated from the Penza Flying Club of *Osoavyakhim*. In 1934 (and up to 1938) she joined a "Propaganda" air team and on 9 March 1936, she met Marina Raskova for the first time. In the fall of 1937, Grizodubova proposed to Raskova an attempt to establish a female long distance flight record. On 24 October 1937, Grizodubova and Raskova flew for 1,443 kilometers (896 miles) non-stop, beating the former record of American Ellen MacLosky of about 800 kilometers (497miles). The following year (having more than 5,000 flying hours) she was selected to be the pilot for a non-stop flight from Moscow to the Soviet Far East. With support from Stalin himself, she was assigned an *Antonov ANT-37* that Grizodubova nicknamed *Rodina* (Motherland).

Polina Osipenko (co-pilot), Valentina Grizodubova (pilot), and Marina Raskova (navigator) in front of the *Rodina*. The *ANT-37* was a converted long-range *DB-2* bomber. It had been developed by P. Sukhoy in 1934 on the basis of the *ANT-35*, the aircraft on which Chkalov and M. Gromos flew to North America via the North Pole. The *Rodina* took off on 24 September at 08.16 for Komsomolsk. Weather deteriorated quickly and the land remained invisible almost until the landing. Temperature dropped to – 36° C inside and – 37° C outside. The new experimental radios stopped working after 12 hours. On 25 September at 10.00 (Moscow Time) the *Rodina* had just enough fuel for a further half an hour, reportedly because the mechanics had forgotten to refill the tanks after the long engine testing. Raskova, in the forward cabin, bailed out at an altitude of 2,300 meters. She forgot the emergency kit and landed in the taiga with no water and only two chocolate bars and some mint candies. Raskova expected that the *Rodina* would land nearby, but the aircraft kept flying for another 15 minutes, force-landing in mire in the middle of a swamp.

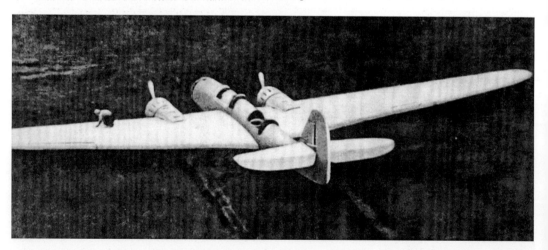

The *Rodina* in the swamp after the force-landing. Valentina Grizodubova is crawling on the wing (the photo was taken from a rescue plane on 4 October 1938). She and Osipenko tried to signal their position with pistols and the emergency radio. A massive research started with many aircraft and hundreds of rescuers. Two search planes collided, killing 16 people. The *Rodina* was at last located eight days after its landing and Raskova finally found the aircraft the next day. The three women were greeted as national heroes. Tens of thousands of people greeted them at the stations during the travel back to Moscow. FAI confirmed the new record: the *Rodina* had covered 5,908 kilometers (3,668 miles) in a straight line and 6,450 (4,005 miles) actual distance in 26 hours and 29 minutes, beating the previous record of Elizabeth Lyon, who had flown for 4,063 kilometers (2,523 miles).

Marina Raskova honored in Moscow for her record. She, Osipenko and Grizodubova were met at Belorussia Station by future president of the Soviet Union, Nikita Sergeyevich Khrushchev (then secretary of the Central Committee of the Ukraine). A parade accompanied them to the Kremlin where Stalin welcomed and invited them to dinner. Raskova sat next to Stalin for several hours. Subsequently, Raskova and her family were awarded their first two-room flat. On 2 November 1938 the three Heroines of the *Rodina* became the first women to be awarded the title of Hero of the Soviet Union and the only women to be decorated with such honorary title before the war. All of them received thousands of letters from girls asking for advices and help on how to become aviators. Both Raskova and Osipenko wrote articles encouraging girls to enter flying schools. As Osipenko died in a flying accident in 1939 and Grizodubova did not want to work with women, Raskova became the idol of many young women who enrolled in air clubs before the war.

Raisa Aronova, before joining Raskova's training air group. "Indeed it was precisely (Raskova – Edit.), with her vivid biography who kindled in me the love of aviation," Aronova recalled. "I admired her record-breaking flights, and after reading her 'Notes of a Navigator' (*Zapiski Shturmana* – Edit.), firmly decided to connect my own life with aviation".[1] On October 1941, Aronova volunteered for Raskova's 122 Air Group and was assigned to the navigators. After six months of training, Aronova was posted to the *588 NBAP*, shortly to be named "Night Witches" by the *Luftwaffe* aces.

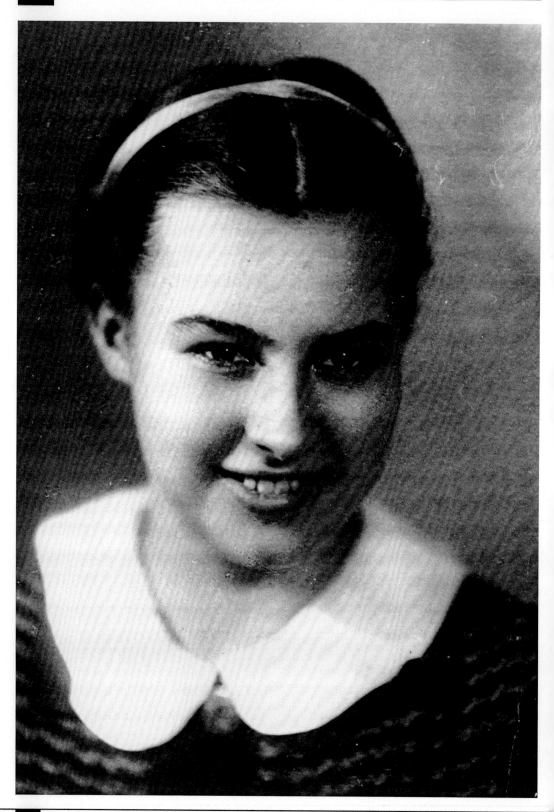

◀◀ Natalya Meklin, future "Night Witch" and Hero of the Soviet Union, as a teenager. She was born in Lubny, in Ukraine, on 8 September 1922. Her father, a Russian soldier, moved first to Kharkov and then later to Kiev. There, she graduated from high school and from a flying club. At 16, she was greatly impressed by the feats of the *Rodina* and recalled how in 1938 she kept pictures of Raskova cut from newspapers and magazines.

Marina Pavlovna Chechneva. Born in the village of Protasovo, near Orel, on 15 August 1922. When she was 12, her father moved near Moscow's Central Airport, to work in a factory. Chechneva was so impressed by the aircraft flying over her house that three years later, she tried to join a flying club of the paramilitary *Osoavyakhim*. She had her father's approval but had to wait until she was 16 to enroll. She learned to fly after school, in the evenings. She graduated from high school and as a pilot almost at the same time. She was determined to become a fighter pilot but air force schools rejected her, so she wrote to Raskova. The heroine of the *Rodina* advised Chechneva to become a flying instructor and perfecting her skills while training candidates for air force schools. Chechneva took the advice and was hired by the Central Flying Club in Moscow until she was transferred to Stalingrad after the German invasion. At last, in December 1941, she was posted to Raskova's 122 Air Group.

Extreme right, Yevgheniya Filipovna Prokhorova, flight instructor, in front of a glider at her aeroclub in 1938. Of average height with an athletic build, Prokhorova was a very talented pilot. She held two world records in gliders and had been the leader of the *Pyaterka*. They performed in many air shows and parades[2]. Many Soviet airwomen who saw combat in the Great Patriotic War, started to fly on gliders. One of them was "Night Witch" Zoya Parfenova-Akimova, future Hero of the Soviet Union. Impressed by the exploits of Raskova, Grizodubova, and Osipenko, while employed as a nurse, she trained to fly first on gliders. She graduated to the *Polikarpov U-2,* the aircraft that would equip the 588th Night Bombers Regiment. Nina Raspopova, another "Night Witch" and future Hero of the Soviet Union, was a glider instructor at the Omsk Flying Club before enrolling in Raskova's Air Group; she became one of the most famous "Night Witches," amassing more than 800 combat missions and being awarded the title of Hero of the Soviet Union.

A female trainee in front of her male instructor. Most airwomen trained in the *Osoavyakhim* (Society of Friends of Defense and Aviation-Chemical Construction), a paramilitary organization. The *Osoavyakhim* trained young people not only in flying gliders and powered aircraft, but even in sharpshooting and parachuting, without sex distinction. However, many airwomen reported how they met considerable opposition in paramilitary aeroclubs. Female trainees recounted many times how their male instructors were "less than enthusiastic" about their participation. Some of the girls gave up but many kept on flying, undaunted, getting at last the respect and admiration of their male instructors. "The commander of the school (of civil aviation, in Khabarovsk – Edit.) said he wouldn't admit us because we were girls," recalled Nina Raspopova, Hero of the Soviet Union, "but the government said they must admit us, so I was enrolled"[3].

Right to left: pilot Olga Yakovleva and her technician M. Timofeev, in front a *Yakovlev UT-1* trainer. The *UT-1* was a very small and simple aircraft for advanced training. Empty weight was only 429 kg. Between 1937 and 1940, 1,241 *UT-1s* were built. Yakovleva used it to train her students who reportedly always passed exams with high or very high marks. Yakovleva was enrolled by Raskova in her air group and assigned to the 586th Fighter Regiment. She was wounded in one arm in 1943 and, after a lengthy rehabilitation, was only permitted to fly the *Polikarpov U-2* in a communications squadron attached to the Kiev Military District, until the end of the war. Subsequently she would be forced to stop flying.

Valentina Lisitsina, climbing on the cockpit of her *UT-1* training aircraft. Just like Yakovleva, Lisitsina, after training in Raskova's air group, was posted to the *586 IAP*. She would earn media coverage for an air combat along with her commander Aleksandr Gridnev during which they claimed two German aircraft while two more *Luftwaffe* fighters collided during the dogfight.

Female pilots participating in an air parade on Tushino Airport, Moscow. Among them Katya Budanova (future fighter ace, second from the right), Olga Golisheva, Mariya Kuznetsova, Olga Shakova, and Raya Belyayeva. They would be posted to the *586 IAP*. Notwithstanding the opposition of air clubs' male directors and instructors (and often by their parents), many girls had persevered and learned to fly. By the start of the war, 100-150 clubs had been established and one out of every three or four pilots was female. Russian women already made up 45 per cent of the Soviet working force (in the USA, percentage was of 27.6). However men who had received flight training were recorded in the military reserve forces, while girls were not.

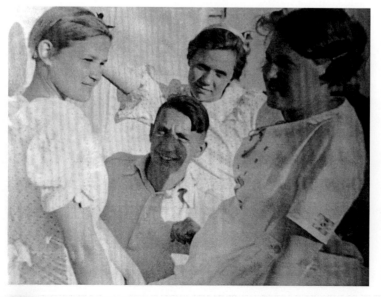

Galina Brok-Beltsova (far left), with some friends. "Galya" was one of the youngest female aviators of the Raskova regiments, as she was born in Moscow in 1925. "I was very sport-minded," she recalled later. "When the war broke out, the government sent out an appeal to the strong, mighty people to join aviation. We were then trained to be gunners or navigators. Without any boasting I can say that we were all mighty, healthy, robust, and patriotic young people"[4].

NOTE

1   R. Pennington, *Wings, Women, & War*, p. 19

2   R. Pennington, p. 33

3   A. Noggle, *A Dance with Death*, pp. 21-22

4   A. Noggle, p. 132

SOVIET AIRWOMEN
OF THE GREAT PATRIOTIC WAR

122 Air Group

Wehrmacht soldiers invading Soviet Union during the first days of *Operation Barbarossa*. At dawn of 22 June 1941, four millions Germans attacked their Communist enemies on a long (2,900 km/1,800 miles) front spanning from the Baltic Sea to the Carpathian Mountains. *Operation Barbarossa* was the largest invasion in the history of warfare. It involved not only Germans, but also troops from other Axis powers (Romanians, Hungarian, Finnish, and even Slovaks). During *Operation Barbarossa* the biggest number of motor vehicles in history (about 600,000) were used, along with 750,000 horses.

German soldiers crossing a river during Operation Barbarossa. The German attack came at the worst possible time for the Soviet armed forces. The Soviets did not have the time to complete deployment of the Red Army and of their air force along the new western border. Actually, in 1939-40, after signing the Molotov-Ribbentrop Pact (also known as the "Treaty of Non-Aggression between Germany and the Soviet Union"), the Russians took possession of a huge part of Central-Eastern Europe: half of Poland, Southern Finland, and – in June 1940 – all of Estonia, Latvia, and Lithuania. Moreover, their aviation units had only just started to re-equip with modern fighters and bombers.

A *Polikarpov I-153* fighter shot down during Operation Barbarossa. When the war started, this antiquated and under-armed biplane represented the bulk of the Soviet Air Force: 1,513 out of 4,730 fighters were *I-153*. German *Messerschmitts* easily had the upper hand against it. At the crack of dawn of 22 June 1941, the *Luftwaffe* made a surprise attack on 66 Soviet airfields close to the border. The Soviet Air Force lost 1,200 aircraft in less than two hours: 800 on the ground and 400 in air battles. The *Luftwaffe Jagdgeschwader* (fighter wing) soon proved lethal. *JG 53* claimed 74 victories in the air and 28 on the ground; *JG 51* was credited with 69 and 129 respectively, while *JG 54* shot down 45 Russian aircraft in the air and 35 on the ground. *Luftwaffe* losses were much lower. By the end of 22 June, the Germans had lost 61 aircraft while 11 were lost by Romanians units.

A shot down *LaGG-3*. There were only two of these modern but troublesome aircraft deployed on the Western Front when the war broke out. Others were hastily sent to the frontline air regiments a few days after the invasion. But the Soviet pilots found the *LaGG-3* very tricky to fly; no other Soviet combat aircraft had problems as serious. Maneuverability was poor and more important, it had the sudden unexpected tendency to stall. Moreover the pilots could not convert to this type and they were soon swept from the sky by the experienced *Luftwaffe* aces flying the much more effective *Messerschmitt Bf 109s*. Soviet losses mounted as Operation Barbarossa continued. On 23 June the Luftwaffe destroyed 755 aircraft, on 24 June, 557; on 25 June, 251. By the 1st of July, the Luftwaffe had already destroyed 4,725 Soviet aircraft. The Red Army also suffered terrible losses: by 30 September, Soviets lost 20,500 tanks and 101,000 cannons and mortars.

In June 1941, only a few Soviet airwomen served in the air forces. But there were several hundred trained women pilots graduated from the *Osoavyakhim* air clubs. In the days immediately following the German invasion, many of these young aviatrixes went to the recruitment centers. They asked to be sent to the front, but they were rejected. "When the war started", recalled Yevgeniya Zhigulenko, Hero of the Soviet Union, "many of my female peers started writing letters to the government. We demanded to be taken into the army. Of course they didn't take us"[1]. So, female flying instructors or simple air club trainees started to write letters to the heroine of the *Rodina* – that they fondly called the "Grandmother of Soviet Aviation," even if she was only 23 or 24 years old – asking her how they could put their skill to the service of the fatherland, or how they could be enrolled to the air force and go to the front.

Marina Raskova. She was a member of the Supreme Soviet and held an air force commission. She knew the chain of military command, and with a suitcase full of letters from young women flyers, she went to the Defense Ministry. "Marina Raskova," recalled Nadya Popova, one of the 'Night Witches' Hero of the Soviet Union, "proposed the formation of a separate women's air regiment, tapping the unconsidered resource of thousands of women who had learned to fly in the sports schools before the war." The Defense Ministry agreed but the idea had to be approved by Stalin himself. Western pre-war gossip suggested that there was a kind of romantic connection between the Soviet dictator and Marina Raskova. What is certain is that they knew each other personally. After the Defense Ministry consented to her proposal, Raskova reportedly met Stalin and proposed the formation of the women's unit.

Stalin in a propaganda picture. Yevgeniya Zhigulenko was told by Marina what happened when she met the Soviet dictator. "You understand, future generation will not forgive us for sacrificing young girls," Stalin considered. Raskova answered: "You know, they are running away to the front all the same… and it will be worse, you understand, if they steal airplanes to go." And – Zhigulenko recalled – there was just such an incident. "There were several girls who had asked to go to the front" and they were rejected. "So they stole a fighter plane and flew off to fight. They just couldn't wait…"[2].

Stalin accepted Raskova's suggestion. Order N° 0099 of the People's Commissariat of Defense of the Soviet Union, of 8 October 1941, directed that, starting by 1 December 1941, three female regiments would be formed. The units should be named *586 IAP* (*Istrebitelnyi Aviatsionnyi Polk*, Fighter Aviation Regiment), *587 BAP* (*Bombardirovochnyi Aviatsionnyi Polk*, Bomber Aviation Regiment) and *588 NBAP* (*Nochnoi Bombaridirovochnyi Aviatsionnyi Polk*, Night Bomber Aviation Regiment). The commanders of air forces and of the Red Army were ordered to equip the three regiments and organize the training of the flying crew and of technical personnel and staff.

The *Yakovlev Yak-1*, the fighter chosen for the 586th , was of mixed construction, fabric and plywood covered. It was simple to build and service, and easy to fly. It earned its designer, Aleksandr Yakovlev, the gift of a Zis car and a prize of 100,000 rubles. It was praised even by *Luftwaffe* experts: "The Yak-1 fighter is presumably the best Soviet fighter. It had a better speed and rate of climb compared to the MIG-3 and comes close to the performance of the Bf 109F... It was appreciably more difficult to hit the Yak-1 from behind than the MIG-3"[3]. Even the best German ace respected it. "The Yak was also a fighter that you could not underestimate," recalled Walter Krupinski, an ace with 197 victories. "It had great speed, could outdive us, outclimb us, and was just as good, if not better, in a turning fight"[4].

Sukhoi Su-2. This single-engine short-range Soviet scout and light bomber, with a crew of two – assigned to the *587 BAP* - was of mixed construction (wood and metal) also. The first version was armed with two pairs of *ShKAS* machineguns in the outer wings. A movable machinegun was mounted in a ball-turret in the back of the cockpit, for rear protection. Its main advantage was its robustness. This rugged aircraft could absorb heavy battle damage (for instance, half of the rudder and tail-plane lacking) and still fly. Its survivability was the highest among Soviet bombers, even higher than that of the celebrated *Shturmovik*, the "flying tank". Shown in the picture is a prototype of the *Su-2*, with lowered flaps and the two blades propeller of a diameter of 2.8 meters (9 feet and 2 inches).

Polikarpov U-2, the aircraft that would equip the night bomber regiment, was the most antiquated aircraft used in combat during the Great Patriotic War. It was "a tiny aircraft made of plywood and percale," recalled the future Chief of Staff, Irina Rakobolskaya, a "biplane trainer with its two tiny cockpits and a low-powered engine that got up a maximum speed of only 100-120 km/h. There was no radio, no... navigation equipment for blind flying, and no armored backrest to protect the pilot against enemy bullets"[5]. To compensate for all those shortcomings, the *Polikarpov* was easy to control, stable and light, did not require prepared airfields, and could land anywhere, even on a village street.

Engineer 3rd Class Olga Kulikova. Soon after authorization by Stalin to form an all female aviation group (later to be called 122 Air Group), Marina Raskova started to gather her staff. For this purpose, she contacted some of the most eminent female aviators, soldiers, political officers, and engineers. Kulikova was one of them.

Another of Raskova's 122 Air Group staff, pilot *Kapitan* Fedorovna Vera Lomako, commander of *Eskadrilya*. Lomako was a well known military pilot. Together with Raskova, she had taken part in several long-distance flights. "I still see her stocky and tall figure," recalled *586 IAP's* pilot, Olga Yakovleva, "wearing a leather coat, boots, and a cap with ear flaps and a grey karakul (lamb's fur). The most striking was her face, a stern face of a veteran. Her brown eyes were sparkling with enthusiasm. Overall, she gave off an aura of daring. She was a genuine fighter pilot and a veteran air force commander"[6]. In autumn 1941 she worked with Battalion Commissar Yevdokiya Rachkevich in some spare rooms at the special services school of *VVS* in Petrovsky Park.

Captain Yevdokiya Rachkevich, a career officer from a peasant family. She was a graduate of the V.I. Lenin Military Political Academy. She was recruited by Raskova. When the volunteers selected by Komsomol, civil aviation, and military, were sent to an assembly point in Moscow (to be interviewed by Raskova), Rachkevich and Captain Lomako saw that they were fed and assigned rooms. Subsequently Raskova assigned her to the *588 NBAP*, the future "Night Witches" Regiment, as political commissar.

Photo group of the young volunteers in Engels (Tatyana Sumarokhova, first from left, and Yevgeniya Rudneva, third from left, in third row). Their recruitment was handed primarily through *Komsomol* channels and by word-of-mouth. Most of them were from Moscow or were studying or working in the city. Pilots were recruited from the military and civil air fleets and from *Osoavyakhim* airclubs, while navigators were recruited from among students at universities and technical schools. Mechanics "were from a very common strata of society: from factories, from working families," recalled *46 GvNBAP* engineer of the regiment, Klavdiya Ilyushina[7].

"At the time the country had a lot of female pilots," recalled "Night Witch" Irina Rakobolskaya, "but ▶▶ unfortunately there were very few women navigators, gunners or mechanics. Those of us who were to train in these fields were taken from civilian colleges"[8]. Rakobolskaya when the war broke out was a third-year student of Moscow University Physics Department and was soon assigned to the navigators group.

Galya Dokhutovich, one of the first to apply to the Central Commettee of the *Komsomol*, requesting assignment to Raskova's Air Group, recalled in her journal about the other volunteers: "They came from all over the capital – from colleges, from offices, from factories. They were of all kinds, lighthearted, noisy, calm, reserved, some with close cropped hair, some with long pigtails; mechanics, parachutists, pilots, and ordinary members of the *Komsomol* who knew nothing about flying." Dokhutovich, who was trained in the navigator group, was subsequently appointed *aide-de-camp* of squadron in the *588 NBAP*.

Another member of Raskova's staff, was Militsa Kazarinova, the sister of Tamara, first commander of *586 IAP*, the fighter regiment. Graduated from the Air Force Academy, she spent ten years in the military serving as an attack pilot and studying air tactics. She even took part in air shows over Moscow. When the trainees arrived in Engels, Militsa and Raskova (and Yekaterina Migunova, Raskova's old friend from the Zhukovskiy Academy and future deputy chief of staff in the 587th) shared a room in the former barbershop, small, cold and drafty. Militsa was named as Raskova's chief of staff, first in the 122 Air Group and subsequently in the *587 BAP*. She was held in awe by the volunteers as she was a military officer and because of her strict character, for her determination and hardness.

The author besides the monument to Marina Raskova, in front of the Red Army House in Engels ▶▶ which had been turned into a dormitory for the 122 Air Group. On 17 October 1941, when the *Wehrmacht* was almost on the outskirts of Moscow, all the volunteers boarded several freight cars on a train bound for Engels, a city on the Volga River, 500 miles southeast of Moscow. The estimated number of the recruits is uncertain. It ranged from 200 to 1,000, according to various authors. The most likely figure is about 300-400. The travel lasted eight days. The trains had no toilets and the girls were given just some bread and herring. "At one station," recalled Kracvchenko, "we saw a lot of fresh cabbage. We jumped off and took it to the train and ate it fresh, just like rabbits. Then Kazarinova (Militsa, an officer of the staff – Edit.) discovered us and made us take it all back"[9]. The group arrived on 25 October in the evening, in the rain and fog; nobody was waiting for them.

Klavdiya Terekhova (married Kasatkina) parachuting. She would be appointed secretary of the party organization of *586 IAP*, with the rank of senior lieutenant. Born in Moscow from a peasant family, Terekhova graduated from a technical school and subsequently entered the Moscow Textile College. "I was a very brave girl," she recalled, "I jumped with a parachute, rode horses, drove a car, I could do everything!"[10]. When the war broke out, she joined the *Komsomol* staff and later volunteered for Raskova's Air Group. "When the girls came to join the army they all looked like girls," she recalled, "with long curly hair and high heels. The first thing to do was make them look all alike, like soldiers, with hair cut short, military boots, and pants. It was really very difficult to make the girls part with their hair and feminine things and put them into men's military clothing"[11].

Olga Yakovleva, future pilot of the *586 IAP*. Before the war she was a flying instructor at the Chelyabinsk Flying Club. When the war started, she wanted to go to the front but instead her superiors tasked her to train a group of girls as replacements for flying instructors sent to the front. But eventually she managed to be assigned to Raskova's Air Group. "And so we arrived in Engels early in the morning. After detraining, we immediately went to the mess. During our trip we were issued dry rations exclusively, so hot food tasted very good to us. Then we formed up and set off for the hairdressing establishment. Here many of us had to part with their braids. We came out with identical 'tomboy' hairdos"[12].

Olga Studentskaya, future pilot of *586 IAP*. After fulfilling the order to report to the garrison barbershop she got a "boy-style" haircut too. "One of our fighter pilot trainees, Olga Studentskaya, had a low voice and a boyish figure," recalled *586 IAP* pilot Olga Yakovleva, "so now she simply passed for a real lad. All kinds of funny things happened to her when she was alone among male pilots. She would be telling us about it and we would giggle until our stomachs hurt"[13]. Studentskaya, when she was serving in the fighter regiment, once took off to practice aerobatics. The elevator control rod became disconnected and so she took the *Yak* back, handling the throttle. She flew until the fuel ran out, then parachuted. She hit her leg on her aircraft, suffering serious injury. She was hospitalized but when she recovered, the doctors did not allow her to fly a fighter; she was transferred to a communication squadron.

122 Air Group's school in Engels. Nowadays, the building is abandoned, but in the fall 1941, it was active day and night. The girls underwent an extremely condensed, intensive training that sometimes lasted fourteen hours a day. Here the girls attended ten courses a day and navigators studied for an additional hour and woke up earlier than other students. In this building pilots also took classrooms before or after drills. The flight training – that normally took three years – was condensed in less than six months. Training for female fighter and dive bomber pilots required a minimum of 500 flying hours, while male pilots were hastily sent to the front with only 65 flight hours.

☆

Marina Raskova supervised all training during the day and even at night as there was a night bomber regiment. "Raskova was the organizer for combat training," recalled Hero of the Soviet Union, Marina Chechneva. "She devoted a great deal of time to checking that we were at our studies, she took exams and tests in many disciplines, not only teaching, but also constantly studying herself"[14]. She rested so little that sometimes she fell asleep on the top of the bed. Still, on occasion, she would take a break from her work, late at night, to play piano, with her dear friend Migunova (they performed Brahms and Schubert). Still at night, as the training proceeded, she discussed with her staff how the personnel should be distributed and who should command the fighter and night bomber regiment. Actually, Raskova kept for herself the command of the 587th Dive Bomber Regiment.

Yevdokiya Davidovna Bershanskaya. Raskova chose her to command the night bombers, but Bershanskaya at first refused. She was an experienced civil pilot, having flown in *Aeroflot* for ten years, and wanted to become a fighter pilot. She tried to protest on the grounds that she had no command experience. There were several days of discussions during which Bershanskaya stubbornly refused. She was at last persuaded to accept the position of commander of the 588th. Hero of the Soviet Union, Nataliya Meklin, recalled the day that Raskova introduced her to them: "Appearing severe, and with a sharp look in her greenish eyes, she was not yet close to, or understood by us. We all tried to pretend that she reminded us of Raskova, but they did not resemble each other externally"[15].

Tamara Kazarinova, older sister of Militsa, first commander of the Fighter Regiment. The selection of a commander for the future *586 IAP* was the most difficult for Raskova. She "could not even identify a single person to whom she could entrust the fighter regiment," recalled Galina Dzhunkovskaya-Markova. At last, Kazarinova arrived in Engels. Some historians suggest that Kazarinova, a pilot who had been awarded the Order of Lenin in 1937, was imposed to Raskova. However, on 9 December 1941, the *586 IAP* was officially created by order of Stalin and Tamara Kazarinova was appointed commander of the fighter regiment.

Yakovlev Yak-1, undoubtedly the best Soviet fighter in service during the first year of war. Raskova managed to get it for her air group, even if (in winter 1941-1942), there was just one fighter (often of old design) for every five Soviet pilots. There were front line pilots waiting to get new aircraft at the aviation company that produced the *Yakovlev* in Saratov. The *586 IAP* got its aircraft on 20-21 February 1942. As usual, only the commander's aircraft had a transmitter radio, the rest had only receivers. But the girls refused to fly aircraft without transmitting radios and Raskova ordered the *586 IAP's* future engineer for special equipment, Irina Yemelianova, to equip all the fighters with transmitters.

Another shot of the *Sukhoi Su-2*. When the 587th Bomber Regiment started to train on the *Su-2*, Raskova's pilots soon complained about its characteristics. *Su-2's* production had started just in August 1939 but Raskova's airwomen regarded it as outdated. Reportedly, the three *Sukhoi* assigned to the *587 BAP*, "smoked, leaked oil, were slow and burned a lot of fuel. Everyone knew that they had been scheduled to be taken out of production which meant that getting spare parts would become increasingly difficult." At the end, Raskova decided to request a newer Soviet bomber type, the *Petlyakov Pe-2*[16].

The *Petlyakov Pe-2* is regarded as one of the best Allied combat aircraft of WWII[17]. Raskova, unsatisfied with the *Sukhoi Su-2*, requested another bomber as a replacement. She was offered the American "Boston" bombers, soon to be delivered thanks to the Lend Lease program, but she refused any foreign-built (or designed) aircraft and choose the *Petlyakov Pe-2*, the newest and most sophisticated Russian bomber of the time. In July 1942, twenty factory-fresh *Petlyakovs* were delivered to the regiment. But soon a problem arose: the *Petlyakov* required a third crew member (a radio operator-gunner). This third member had to be strong. To recharge the antiaircraft machinegun using the left arm, it took a force of 60 kilograms. Moreover, as the *Pe-2* was so much more sophisticated than the *Sukhoi*, it required four more technicians for each ground crew to maintain it. However there was no more time to train other women so Raskova was forced to admit men (gunners and mechanics) into the *587 BAP*. At that point, it ceased to be an all-female regiment.

When the women of the *587 BAP* learned that they would fly the *Petlyakov*, many became worried. Male pilots took it as a personal insult. The *Pe-2* was demanding in flying technique and did not allow slow pilots' reactions. "Strong pilots liked this airplane," remembered one of the instructors who trained the women pilots. "Weak ones feared it. Of course, for a woman, flying the *Pe-2* was a real achievement"[18]. But men too, found it difficult. "The aircraft is too complicated in handling, especially on take-off and landing," wrote Col. Pestov, of *95 SBAP*, one of the first *polk* equipped by the *Pe-2*. "Its operation requires pilots of above-average skill. An ordinary pilot finds it difficult to become familiar with the aircraft"[19].

Lilya Tormosina, pilot. On 10 March 1942, during training of the *588 NBAP*, a fatal accident happened. Tormosina flew a *Polikarpov* with her navigator Nadiya Komogortseva, along with three more *Po-2s* during the night. Komogortseva lost her commander, Nadezhda Popova, and she crashed.

Nadiya Komogortseva, navigator of Tormosina. "Komogortseva got lost," recalled Yekaterina Polunina, "It was at night, there was a lot of snow, and she ran out of fuel." They crashed to their death on 10 March 1942, during a training flight[20].

Aniya Malakhova, pilot, crashed on 10 March 1942 with her pilot Marina Vinogradova. "We were very stressed by our flying conditions," recalled Nadezhda Popova. "We were without instruments to help us orient ourselves. At that time the equipment was very primitive, and inexperienced pilots become disoriented"[21].

Marina Vinogradova, navigator of Aniya Malakhova. They were killed during the training flight of 10 March 1942. That night, recalled Nadya Popova: "It began snowing heavily. Two aircraft crashed, and we lost four people that night, there were the first losses in our regiment."

Next page, Nadya Popova. On 10 March 1942, she was the flight commander of the training flight. Accordind to Polunina, "Popova was to blame." But she defended herself. "Some thought that it was my fault because I didn't teach them well. When I landed near the bombing range, I saw Lilya (Tormosina – Edit.), my friend, lying on the ground under the aircraft. Raskova asked me, 'Where are your pilots – dead! Why are you here, and where are they? Dead! You are flying together, and why did it happen that you are here and they crashed?' I was flight commander, and they blamed me for not instructing them properly. When something like this happens, they always look for a scapegoat. I was nineteen years old"[22].

Rufa Gasheva (right) and Katya Ryabova (navigator), both future Heroes of the Soviet Union. Gasheva was the navigator of pilot Ira Sebrova during the flying accident. By a miracle, Sebrova and Gasheva survived. Their plane touched the ground and was damaged, but Sebrova, thanks to her expertise, managed to land. She and Sebrova walked away from their aircraft and come back to base at Engels on foot.

Ira Sebrova. She was involved in the flying accident of 10 March 1942. Sebrova, even before enrolling, was already an experienced pilot. She started training as a locksmith, working as a mechanic and repairing sewing machines (at a cardboard manufacturing plant). She graduated from the Kherson Flying School and was a flight instructor at the Frunze District Flying Cub in Moscow.

588 NBAP airwomen. Back row, third from left, Ira Sebrova and to her right, Natalya Meklin. In front of Sebrova, are four future Heroes of the Soviet Union: Marina Chechneva (in white suit) and (left to right), Yevgeniya Rudneva, Dusya Nosal, and Yevdokiya Pasko. In front row, left to right, Political Commissar Yevdokiya Rachkevich, Commander Yevdokiya Bershanskaya and Irina Rakobolskaya, chief of staff. The flying accident of 10 March delayed the 588th's scheduled departure for the front. Originally, the night bomber regiment should have been the first regiment to enter combat. Instead it was the fighter regiment, assigned on 16 April 1942 to active duty. Only on 23 May 1942, after seven months of training, the 588th would leave Engels to a frontline airfield. Last to leave the training base was the 587th, which was delayed by the change of aircraft.

NOTE

1   Reina Pennington, *Wings, Women, & War*, p. 26

2   Pennington, p. 26

3   Yefim Gordon and Dmitry Khazanov, *Yakovlev's Piston-Engined Fighters*, p. 16

4   Colin D. Heaton and Anne-Marie Lewis, *The German Aces Speak*, Zenith Press, Minneapolis USA, 2011, p. 32

5   Kazimiera Cottam, *Women in Air War*, p. 115

6   Noggle, *Women in Air War*, p. 240

7   Noggle, p. 49

8   Noggle, p. 37

9   Pennington, p. 41

10   Noggle, p. 190

11   Noggle, p. 191

12   Cottam, *Women in Air War*, p. 239

13   Cottam, *Women in Air War*, p. 239

14   Pennington, p. 44

15   Cottam, *Women in Air War*, p. 122

16   Pennington, p. 51

17   Jeffrey Ethell, *Aircraft of WWII*, p. 152

18   Pennington, p. 53

19   Yefim Gordon, *Soviet Airpower*, p. 367

20   Pennington, p. 49

21   Noggle, p. 82

22   Noggle, p. 82

SOVIET AIRWOMEN
OF THE GREAT PATRIOTIC WAR

Night Witches

Unit designations: 588th Night Bomber Aviation Regiment - 46th Guards Night Bomber Aviation Regiment

Dates of service: 27 May 1942 - May 1945 (disbanded on 15 October 1945)

Main operative areas: Donetsk, Mozdok, Terek Valley, Kuban, Krasnodar, Novorossiyks, Kerch, Sevastopol, Minsk, Warsaw, Berlin

Commander: Yevdokiya Bershanskaya

Aircraft flown: *Polikarpov U-2, Po-2*

Combat missions: more than 24,000

Heroes of the Soviet Union: 24

Female pilots: 61

Female navigators: 63

Female staff and political officer: 24

Female mechanics, armorers and engineers: 99

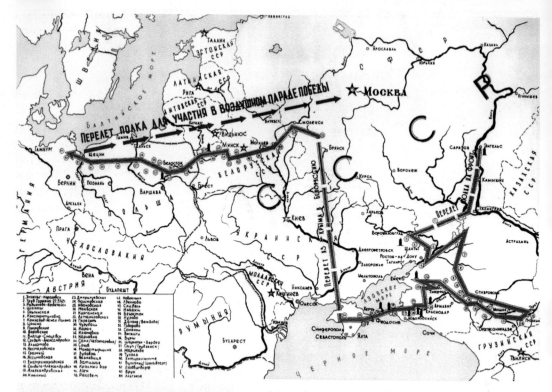

Map of movements and bases of the "Night Witches". The 588th arrived to the front on 27 May 1942[1]. The night bomber regiment first saw combat on the Southern Front, bombing the crossings of Mius River in Ukraine and of the Don River in Russia. Subsequently it fought in Southern Russia: Trans-Caucasus, Kuban, Taman Peninsula, and Crimea. In 1944 it fought in Belarus and Poland. The following year, it was in Prussia, ending the war in Germany near the Oder River and Berlin.

Yevdokiya Bershanskaya, commander of the *588 NBAP*, later to become famous as the "Night Witches" regiment. A civilian fleet pilot with ten years of experience before the war, thirty-year old Bershanskaya was the oldest among the female volunteers. She was the only woman to remain in command of a women's regiment throughout the war. Promoted to the rank of *Kapitan* and appointed by Raskova as the commander of the night regiment, she had to abandon her dream of becoming a fighter pilot and had to adjust to a completely different level of combat responsibility[2]. (Archive of Anatoly Plyac)

Left to right: *Mayor* Irina Rakobolskaya, navigator, chief of the staff, and deputy commander, and *Kapitan* Yevdokiya Rachkevich. As the deputy commander, Rakobolskaya stayed at an advanced temporary airfield at night while the pilots and navigators fulfilled their bombing missions. She had a special map that showed what time each crew had to fly over the target and return. She was so near to the front that she could check each aircraft up to the target. She herself flew 23 combat missions. Rachkevich, former political worker and member of Raskova's staff in the 122 Air Group, was the regiment's commissar.

The *588 NBAP* airwomen assembled on the airfield. "We were the only regiment in the whole Red Army without any men serving in it," recalled *Mayor* Irina Rakobolskaya. "We started the war with two squadrons and finished the war with four"[3]. "When we first went to the front, we had 112 people, two squadrons each with ten aircraft. By the end, I don't know, about 300, no more"[4]. There were about one fourth pilots, one fourth navigators, and the rest were mechanics, armorers, engineers, staff, and political officers. (Archive of Anatoly Plyac)

The night bomber regiment was the worst equipped of Raskova's three regiments. The "Night Witches" flew in the *Polikarpov U-2* (later *Po-2.*) It was a two-seater, single-engine biplane made of wood and painted fabric. The *U-2* was originally designed in 1927 as an agricultural and training aircraft. It was equipped with a *Shvetsov M-11* five-cylinder radial engine of 100 hp. It had an open cockpit and no brakes. The pilot sat in the front seat while the navigator/bomber in the rear. The Soviets used this aircraft extensively during the war. It was very difficult to shoot down for German fighters, as its cruising speed (60 mph) was lower than the stall speed of the German fighters *Messerschmitt Bf 109* and *Focke-Wulf Fw 190*. The *U-2* could land almost anywhere and a village street could be used as an airstrip. (Archive of Anatoly Plyac)

"Night Witches" *Polikarpov U-2s* in daylight flight. At the beginning the airwomen "did not fly in formation with a leader but instead flew one after another in a line toward the target," recalled Irina Rakobolskaya. "We then looped back to the field to rear, took off again, and flew another mission with the same pattern. There were no radio in the aircraft so no communications while the planes were in the air. That was the pattern of our particular night mission"[7]. But the Germans soon understood this tactic and adopted countermeasures, concentrating all their *flak* and searchlights against every single bomber, managing to destroy or impeding it from bombing accurately. "Later on we devised new tactics for our missions," added Gelman. "We flew two planes at a time to the target. The first attracted all the searchlights and antiaircraft guns, and the other would glide in over the target, with its engine idling so the Germans couldn't hear it, and bomb the target. With all the attention on the first plane, the second could make a successful attack"[8].

◀◀ Photo group of *588 NBAP/46 GvNBAP* airwomen. The *588th* left Engels for combat duty on 23 May 1942. The night bomber regiment had been first assigned to the 4th Air Army on the Southern Front, then in Ukraine. Marina Raskova led the 20 *Polikarpovs* during the travel. The trip lasted two days. They stopped at an intermediary airfield to refuel and rest. At last, they landed at Trud Gornyaka, near Morozovskaya, in the Donetsk Basin. "The first base was very small," remembered Polina Gelman, Hero of the Soviet Union. "There was a large cowshed on a farm close to the airfield," recalled another Heroine of the Soviet Union, Marina Chechneva. "There weren't any cows in it, of course, and most of the traces of the previous occupants had been removed but the smell was pretty vile. We got cans of disinfectant and lots of hot water and scrubbed and scrubbed until it was fit to sleep in. But we never quite got rid of that smell"[5]. But the Soviet commander did not hide his bitter disappointment. D.D. Popov, the commander of the 218th Night Bomber Aviation Division (to which the *588 NBAP* had been posted) commented to his superiors: "We have seen everything now. They're giving us some sort of little girls, and in Po-2 boot. I've received 112 little princesses. Just what am I supposed to do with them?"[6]. (Archive of Anatoly Plyac)

Commander Yevdokiya Bershanskaya (extreme right), in flight suit, giving the last briefing to the aircrew before a sortie. On 8 June 1942, the *588 NBAP* had its baptism of fire. The target was a German headquarter near Voroshilovgrad (now Luhansk or Lugansk), a city in southeastern Ukraine. Only three aircraft were to take part on the mission, flown by the most experienced crews. Commander Bershanskaya herself would fly the lead *Polikarpov*. Olkhovskaya and her navigator Vera Tarasova would take off two minutes later, followed by Anya Amosova in the third aircraft. Bershanskaya flew straight to the target. "I could clearly see the buildings and I knew that if I hit the target then Luda (Olkhovskya – Edit.) behind me, would be able to aim at my fires that I started," she later recalled. "I was right over the target... I yanked the release wire and dived away

from the searchlights and steered off for home. I saw flames coming from one of the buildings and thought that Luba would have a beacon to aim for now."[9] Bershanskaya landed back safely. Anya Amosova and her navigator followed fifteen minutes later. But Olkhovskaya and Tarasova did not come back.

Vera Tarasova, navigator of Lyubov Olkhovskaya, was reported as missing in action on her very first mission. Only after the war it was discovered exactly what had happened to her. Arriving over the target after the bombing of Bershanskaya, the searchlights had illuminated her aircraft and the heavy *flak* shot them down in German-held territory. The following morning Soviet villagers found them before the *Wehrmacht* patrols reached the *Polikarpov*. The aircraft looked intact but the two girls had bled to death from the wounds. When the Germans arrived, they dragged the bodies from the cockpits. They took their revolvers, maps, and few personal objects, and went away. The villagers washed the blood from their faces and buried them just outside of their village[10].

Lyubov Olkhovskaya, the first "Night Witch" pilot to fall during the Great Patriotic War. She held the rank of *Leytenant*. She was remembered by her comrades as rather stern. "Sometime she would chide some of the more untidy girls about the state of their beds," recalled Chechneva. "Some of the girls thought that she was unnecessarily strict about that and there was a little resentment. It didn't seem to matter now. The picture I shall always carry in my mind is of Luba milking a cow at the farm to which our cowshed belonged before she flew the last mission and joking about the Flying Cow as she handed the warm milk around to us"[11].

Mechanic of armament Nina Karasyova-Buzina, servicing the defensive *ShKAS* (*Shpitalniy-Komaritskiy Aviatsionnaya Skorostrelny*) machinegun of the *Polikarpov U-2*. The *ShKAS* appeared in the early 1930s and soon replaced all other Soviet machineguns. It fired 1,800 rounds per minute in unsynchronized form. Buzina was born in 1923 in the village of Kluchyiovo, in the Tula region. She went to work in a plant after nine grades of school. When the war started, she responded to the *Komsomol* appeal for volunteers to the front and Marina Raskova interviewed her. "I was warned that the service I was volunteering for would be very difficult because I would have to carry heavy bombs to the aircraft, work in freezing conditions, and probably stand in cold water day and night with little rest." Nevertheless she joined Raskova's Air Group. "At first I was just an armorer, then a mechanic of armament; then I became a senior technician in armament. A technician not only arms the aircraft but has the added responsibility of overseeing the other armament personnel and their work"[12].

Senior Lieutenant Zoya Ivanovna Parfenova-Akimova, left, being congratulated by her superior. In the middle, Marina Chechneva. Parfenova was born on 21 June 1920, in Alatyr (future Chuvash Autonomous Soviet Socialist Republic) in a working class family. She lost her father when she was a child. She became a nurse and attended flying lessons in the evenings. Parfenova became the first woman pilot at Alatyr and worked as a flying instructor when the Germans invaded. When she learned that Raskova was forming an all-female unit she volunteered and was assigned to the 588th. After her unit became operational at the front, Parfenova flew almost every night, bombing concentrations of enemy troops and equipment in the vicinity of the Mius River, the town of Taganrog, Don River, and North Caucasus. While the Germans were advancing towards the Volga and the Caucasus, Parfenova and the other "Night Witches" supported the retreating Red Army with reconnaissance, in addition to routine bombing mission. (Archive of Anatoly Plyac)

Navigator Yevgeniya Rudneva, future Hero of the Soviet Union, at the beginning of her career. She was an astronomy student when she volunteered for aviation. At first it was difficult for her to acquire military skills but she was persistent; she quickly improved. By September 1942 she became the regiment's chief navigator and her name appeared in the Red Army's bulletins. On 11 September she was commissioned and on the 13th of the same month she received her first award, the Order of the Red Star. (Archive of Anatoly Plyac)

Notwithstanding its successes, in September 1942, the *588 NBAP* had to retreat to North Caucasus, in Grozny Region, pushed back by the summer German offensive "Case Blue" (*Fall Blau*). It was later renamed Operation *Braunschweig*. It was the *Wehrmacht* plan for the 1942 strategic summer offensive in southern Russia, between 28 June and 24 November 1942. Its aim was to overrun the Caucasus and seize control of the Caucasian oilfields from the Soviets. More than 90% of Russia's oil extraction capacity was located in the Caucasus area. In 1940, the Maikop region produced 19 million barrels of oil annually, the Grozny area 32 million barrels, and Baku 170 million barrels. In May 1941, a German High Command study had stated that monthly military requirements for its armed forces were approximately 7.25 million barrels. With no new oil delivery, German stocks would be rapidly exhausted. The study concluded that this shortfall could only be made up with petroleum from Russia. This was a prime element in Hitler's decision to attempt to capture the region. The picture shows a German 7.5 cm *Gebirgsgeschütz 36* cannon in front of the Caucasus mountains. The *GebG.36* was the standard light mountain gun of the German mountain divisions.

◄◄ A *Polikarpov U-2* taking off at night. Note the bomb suspended under the wing. "The aircraft carried different types of bombs," recalled mechanic of armament, Junior Lieutenant Olga-Yerokhina-Averyanova. "One small one made a crackling sound when it hit and it was very frightening to those on the ground"[13]. The bombs weighed 25 (55 lbs), 32 (70 lbs), or 100 kilos (220lbs) each. "We lifted them into place manually," recalled mechanic of armament Nina Karasyova-Buzina. "Some nights we lifted 3,000 kilos (6613 lbs – Edit.) of bombs"[14]. During the summer of 1942, the "Night Witches" flew many sorties trying to stop the German offensive aimed at reaching the oilfields in Southern Russia. The regimental log of the night bomber regiment reported:

11 July   Railway station destroyed and fuel tankers blown up in a great explosion after four attacks.
25 July   Helped destroy crossing of the River Don.
26 July   Flew 47 sorties, destroyed motorized unit and personnel trying to cross Don.
27 July   Entire regiment again flew, destroyed Don Crossing and caught German troops attempting to cross in boats and rafts. (Archive of Anatoly Plyac)

German troops on the Caucasus. After the capture of Rostov-on-Don, during summer 1942, the tank units of Ewald von Kleist moved across the Caucasian Mountain Range while troops of the 4th German Mountain Division, manned with Tyroleans, captured the passes that led to Mount Elbrus, the highest mountains of the Caucasus. The "Night Witches" were located few kilometers from them.

Terek River Valley, in North Caucasus. The Germans occupied the left bank of the river, and the Soviets the right one. The "Night Witches" airfield was located in the Sunzha Valley, surrounded by high peaks in the Terek region. The flights were difficult; the airwomen had to overfly deep valleys and steep gorges often in unpredictable weather against highly defended targets. North Caucasus was an extremely demanding front for the "Night Witches" because of its dangerous updraughts and downdraughts, as well as fog. Wind shears were so powerful that they could smash an airplane stronger than their fragile biplanes.

Two unknown "Night Witches" waiting for their comrades-in-arms to come back from a daylight flight. The *588 NBAP* airwomen, knowing it was considered suicidal to fly their slow, antiquated biplane without the cover of darkness, were sometimes ordered to take off during the day. "Our baptism of fire was harsh," recalled Irina Rakobolskaya. "Soviet troops were retreating toward the Caucasus and our Po-2s were based only about 20-30 kilometres from the front line. On several occasions, German tanks came quite close to our airfield, so, in spite of the huge risk, we were compelled to reconnoiter the dispositions of enemy troops in daytime".

Dusya Nosal, the first Hero of the Soviet Union of the "Night Witches." On 2 September 1942, on her 100th mission, Nosal managed to hit a train at Ardon Station on the foothills of Caucasus. The train carried ammunition that exploded and spread fire to the nearby fuel tanks. She was born on 13 March 1918 in a peasant family, in the village of Burchak, Ukraine. She studied in a pedagogical institute and taught in Nikolayev while attending a local flying club. In 1940 she graduated from Kherson Flying School and was hired by Nikolayev Air Club as an instructor. Shortly after the German invasion she was in Brest, Belarus, with her husband to give birth to her son. The Germans bombed the maternity hospital and killed her baby. She was rescued from the ruins and volunteered for flying at the front. She was placed under the command of Marina Raskova, who was forming her 122 Air Group. When she hit the train in Ardon, Nosal wrote a letter to her husband who was in the Urals to tell him of her successful bombing. A week later she was awarded the Order of the Red Star; on 30 December she received the Order of the Red Banner. While in the Caucasus, Nosal flew constantly four to five (or even more) missions each night, volunteering for the most dangerous missions.

Five "Night Witches" of the first squadron, concentrated in planning missions. Left to right: Lidya Svistunova, Tanya Makarova, Olga Kliveva, Marina Chechneva, and Yevgeniya Zhigulenko. As the airwomen became more experienced, they began to achieve more decisive successes. On the night of 25 October 1942, the regiment hit a fuel depot at the airbase of Armavir. Reportedly, six *Junker Ju 88s* and *Heinkel He 111s* of *Stab II./KG 51* were destroyed. Only one German twin-engine bomber avoided destruction. Subsequently the *KG 51* had to retreat to the Kerch Peninsula. (Archive of Anatoly Plyac)

A *Junker Ju 88A* of the *KG 51*, the same unit bombed by the regiment at Armavir Airbase on 25 October 1942. This particular aircraft belonged to *Hauptmann* Klaus Häberlen, *Kapitän* of *Staffel 10* of *KG 51*. In addition to the Edelweiss (emblem of *KG 51*), this aircraft shows the coat of arms of the City of Memmigen. *Kampfgeschwader 51* "Edelweiss" (*KG 51*) (Battle Wing 51) was a *Luftwaffe* bomber unit active during World War II. It was equipped with *Dornier Do 17s*, *Heinkel He 111s* and *Junkers Ju 88s* light and medium bombers. It was named after the Edelweiss flower. *Stab/KG 51* was formed in 1939 and participated in the "Phoney War," the invasion of the Low Countries and France, the Battle of Britain, the Balkan Campaign, and then to Operation Barbarossa, the invasion of the Soviet Union. On 29 July 1942, the *Geschwader* flew its 15,000[th] bomb sortie.

Heinkel He 111, one of the two types of aircraft destroyed by the "Night Witches" on 25 October, at Armavir. This type equipped the *Geschwader* since 1939. Actually, according to other sources[15] *Stab/KG 51* lost just one aircraft – a *He 111P* – when the airfield was bombed on 25 October. Subsequently, the *Geschwader* was relocated to Sarabus, in the Crimea, and, afterwards, to Rostov. *Stab/KG 51* kept on fighting to support the German offensive at Kursk. It was repatriated to Southern Germany to convert to fighter-bomber operations. Flying *Messerschmitt Me 410* and later the *Messerschmitt Me 262* jets, the unit fought for the defense of the Reich and finally surrendered to US Forces near Holzkirchen, on 8 May 1945.

Stab/KG 51 "Edelweiss" early type. This badge combines the three *Gruppen* emblems, inspired by the mountain flora that grew around Landsberg where that *Luftwaffe* unit was based.

The Edelweiss, the emblem of the *KG 51*. The color of the shield was blue. Since its formation, this *Luftwaffe* unit had this Alpine flower as its badge. It identified the aircraft of *KG 51* until the end of the war, appearing even on the *Messerschmitt Me 262* jets.

Starshiy Leytenant Serafima Amosova-Taranenko (first to right), deputy commander of *588NBAP/46 GvNBAP*, tasking "Night Witches" crews. Left to right: Nadya Popova (pilot), Nina Danilovna (navigator), Meri Avidzba (navigator), Lyudmilla Klopkova (pilot), Katya Ryabova (navigator), Ira Sebrova (pilot), Yevgheniya Glamadzina (navigator), Taisya Fokina (pilot), Galina Bespalova (navigator), Maguvba Syrtlanova (pilot), Klavdiya Ryzhkova (pilot). "Nobody knows the exact day when they started calling us night witches," recalled Serafima Amosova-Taranenko. "We were fighting in the Caucasus near the city of Mozdok... We were bombing the German positions almost every night, and none of us was ever shot down, so the Germans began saying these are night witches, because it seemed impossible to kill us or shoot us down"[16].

German ace Alfred Grislawski. After the war, it was generally assumed that the nickname "Night Witches" was a Soviet propaganda invention, but German pilots who served in Northern Caucasus stated that they coined the nickname. "It was we pilots in the *III./JG 52* who invented the name," revealed Grislawski, who served as an *Oberfeldwebel* in the Caucasus in 1942. "And I can assure you that it was an expression of respect we felt towards those courageous women"[17]. Alfred Grislawski was born in Wanne-Eickel, Germany on 2 November 1919. He was one of the most successful *Experten* on the Eastern Front. He was credited with 133 victories (109 claims recorded over the Eastern Front), claimed in over 800 combat missions. He died in Herne, Germany 19 September 2003.

Pilot of *9 Staffel* of *JG 52*, "Top Gun" Alfred Grislawski in the Crimea, Soviet Union, 1st July 1942. In mid-July 1942, *JG 52* started to re-equip with the new *Messerschmitt Bf 109 G Gustav*. *III./JG 52* pushed towards the Caucasian oil fields in the south during August–September 1942. In August 1942 *Oberfeldwebel* Grislawski was assigned to *7./JG 52* based in the Caucasus. In September, he claimed 16 victories over the Terek bridgehead. On 5 November he downed four *Ilyushin Il-2s* but was shot down in his *Bf 109 G-2* and belly-landed with a few bruises.

German *Experte Hauptmann* Johannes "Macki" Steinhoff. He was another of the pilots who experienced the nuisance bombings of the *588 NBAP*. "We simply couldn't grasp that the Soviet airmen that caused us the greatest trouble were in fact women," recalled Steinhoff, who was *Kommandeur* of *II./JG 52* in the Caucasus, between September and November 1942. "These women feared nothing. They came night after night in their very slow biplanes and for some periods they wouldn't give us any sleep at all"[18]. Steinhoff was born in Bottendorf, Province of Saxony, on 15 September 1913. He was one of very few *Luftwaffe* pilots who survived fighting through the whole war. He was also one of the highest scoring pilots with 176 victories, and one of the first to fly the *Messerschmitt Me 262* jet fighter in combat. He died on 21 February 1994, in Bonn.

Left, Senior Lieutenant pilot Nina Raspopova, Hero of Soviet Union. Actually, the "Night Witches" were not so fearless like Steinhoff believed. "Don't' believe those who say they had no fear in the war," she later recalled. "I did fear the war, and death - feared each combat mission. After bombing and having escaped the enemy's fire, I couldn't pull myself together for ten or fifteen minutes. I was shivering, my teeth were chattering, my feet and hands were shaking, and I always felt an overwhelming striving for life. I didn't want to die. I dreamed of a small village house, a piece of rye bread, and a glass of clear river water"[19].

Pilot Larisa Rozanova-Litvinova (right) also mentioned the dire fear of flying a bombing sortie. "When you leave behind the area of the target, the sea of antiaircraft fire, and the searchlights, the next instant you start shivering – your feet and knees start jumping – and you cannot talk at all because you are wheezing in your throat.  This was a normal reaction after each flight. In a few minutes you'd recover"[20]. (Courtesy of Larisa Rozanova-Litvinova's family).

Left to right: pilots Mariya Smirnova and Dina Nikulina, Yevgeniya Rudneva (navigator), Ira Sebrova (pilot), Natalya Meklin (navigator/pilot). Raspopova was not the only "Night Witch" to fear death on each sortie. "We never became accustomed to fear," confessed later Heroine of Soviet Union, Mariya Smirnova. "Before each mission and as we approached the target, I became a concentration of nerves and tension. My whole body was swept by fear of being killed. We had to break through the fire of antiaircraft guns and also escape the searchlights. We had to dive and sideslip the plane in order not be shot down. All this affected my sleep enormously. When we returned from our missions at dawn, I couldn't fall asleep; I tossed in bed and had anxiety attacks. We slept two to four hours each day throughout the four years of war"[21].

German 150-centimetre (4,9 feet) diameter *flak* searchlight-34 or -37. It was probably this improved type of searchlight (compared to the former 60-centimeter diameter type) that the Germans started to use to face the sorties of the *588 NBAP*, while based at Assinovskaya. "In Mozdok, in the Caucasus, where we flew missions attacking the headquarters of the German staff, they had the most powerful searchlights we had yet encountered," recalled Polina Gelman. "If a searchlight caught our planes in its beam, we couldn't see anything – we were blinded. The pilot flew with her head very low in the cockpit because she could not see anything outside, and when we managed to get out of the beam we were still blinded for a few moments"[22]. The *flak* searchlight in the picture used parabolic glass reflectors and had a detection range of about 8 kilometers for targets at an altitude of between 4,000 and 5,000 meters, so it was absolutely powerful for aircraft that flew at height between 600 and 1,000 meters. It required a crew of seven to operate it.

Polina Gelman, future Hero of Soviet Union, at the beginning of her career. When the war broke, she was in her third year at the Moscow State University. At the end of May 1942 she was transferred to a base along the Mius River, in the Donetsk coal fields, in Eastern Ukraine. In the picture, she is wearing just the Parachute Badge and the first Order of the Red Star.

Galina Dokhutovich, navigator of *588 NBAP*. Born in 1921, she attended high school with Polina Gelman, in Gomel (*Гомель*, the second largest city of Belarus, on the bank of the Sozh River). Dokhutovich, a girl with "many talents," got very high marks at school. She won literary prizes, and excelled in gymnastic and music (in one year covered a four-year course, not having a musical instrument). She and Gelman joined a flying club and Dokhutovich soon became the best trainee of the group and the first to fly solo. When the war broke out, she volunteered and was enrolled by Marina Raskova in the navigation group. But to her bitter disappointment, she was at first appointed *aide-de-camp* of a squadron. Dokhutovich insistently requested to fly as navigator. In the summer 1942, she met with a serious accident. After returning from a sortie, she was lying down at the edge of the airfield in the dark when a refueling truck ran over her. Galya suffered serious injuries to her back. Nevertheless she still longed for flying. "Promise me that when I return you'll not re-appoint me aide-de-camp," she told chief of staff, Irina Rakobolskaya. She was hospitalized for six months[23].

A "net" of German *flak* searchlights. The searchlights were placed according to a geometrical pattern, so that the aircraft could be caught in the cross-fire of several beams. It was more difficult for the aircraft to get out of inclined beams, while it was easier for the operators to follow the aircraft path. "The numerous searchlights caught and held us in their beams as spider webs hold a fly," explained Gelman. "They followed us even after we crossed the front line, and the guns followed us also... It was difficult to even maintain the aircraft in level flight, because we flew only by visual references."[24].

Marina Pavlovna Chechneva. She was born on 15 August 1922, in the village of Protasovo, in the Orel region. In 1934 she moved to Moscow where her father worked in a factory near Moscow Central Airport. When she was 16 she joined a flying school and learned to fly after school. One of her instructors was Valeriya Khomyakova, later a famous fighter pilot. Marina herself became a flying instructor at the Central Flying Club in Moscow. Exactly one month after the German invasion, on 22 July 1941, her flat in Moscow was destroyed by an incendiary bomb. She was transferred to Stalingrad with her club and in December she was posted to Raskova's 122 Air Group. Chechneva was assigned to the night bomber regiment and became one of the bravest pilots of her unit. She was given the most difficult missions. Marina was selected to try out the new tactic of bombing in two-plane formation near Mozdok, in the Caucasus.

Senior Lieutenant pilot Nina Raspopova, Hero of Soviet Union (left), and Larisa Radchikova. Raspopova was shot down twice during the Great Patriotic War. The first time during a mission on the Terek River, near Mozdok, while the German offensive aimed to cross Caucasus and conquer the oil wells in Northern Georgia. "On December 9, 1942, our regiment was given an assignment to not let the enemy ferry across the Terek River. My navigator, Larisa Radchikova and I completed the first mission, but on the second one we were caught by enemy searchlights after we had dropped our bombs", she later recalled. Her biplane was hit and they were wounded. She had to force land in the neutral zone. "I was bleeding all over. Large splinters were sticking out of my body. My navigator was wounded in the neck, and even after she was operated on, hear head was set to one side." Notwithstanding the wounds, the two girls walked to the Soviet lines and after several hours they arrived at a field hospital. "We were opposite a deep pit and watched dead bodies covered with white cotton sheets being thrown into that huge communal grave... As long as I live, I'll never forget mortally wounded soldiers whispering to us to jump the line and go ahead of them for surgery, because their minutes were numbered." After surgery, Raspopova was bedridden for two months. "When I returned to duty and was assigned a mission, it was terribly difficult to return to combat"[25].

Another picture of Terek River, near Mozdok. For six months the "Night Witches" were based in the Sunzha Valley, in the Terek River area. During autumn 1942 the "Night Witches" were often tasked to bomb the German strongholds on the banks of the river and their crossing. Based near the Terek River, there were German bombers from *Fliegerkorps IV* that attacked the Grozny oil refineries. Hitler believed that his *Wehrmacht* could capture them.

The *Polikarpov* had not been designed for blind-flight, it had no radio and only a limited number of primitive instruments. The new theatre of war often required them to fly in all sorts of adverse weather conditions. "When we were flying in the Northern Caucasus," recalled Mariya Smirnova, "we would take off in clear weather and often return in dense fog that reached from the ground up to fifty meters. We found the location of the airdrome by orientation, for we knew all the terrain landmarks. On those foggy nights, the ground personnel would shoot a red flare to indicate the landing strip and a green one if they thought the aircraft was not in position to land. Landing in thick fog, I would enter that milky sheet and when the cockpit began to darken, it was a sign that the land was close. Then I would pull the nose up and sink to the ground for a landing"[26].

Junior Lieutenant Yevdokiya Nikulina, pilot, and Senior Non Commissioned Officer, Yevgeniya Rudneva, navigator, future Heroes of Soviet Union, in front of their *Polikarpov U-2*. After the death of Olkhovskaya during the 588th baptism of fire, Nikulina was appointed commander of Nr. 2 Squadron. Together with Rudneva, they bombed troops, tanks, vehicles, artillery positions, and bridges on the Terek River. In Mozdok, Rudneva managed to hit and destroy the headquarter of *Wehrmacht* commander Baron Ewald von Kleist. Rudneva, by September 1942, was commissioned and became the regiment's chief navigator. On 13 September she was decorated with the Order of the Red Star.

Baron Paul Ludwig Ewald von Kleist, the German General whose HQ was hit by Rudneva. Von Kleist commanded the First Panzer Army that was part of Army Group A. During Operation Blue, this unit spearheaded the attack into the Caucasus, aimed at capturing Grozny and the Baku (current capital of Azerbaijan) oilfields. At first, von Kleist succeeded in the attack and Rostov, Maikop, Krasnodar, and the entire Kuban region, were captured. However, in September 1942, Army Group A's offensive was stopped in the Caucasus. After Hitler briefly took personal control of Army Group A, he appointed von Kleist to command it on November 21, 1942. As von Kleist took command of Army Group A, Colonel General Eberhard von Mackensen took the reins of the First Panzer Army. In December 1942, as the German Sixth Army was already being crushed in the Battle of Stalingrad, the Red Army launched a successful offensive against Army Group A. The First Panzer Army was evacuated through Rostov in January 1943 before the Soviets could cut it off in the Kuban.

Another picture of Ewald von Kleist (far right). He was born on 8 August 1881 in Braunfels. Von Kleist was an aristocratic. He was educated in a German military school. Graduated in 1900, he served as a lieutenant of hussars and a regimental commander in World War I. Subsequently he served as a commander of a cavalry division. In April 1941, Kleist commanded *1st Panzergruppe*, which spearheaded the Blitzkrieg-style invasions of Yugoslavia and Greece. With this formation he also participated in the subsequent Operation Barbarossa as part of Army Group South. On 14 August 1941 (and until 3 June 1942) he was given command of the Italian Expeditionary Corps in Russia (*Corpo di Spedizione Italiano in Russia*, the CSIR). Between 20 October and 2 November 1941, Kleist employed the CSIR in the assault on the city of Stalino (now Donetsk), an important steel center in Eastern Ukraine, and in occupying the nearby towns of Gorlowka and Rikovo. Captured by Americans, he was delivered to the Soviets after the war. Charged as a war criminal, he was given a ten year sentence. He died on 13 November 1954 in Russian captivity.

Another picture of Rudneva and Nikulina. The two "Night Witches" became very close friends. Together, Rudneva and Nikulina flew about 450 mission sorties. Nikulina was awarded for the first time on 27 September 1942. Rudneva, up to 19 October 1942, had accumulated 256 sorties. This "destructive" woman blew up ammunition dumps, fuel depots, a river crossing, and damaged other targets. She also hit transport motor vehicles. For these feats she had been awarded the Order of the Red Star. In this picture, Rudneva holds the rank of *Starshy Leytenant* while Nikulina has the Order of the Red Banner pinned on her left chest and the Order of the Great Patriotic War on her right chest.

Left to right: Regimental Commander Yevdokiya Bershanskaya, navigator Yevdokiya Pasko, and pilot Zoya Parfenova. Pasko and Parfenova became one of the outstanding crews of the "Night Witches." They were one of the first to be decorated in the regiment, in September 1942, with the Order of the Red Banner. Together they flew two to nine sorties per night. Note the oversized flight suit of Pasko, who was rather petite. During the fighting near Mozdok, Parfenova, with Serafima Amosova crew, destroyed an important enemy bridge on the Terek River.

Antonina "Tanya" Grigoryevna Efimova, navigator of *588 NBAP*. She died of illness in December 1942 while the "Night Witches" were based in Northern Caucasus. Very little is known about her.

Flight Commander Nadya Popova (left) and her navigator, Katya Ryabova, planning a sortie. Popova wears her Order of the Red Banner, while Ryabova has her Order of the Red Star, pinned on her left chest. Their superiors considered them complementary. In May 1942, they flew to the front together. Ryabova was a second year student of mechanics and mathematics, while Popova, as a teenager, had dreamed of becoming a singer or an actress. Popova was regarded as one of the best pilots in the regiment. She helped Ryabova

in becoming a very competent navigator. On their first mission, they hit an enemy ammunition depot. Subsequently they managed to bomb and destroy an important bridge on the Don. During summer 1942, as the front line moved chaotically, they were often requested to fly reconnaissance sorties in daytime. These missions were extremely dangerous because they were flown at low levels to avoid interception by German fighters, but in this way they became easy target for *flak* or even rifle fire.

One of the outstanding "Night Witches" was Natalya Meklin. A fervent patriot, as soon as she learned that Raskova was recruiting volunteers for female regiments, she rushed to the recruitment center. She requested to be posted as a pilot but due to her insufficient flying experience she was assigned to the navigators' group. At first she was navigator of the deputy squadron commander Mariya Smirnova, regarded as a strict and demanding pilot.

★

Mariya Smirnova. Her first mission with Natalya Meklin was memorable. They took off in the dark. The airstrip was marked only by three camouflaged lanterns, the "Flying Mice." They were exposed only during landings and take offs. Their task was to bomb a railway station to prevent the Germans from bringing reinforcements to the front line. They found it very difficult to see the reference points. The only lights were the flashes of the firing guns and flares. Nevertheless they dropped their bombs and reached the airfield after evading *flak*.

Natalya Meklin (right) and Ira Sebrova. Sebrova, born in 1914, was one of the most experienced "Night Witches". She usually brought her aircraft back without damage or bullet holes. She had her baptisms of fire in North Caucasus. In that remote and demanding area she was able to hit a fuel depot, motorized transports, and bridges. She was decorated for the first time with the Order of the Red Banner. Once she had to bomb enemy *flak* batteries near Mozdok. Her task was to draw attention of the anti-aircraft defense to allow the other "Night Witches" to hit the target. They took off in clear sky but soon mist arrived from the east, hiding the airfield completely. But thanks to her expertise, Sebrova, after hitting the target, managed to fly across the fog and landed without incident. On another occasion she had to take off in bad weather and encountered heavy snowfalls half way. Nevertheless, her navigator dropped the bomb through an opening between the clouds. When she came back, it was pitch black, but her navigator dropped a flare and she saw the highway and the Sunzha Valley, and they landed on their airfield successfully.

Fighting in Mozdok. Reportedly, in this Soviet propaganda picture, Soviet soldiers capture Germans troops among the ruins of the city on left bank of the Terek River. Actually, the *Wehrmacht* conquered Mozdok on 25 August 1942. But at that point, the Axis offensive (Rumanians also participated in the operation) had to stop due to overstretched supply lines. Moreover the Axis Forces were heavily weakened by reinforcing troops fighting in Stalingrad.

Two "Night Witches" preparing to take off in a *Polikarpov U-2*. The strain of air combat is clearly visible on their faces. "There is a superhuman psychic overstrain when you are blinded by the searchlights and deafened by the explosions of antiaircraft shells and dire all around you," recalled Yevgeniya Zhigulenko. "Your concentration over the target is so intense that it results in a complete loss of your whereabouts – a disorientation. You cannot tell the sky from the ground. Many of our crews crashed in that way"[27]. Pilot and flight commander Larisa Rozanova-Litvinova also mentioned the enormous stress of air combat: "Each mission was a constant overstrain. We inhaled the gunpowder, choking and coughing, unable to breathe, from the anti-aircraft gunfire bursting around us. It sometimes lasted fifteen minutes until we completely escaped the searchlights".

Yevgeniya Andreyevna Zhigulenko, navigator-bombardier of the *588 NBAP*. While based in Assinovskaya, she was tasked with her pilot Polina Makogon to bomb a bridge that the German were constructing from the left bank of the Terek River. "From... an altitude of 1,200 meters (3930 feet)... the small bridge seemed a thin thread. To hit it a pilot has to concentrate all her energy and vision, and more than that, to know exactly her speed, altitude, and course for a full minute before the bomb was dropped. When the target became discernible and was under the wing of the aircraft, I cried to the pilot to hold to the left because we were drifting with the wind. Our bombs missed the target. The antiaircraft guns were firing, and the searchlight lit up the sky around us. I was sweating and could feel a strip of sweat rolling down my back. We turned from the target, giving way to following aircraft, in the turn we fell into a stall and were nearing a crash, but she (*Makogon* – Edit.) managed to recover..."[28].

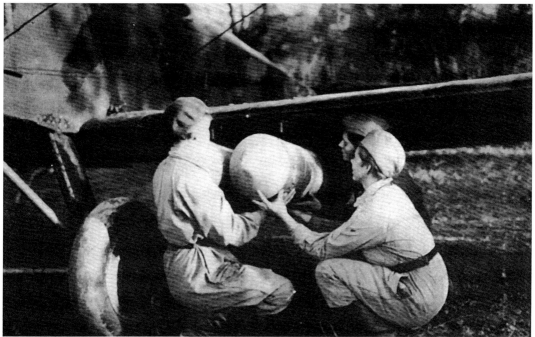

Armorers and mechanics of armament preparing and attaching the bombs for a sortie. "We attached the fuses to the bombs, which armed them, and only then attached the bombs to the aircraft," recalled mechanic of armament Nina Karasyova-Buzina. "We worked all night, then had a two to three hour rest and returned to the planes in the morning to examine the bomb racks under the aircraft". The racks were so low to the ground that the armorers had to kneel to examine and attach the bombs[29].

The "Night Witches" managed to fly a record number of missions thanks to a new method that technicians adopted for maintaining and servicing aircraft. According to the regulations, every mechanic and armorer had to service their own airplane. "If each mechanic only worked on her own plane, we could only manage two flights per night," recalled Rakobolskaya. But as the aircraft came back with intervals of several minutes, the technician of the aircraft that had not still landed were available to help their colleagues. This new system was like a factory with a "well-functioning conveyor belt," noted Rakobolskaya. In this way, the "Night Witches" managed to rearm and refuel an aircraft in just five minutes. During the nights of August and September 1942, each crew could fly five to seven or eight sorties per night. At times the 588th amassed 80 to 90 combat sorties per night.

In December 1942, the regiment, originally formed with two squadrons, was instructed to form a third one. So, some of the navigators that wanted to become pilots, like Natalya Meklin, were retrained as pilots. Thanks to reorganization, pilot Tanya Makarova was commissioned and appointed Nr. 2 Squadron commander.

Tanya Makarova in civilian clothes. Before enrolling, Makarova was a flying instructor in the Military School of Basic Training and held the rank of sergeant. All her trainees were admitted to school for fighter pilots.

Soviet soldiers on *T-34-8* tanks. In autumn 1942, the *Wehrmacht* units involved in North Caucasus were forced to transfer part of troops and equipment for the armies besieging Stalingrad. So weakened, the German offensive aimed to capture the local Soviet oil wells in Northern Caucasus was stopped in Chechnya by Red Army's North Caucasian Strategic Defensive Operation (25 July 1942 - 31 December 1942). The immediate and subsequent Soviet North Caucasian Strategic Offensive Operation (1 January 1943 - 4 February 1943) pushed back the Germans westwards in the Kuban steppes. The "Night Witches", who operated always very close to the front, followed the retreating Germans. "Our main airfield was usually situated forty kilometers to the front," recalled Rozanova-Litvinova, "our auxiliary field twenty kilometers from the front".

"Night Witches" on Krasnodar Airfield, spring 1943. The *588 NBAP* was transferred to the Kuban and based near Krasnodar. They stayed there until September 1943. Here the flying conditions were similar to those already experienced in North Caucasus, with extreme weather conditions and rough terrain. (Archive of Anatoly Plyac)

Yulya Fedorovna Pashkova, she was one of the three aviatrixes perished in mid-air collision, on 1 April 1943. She is still a little known historical caracter.

Lidya Svistunova, a young replacement navigator, was killed in a collision on 1 April 1943, while flying with Polina Makong, in spring 1943. In the night of 1 April 1943, they were flying back from a mission when collided with another aircraft in the air. According to Rakobolskaya, the collision occurred in Poland: "In one episode over Poland, polina Makong was killed when her aircraft collided with a German night fighter".

Polina Makogon, pilot, and Lidya Svistunova, navigator. Makogon initially was the pilot of Yevgeniya Zhigulenko. "I flew as navigator with pilot Polina Makogon," recalled Zhigulenko, future Hero of Soviet Union, "who was only twenty-five, but I, being nineteen, considered her to be quite old. Our flights together made me believe everyone was born under her own star, lucky or tragic; but we are all destined to our own fate, a fate impossible to change no matter what the circumstances". And the fate of Makogon was doomed. While still pilot of Zhigulenko, reportedly, she escaped death three times. The first episode happened in the Caucasus. The runway ended abruptly in a steep precipice. The *Polikarpov* had just left the ground when the engine died. The biplane, that was not equipped with brakes, returned to earth, running toward the abyss. By a miracle, it stopped a short distance from the cliff. The second episode occurred while they tried to bomb a bridge that Germans were building across the Terek River. The reaction of the *flak* was so violent, and the searchlights so bright, that Makogon lost control and the plane stalled, nearing a crash and recovering at the last moment. The third time their *Polikarpov* was hit on the Caucasian foothills. They had to force-land. Worried that Makogon had not seen a steep hill to their right, Zhigulenko shot a flare. "It was strictly forbidden – the enemy could spot us," recalled Zhigulenko. "But our lives were at stake, so I violated the order; I had a strong urge to live. In the light of the flare Polina could see the hill, she made a quick turn to the left, and we escaped the crash". (Archive of Anatoly Plyac)

Polina Makogon

Yekaterina "Khivaz" Dospanova. She was the navigator of Pashkova the day that she was killed. She had a broken leg and other injuries. She was believed dead so she was put with the other corpses. When the soldiers took her by the hands and feet to take her away and bury her, they felt her hands were not cold and so they realized that she was not still dead. She had broken legs but she was still alive. She was hospitalized but her legs were badly casted so they had to be broken twice. Still Dospanova came back to the regiment, but was not allowed to fly operational sorties. After the war, she was declared invalid of 2nd degree and went back to Kazhakistan. (Archive of Anatoly Plyac)

Lyudmilla Klopkova, pilot. In spring 1943 she teamed with Galya Dokhutovich, to form one of the most successful "Night Witches" crew. On 20 April 1943, Dokhutovich wrote in her diary: "Lyusya Klopkova and I flew six sorties to Krymskaya. During the first one we blew up a fuel depot. The huge fire burned all night and the girls kept congratulating me".

Galya Dokhutovich was the former *aide-de-camp* who was run over by a refueling truck. After six months at hospital, she went back to the regiment in December 1942. "I doubt whether it would be possible to get a better reception anywhere else," she wrote in her diary. "It was like going home to my own family!" Notwithstanding the severe injuries ("I feel awful. I try to stand the pain, but I am afraid my endurance has its limits," she wrote), she had started flying sorties again[30]. Galya Dokhutovich was one of the very few who revealed how military women and men developed liaisons, sometimes imposed by men. "Everything around me is so disgusting. Even the best senior commanders are debauched scoundrels!" Dokhutovich wrote. "The way that the best and worst characteristics can be combined in the same person is really terrible and absurd"[31]. Six weeks after writing this entry, on 31 July, 1943 (at 22.18, Moscow time), Dokhutovich was shot down and killed with her pilot, by *Luftwaffe* night fighter ace Josef Kociok.

Left to right: Irina Rakobolskaya, Irina Sebrova, Yevdokiya Bershanskaya, and Natalya Meklin. Sebrova was one of the most experienced "Night Witches." She was 27 when she was enrolled by Raskova. She flew many bombing sorties in North Caucasus but always came back with her aircraft virtually undamaged. "After some missions in the Ukraine area (at the beginning of 1943 - Edit.), we changed our airdromes to the banks of the Sea of Azov. We were bombing the so called Blue Line on the Kerch Peninsula. It was difficult because there were strong German positions. Most of their military fortifications were concentrated on this line. In this area we lost our best pilot, Dusya Nosal"[32].

Yevdokiya "Dusya" Nosal. On the night of 23 April 1943 Nosal took off, for the first time, with Irina Kashirina. Kashirina was a former mechanic who had retrained as a navigator. On their second mission (Nosal's 254th) they had to bomb enemy troops on the hills between Novorossiysk and Malaya Zemlya beachhead, occupied by the Soviets. As she turned for home, southwest of Novorossiysk, a German fighter shot at the aircraft, smashing the pilot's cockpit and hitting Nosal in the head. Nosal was killed instantly and fell onto the instrument panel and the stick. The plane fell out of control. However, Kashirina managed to recover the aircraft just before it hit the sea and took it back to the airfield. Nosal was buried in the Cossak village of Pashkovskaya, near Krasnodar, where a museum was dedicated to her. Nosal was the first "Night Witch" to be awarded the Gold Star and title of Hero of the Soviet Union posthumously on 24 May 1943. School Nr. 58 in Krasnodar and the school in Burchak (her native village) were named after her. A bust was placed in Victory Square in Mikhaylovka (Zaporozhye Region).

Wolf Ettel, one of the outstanding aces of *JG 3*, was the German pilot who shot at Dusya Nosal's aircraft, killing her. Ettel was credited with 124 air victories in just 250 missions, with a rate of kill/missions of 1 out of 2, better than that of Erich Hartmann (the highest scoring fighter ace in the history of aerial warfare) that was 1/4. He was born on 26 February 1921 in Hamburg. In spring 1942, with the rank of *Leutnant*, Ettel was posted to the fourth *Staffel* of *JG 3,* then based on the Eastern Front. On 24 June, he gained his first two victories when he shot down two Russian *Il-2 Sturmovik* ground-attack aircraft. He recorded his 30th victory on 7 October. On 31 October, Ettel shot down three enemy aircraft (32-33). When *4./JG 3* was relocated to the Kuban bridgehead in February 1943, Ettel had 36 victories to his credit. His score grew steadily. He claimed 36 victories in April, including five shot down on 11 April (66-70) and four on 22 April and 23 April. During this last day, Ettel claimed a *Polikaropv U-2* (the aircraft piloted by Nosal) exactly in the place where Nosal's aircraft had been machinegunned by a German fighter[33], falling out of control almost up to sea level. The time of his air victory is 05.30, that is still night in that season.

Ettel recorded his 120th victory on 11 May 1943 but was shot down by *flak*. He belly-landed his *Bf 109 G–4* "White 10" in no-man's land and returned to German lines despite Russian troops bombarding him with rifle fire and grenades. Later that night, Ettel led a combat patrol back to his damaged aircraft to salvage important equipment. He was awarded the *Ritterkreuz* on 1 June in recognition of this feat. On 5 June 1943, Ettel was appointed *Staffelkapitän* of *8./JG 27* and relocated to the Mediterranean Front. He shot down a *RAF Spitfire* fighter over Sicily on 14 July. On 16 July, he shot down two *USAAF B-24* bombers and a *Spitfire*. But, the following day, he was himself shot down and killed by Allied *flak*, while attacking British troops around Catania. His *Bf 109 G-6* (W.Nr. 18 402) crashed near the village of Lentini. Ettel was posthumously awarded the *Eichenlaub* (Nr 289) on 31 August.

Far right, Irina "Ira" Kashirina. A former mechanic, she was appointed navigator just the day before Nosal was killed, after a navigation course. She had some flying lessons before the war. "After dropping our bombs," she recalled later, "we turned to go home. Ahead of us and to port appeared a flash, and I noticed a German fighter." Kashirina tried to warn Dusya, but a ball of fire exploded in the pilot's cockpit. Nosal hung her head and the biplane rolled on to its back, diving almost vertically. It seemed a brilliant evasive action but the dive continued and the pilot did not react. In the *Polikarpov* there were duplicate aircraft controls. "Then I took over the controls,"continued Kashirina, "but the pedal was jammed." Kashirina, with one hand holding up the pilot's head by the collar of her flying suit and with the other attempting to control the aircraft, managed to level the aircraft at 500 feet. "I put the aircraft into a turn to fly back. Dusya kept sliding down into the cockpit, leaning against the control stick. I kept pulling her up by the collar. In this manner, I brought the machine back..."[34].

After Dusya Nosal was killed, her friends wrote on this *Polikarpov*: "To avenge Dusya". Few days later, during the night of 28-29 April, the "Night Witches" bombed with extreme precision – as remembered by *Luftwaffe* ace, *Wilhelm Batz*[35] – the spot along the front line where the 56th Soviet Army had chosen to open a breach on the morning of 29 April. The airwomen supported the Soviet offensive in the Kuban region aimed to break the German fortified "Blue line" that extended from the port on the Black Sea, Novorossiysk and the one on the Sea of Azov, Temryuk.

German *Luftwaffe* fighter ace, Major Wilhelm "Willi" Batz. He was born on 21 May 1916 in Bamberg. *Willi* Batz shot down 237 enemy aircraft during 445 combat missions. He achieved almost all his victories over the Eastern front. He was shot down four times and wounded three times. Batz was awarded the Knight's Cross of the Iron Cross with Oak Leaves and Swords. He died on 11 September 1988 in Mauschendorf/Ebern (in Unterfranken).

Irina Kashirina, mechanic/navigator and Sofiya Ozervkova, engineer. They are both wearing, on the right chest, the Guards Badge. Kashirina on her left has the Order of the Red Banner, awarded to her on 30 April 1943[36]. The feat of Kashirina who came back to the airfield even though the pilot was dead, reveal the way the *46 GvNBAP* managed to have female replacements even if no new pilots or navigators were posted to the regiment. "We began ourselves to retrain our own personnel as replacement," recalled chief of staff Irina Rakobolskaya. It was possible as the *U-2* was a training aircraft, with linked controls in both cockpits. Often the pilots let navigators practice flying the biplane. The *Polikarpov* was very simple to pilot so the navigators quickly became long-legged pilots. The "Night Witches" devised a formal system, organizing retraining courses. "First we retrained one or two people, then we organized a group," recalled Rakobolskaya.

Navigator trainees learning how to read maps and use them in combat. Yevgeniya Rudneva, extreme right, standing, is the navigation instructor. Already by September 1942, thanks to her thorough knowledge of mathematics, geography, and astronomy, she was promoted as the regiment's chief navigator. As such, Rudneva was not expected to flew many sorties but rather to monitor the work of navigation on the ground, and initiate all the new navigators into their duties. The first navigators group, made up of former armorers, was created in 1942. Rudneva was posted as instructor and designed the course.

Natalya Meklin (left) planning the forthcoming sortie. While a navigator of Sebrova, returning from missions, Sebrova would pass the controls to Meklin. Natalya, who had some flying experience, was, along with three other navigators, allowed to retrain as a pilot, since the regiment was experiencing a shortage of pilots. On 18 May 1943, less than one year after the regiment's arrival to the front, Meklin flew her 381st sortie as a pilot[37].

Navigator retrained as pilots. Left to right, Yevdokiya Nikulina and Ira Sebrova. Second from the right, Polina Gelman. "We turned navigators into pilots," recalled Rakobolskaya, "and trained new navigators from among the mechanics, and made armorers of the girl volunteers who were just arriving at the front... The regiment flew combat missions at night, and the training groups worked during the day"[38].

Serafima Amosova (second from left), deputy commander, is showing Dina Nikulina (to her left) and Yevgeniya Rudneva (far right) a location on the map. Extreme left, Tatyana Sumarokhova. Nikulina was awarded the Order of the Patriotic War II Class on 12 May 1943. She was seriously wounded in her leg on 22 July 1943. That night the regiment had been tasked to bomb the German fortified Blue Line, full of searchlights, coaxial machine-guns, and *flak* batteries. While returning near the vicinity of the village of Kievskaya and Trudovaya, her aircraft was hit and set on fire. She managed to extinguish the fire twice by side-slipping, but there was the danger that the aircraft could explode if the fire reached the fuel tank. Nikulina decided to force-land on the shoulder of a highway. A group of soldiers passing by noticed the aircraft and came to their aid. She spent two months in a hospital in Krasnodar.

German 150 cm *Flak Searchlight*. It could detect targets 8 km (4.97 miles) far at an altitude of 4000-5000 meters (13119-16398 feet). It used a 4.9 feet searchlight parabolic glass reflector, powered by a generator around a 8 cylinder engine. The searchlight was attached to the generator by a cable 200 meters (656 ft) long. It required a crew of seven men to operate. Searchlights were deployed forward of the antiaircraft artillery in a grid with 5 km between each light. Sound locators (later replaced with radar) helped them to find targets.

Flak sound locator. The RRH (*Ringtricherich-tungshorer*, acoustic monitoring device) was used before radar were supplied, to detect the approaching enemy aircraft. It featured an acoustic horn (much more accurate and sensitive than the human ear) to detect the sound produced by plane propellers. The sound was amplified acoustically (on early types) or electrically. The detection range was of 5-12 km depending on weather and wind direction. The sound locators were effective mostly at determining direction and when used to track the noises from a single aircraft.

Yelena Salikova (right), and Anya Visotskaya, navigator of Yevgeniya Krutova on the night of 31 July 1943. On the night of 31 July 1943, the regiment was tasked to bomb German troops in the village of Krymskaya, along the Blue Line. Salikova directed her pilot over the Kuban River to the Cossack village.

"Halfway to the target," recalled Larisa Rozanova-Litvinova, who was flying behind her, "I could see four searchlights turn on... But I could also see a white spot caught by the searchlights." It was the aircraft of Krutova and Salikova. "But in a few seconds that white spot turned into red. I knew well what that meant: an aircraft was burning. I calculated it was the first plane that took off from our airdrome. The strangest thing was that no antiaircraft shells were exploding in the air, the anti-aircraft guns were silent, but still it was set on fire." It was 22.18 (Soviet time). Visotskaya that night was flying with Dokhutovich as a navigator[39].

Yevgeniya "Zhenya" Krutova was a close friend of Yevgeniya Rudneva. "Zhenya and Lena Salikova burned to death before my very eyes," wrote desperate Yevgeniya Rudneva in her diary. "Zhenya, Zhenya... I saw how death stole toward Zhenya, but what could I have done?! We were already over the target, but I sent Klava (Klavdiya Serebryakova – Edit.) to bomb the nearest searchlight, one of the seven that held Zhenya's aircraft. At first she took evasive action, then her wings began to burn, but she glided and was not falling. Just before landing they sent up red flare. My wing obscured the blazing aircraft, and all I saw was that flash in the air from the explosion on the ground. It happened on enemy-held territory, near Kievskaya. I wondered if they had time to escape and whether there were any survivors to escape!" Unfortunately both girls had perished[40].

Oberfeldwebel Josef Kociok, from *10./(NJ)ZG 1*. He was the night fighter ace who on 31 July 1943 shot down the aircraft of Krutova and Salikova. At 21.15 (German time), flying his *Messerschmitt Bf 110,* Kociok shot them down over Krymskaya, at 1,200 meters (3,935 feet). The *Polikarpov* biplane was mistakenly identified as a *R-5* (actually the *R-5* was very similar to the *U-2*, the main difference being the engine was inline and not radial). The picture was taken on 15 May 1943, soon after Kociok shot down four Soviet-built *DC-3s*.

Kociok's *Messerschmitt Bf 110*. Kociok flew this aircraft on 31 July 1943. It was not yet equipped with radar so it relied on searchlights to locate the enemy aircraft. The crew of this aircraft consisted of two people. On this *Bf 110*, the 20 mm *Oerlikon* cannons *MG FF* had been replaced by the *MG 151/20* of the same caliber but more effective. It was enough to hit a single engine aircraft with four rounds to destroy it while to down a four-engine American bomber it took 18 to 25 rounds. The picture was taken in Bagerovo, the same airfield from where the aircraft took off to attack the "Night Witches" in summer of 1943.

Aniya Visotskaya, pilot. She was flying the second aircraft on the night of 31 July when they arrived over the target. "The four searchlights were switched on again and caught the second of our aircraft," continued Rozanova. "Usually as we approached the target there was a sea of fire from the anti-aircraft guns, and now for the second time the guns were silent… We saw the second plane set on fire too, and I saw in the sky the smoke trail of a fighter. I realized that a German fighter had shot down two aircraft." It was 22.00, German time, and Kociok had scored his second victory of the night, his number 26. "Then Dudina (Anna, another pilot – Edit.) flew in and reported that at 23.00 hours yet another aircraft had burned down. Whose? According to the take-off sequence, it would have been either Visotskaya's or Rogova's"[41].

Galina Dokhutovich, navigator of Visotskaya. She was on the second aircraft that Kociok shot down. Rudneva was very fond of "Galya" Dokhutovich. "The person whom I've always admired is my beloved Galochka. She has lived through so much; she is so brave, such a wonderful person! Galya is one of my colleagues," Rudneva wrote on her diary on 26 April 1943[42]. Not seeing Dokhutovich coming back, Rudneva felt desperate. "I kept running up to every landing aircraft, but there was no Galya (Dokhutovich –Edit.) My Galya didn't come back!"[43].

Sofiya Rugova, pilot. She flew the third aircraft shot down over Krymskaya on 31 July. It happened at 23.05, just five minutes after the fall of the second. Rozanova, almost over Krymskaya, at last, could witness the tragic end of two more of her friends: "While we were gliding over the target, I could see the third plane on fire, turning over and over in the air, somersaulting down, the flares exploding one after another in the cockpits. We realized that our friends were dying".

Yevgeniya Sukhorukova, navigator of Rugova on 31 July 1943. She burned alive in the rear cockpit of their *Polikarpov*, hit by German ace Kociok."Flares blew up in Rogova's rear cockpit; her aircraft kept falling chaotically"[44].

Yevdokiya Bershanskaya (left) and navigator Larisa Nikolayevna Rozanova-Litvinova. Rozanova recalled how she felt when she saw the two first *Polikarpovs* falling on the night of 31 July 1943: "A bitter tickling in my throat, incapable of breathing. Goosebumps were jumping along my back, and I could hardly feel my feet - they were as if made of cotton-wool. We saw the second plane set on fire too, and I saw in the sky the smoke trail of a fighter... My legs wooden, my teeth clenched... I was so frightened I couldn't even think of escape"[45].

Irina Kashirina was the navigator of the fourth *Polikarpov* shot down, flown by Valentina Polunina. She was the same navigator who, several weeks before, flew the aircraft back after her pilot, Dusya Nosal, had been killed.

Valentina Polunina, pilot of the fourth aircraft which fell on the night of 31 July 1943. According to Rudneva, her *Polikarpov* was hit by German *flak*. "Polunina was hit by an anti-aircraft machine gun. The first three were shot down by fighters"[46]. But, according to Amosova, all of the four *Polikarpovs* were shot down by *Luftwaffe* night fighters. "The anti-aircraft guns stopped, and a German fighter plane came and shot down four of our aircraft as each one came over the target".

Josef Kociok (left) and his radio operator, *Feld-webel* Alexander Wegerhoff, on 1 August 1943, beaming with happiness after their successful night of air combat on the Kuban. Actually, during the night of 31 July 1943, Kociok claimed three *Polikarpovs*. He was the only German pilot to claim Soviet night bombers[47]. It could be a case of under-claiming. In several cases, the aerial destruction of Soviet airplanes was not credited to German pilots, which were submitted to a strict system of verification. Or the victory claim could not be confirmed.

Josef "Sepp" Kociok poses proudly by the tail of his *Messerschmitt Bf 110*. He points out the last three marks of the air victories numbers 25, 26 and 27 that he has just achieved during the night of 31 July 1943. He is wearing the coveted Knight's Cross of the Iron Cross, his last award, received a few hours before shooting down the three "Night Witches'" aircraft. He had received the *Eisernes Kreuz* (Iron Cross), 2nd Class on 1941, the *Eisernes Kreuz* 1st Class, on 1942. On 1 June 1943 he had received the *Ehrenpokal der Luftwaffe*; on 2 December 1942 the *Deutsches Kreuz* (German Cross in Gold) and in 1943 the *Frontflugspange* (Combat Flying Clasp for Fighter Pilots in Gold), which was awarded only after 110 combat missions.

Exactly eight weeks after killing six (or eight) "Night Witches," on 26 September, Kociok intercepted a Russian *DB-3* bomber, 20 km south of Kerch. Kociok fired from pointblank range, hitting the Russian bomber but soon after he collided with the aircraft. He and Wegeroff parachuted out. However, Kociok's chute did not open and he fell to his death. He was buried with full honours in the military cemetery of Kerch.

Serafima Amosova in foreground, left, with navigators Nina Danilova and Galina Bespalova. "When we landed and reported that we were being attacked by German fighters", Amosova recalled, about 31 July 1943, "they would not let us fly again that night. We lived in a school building with folding wooden beds. You can imagine our feelings when we returned to our quarters and saw eights beds folded, and we knew they were the beds of our friends who perished a few hours ago. It was impossible not to cry. It was a great loss and pain but none of us surrendered, and we were full of anger and decided to pay the enemy back for the loss of our friends"[48]. Danilova holds the barrel of a 7.62 mm Nagant Model 1895G revolver. This pistol, actually designed in the early 1890s by the Belgian brothers Emile and Leon Nagant, was widely used and produced in the USSR during the Great Patriotic War. In the Soviet Union, production ceased in the 1950s. (Archive of A. Plyac)

"Night Witches" honouring the memory of Dusya Nosal. During the summer and fall of 1943, sixteen "Night Witches" were killed in combat in Kuban and Taman peninsulas. It is recognizable, first from the left, Zoya Parfenova. Parfenova was nearly killed during a mission over the famed Blue Line, which involved dreadful weather, powerful anti-aircraft artillery, and élite *Luftwaffe* air regiments. During a mission to bomb enemy troops near the village of Slavyanskaya, the mechanism of the bomb release of her biplane was damaged by *flak*. But Parfenova managed to fly back and land on her airfield with the bombs still attached. During the final attack to the Blue Line, she flew combat missions to Chushka Spit, to bomb the still resisting Axis troops. (Archive of A. Plyac)

The *46 GvNBAP* in early September 1943, before the attack to Novorossiysk. Standing, touching her hair, is pilot Nadya Popova. She is wearing, on her left chest, the Guards Badge and the Order of the Great Patriotic War 1st Class. In front of her, sitting, with a black cap, is pilot Ira Sebrova, future Hero of the Soviet Union. Far right, Vera Belik, still with cotton in her ears. "During the battle at Novorossiysk, a city on the Black Sea," Popova recalled later, "our regiment was located about twenty kilometers from the city, in a resort area behind a low hill. While we were stationed here we fulfilled two combat missions in cooperation with the naval fleet... A part of our navy troops occupied a small territory of the city on the sea coast, and they had sent a radio message that they had no water, ammunition, medical supplies, or food and asked for urgent assistance..." Popova and Ryabova took off and when they were near to the city, they muffled the engine and descended to low altitude, dropping the cargo of supplies to the Soviet marines. Other "Night Witches" followed, dropping food and ammunitions as well, allowing the marines to resist. (Archive of A. Plyac)

In this second picture, far left, bent and in dark overall, is deputy commander Serafima Amosova. During the night of 15-16 September, the "Night Witches" took off to support the offensive of the Red Army aimed to free Novorossiysk. At the command post of their airfield there were Ivan Yefimovich Petrov, Commander of the Independent Maritime Army, Konstantin Andreyevich Vershinin, Commander of 4th Air Army, and Yermachenko, Commander of Naval Aviation of the Black Sea. "Throughout the night, our aircraft," recalled Amosova, "neutralized the remaining centers of enemy resistance. At daybreak we received an order to bomb the HQ of Nazi troops, located in the center of Novorossiysk. So we took again. As a result of this raid, the HQ was destroyed"[49]. (Archive of A. Plyac)

Nadya Popova (left) and Larisa Rozanova-Litvinova. Nadezhda Vasiliyevna Popova was born on 17 December 1921, in Shabanovka (now Dolgoye) in Orel Region, Russia. Her parents were of working class. She grew her up in the Donetsk (Ukraine), in the area of the coal fields, where she first flew her combat missions with *46 GvNBAP*. As a teenager, she had no interest in aviation. She desired to become an actress and performed in amateur shows, singing and acting. She decided to become a pilot after a small aircraft landed in Donetsk near her house. She flew solo when she was just 16. She got a Voroshilov Sharpshooter Badge and after graduation, she trained at the Donetsk Flying Club. To be posted to Kherson Flying School in Ukraine she needed the help of the Hero of Soviet Union, Polina Osipenko. She graduated from Kherson in 1940 and became a flying instructor. Meanwhile her brother was killed at the front and they had to abandon their house because of the German invasion. She then requested Komsomol for assignment to the air force and was henceforth posted to the 122 Air Group. (Archive of A. Plyac)

Nadya Popova and Natalya Meklin. "I was shot down several times," recalled Popova, "my aircraft was burning and I made some forced landings, but my friends used to say I was born under a lucky star; I was never even wounded"[50]. In this picture, Popova already wears the Gold Star of Hero of the Soviet Union (awarded to her on 23 February 1945), while Meklin wears two Orders of the Red Banner. (Archive of A. Plyac)

Some unidentified "Night Witches" reading newspapers before a mission. The Soviet women pilots were highly educated and cultured, and loved to read books and newspapers. "The pilots, navigators and technical staff all came from universities and colleges," recalled Captain Klavdiya Ilyushina, engineer of the regiment. From late August to October 1943, eight *Polikarpovs* with their pilots and navigators operated with the Black Sea Fleet to support Soviet marines trying to re-capture Novorossiysk. Meanwhile, the other "Night Witches" fought along with the Red Army to retake the Taman peninsula. (Archive of A. Plyac)

In October 1943, the 46th Night Bomber Regiment was awarded the "Taman" honorary designation for its combat service in that region of southwest Russia. That was the usual procedure in the Soviet armed forces, to give the appellation of a city or a locality to a regiment that had distinguished itself for feats in battle in that region. In the picture, Yevdokiya Bershanskaya salutes the deployed regiment, followed by Yevdokiya Rachkevich, navigator and political commissar of the regiment. (Archive of A. Plyac)

Yevgeniya Zhigulenko. She started as a navigator but later managed to be retrained as a pilot. During the fall of 1943, the "Night Witches" experienced some of their most demanding sorties, supporting the Red Army in its amphibious operations in the Crimea. "The Soviet Army began advancing into the Crimean Peninsula," recalled Yevgeniya Zhigulenko. The 46th was tasked to stop enemy bombers from taking off to attack their airfields every few minutes. Zhigulenko and her navigator had to drop small firebombs on the German airstrip to indicate the target to other planes. Afterwards they decided to "fly on five kilometers to the fascist weapon storage area and bomb it. We dropped bombs and set the building on fire... Then the guns all fired along with searchlights... When I saw the storage building flaming above me and the moon below me, I knew we entered a stall. The plane was shaking, losing flying speed and altitude... I called to my navigator to give me directions, but there was no reaction. I turned in my seat and to my horror found no navigator." With the fuel line hit, losing height and speed, still Zhigulenko managed to cross the Strait of Kerch and to land on the seashore. At that moment she heard her navigator's voice: "While we were stalling, her seat had fallen to the bottom of the cabin, and her leg had stuck into the broken floor"[51]. (Archive of A. Plyac)

Navigator Olga Timofeyeva Golubeva-Teres. Golubeva worked at first as an instrument technician. Subsequently she requested to be trained as a navigator. According to Golubeva-Teres' flight log, she and her pilot Nina Ulyanenko, on 6 December 1943, flew seven sorties over the Kerch Strait. Weather conditions were typical of Russian early winter: heavy, dark clouds, wet snow, and fog. The crew had virtually no navigational reference points. They flew five missions dropping supplies only with the help of a flashlight operated by the Soviet troops. They were subsequently ordered to bomb Eltigen, for their seventh mission, as the marines had broken through Mitridat Mountain. Golubeva-Teres recalled, in her book[52], how Ulyanenko had "nerves of steel, tremendous willpower, and remarkable self-control"[53]. When the "Night Witches" moved north, Golubeva become Zoya Parfenova-Akimova's second navigator and they flew some joint missions over Poland, before Parfenova was wounded. (Courtesy of Olga Golubeva's family)

Zoya Parfenova-Akimova. At the end of the war she had amassed a total of 2,035 flying hours and 715 combat sorties. Her decorations included the Order of the Red Star and the Order of the Patriotic War 1st Class, two Orders of the Red Banner, the Medal for the Defense of Caucasus (in the picture, far right) plus, of course, the Gold Star of Hero of the Soviet Union (awarded on 18 August 1945) and the Order of Lenin.

Left to right, Anya Bondareva and Tatyana Kostina. They were both navigators of the *46 GvNBAP*. Kostina survived the war but very little is known of her after the end of the conflict. Bondareva took off during the night of 27-28 January 1944 for a sortie, with pilot Taisya Volodina, but they never came back and were reported as missing in action. Nothing was known of them until, on 10 March 1944, "their aircraft, which was smashed into bits, was found by a peasant in the flood near Chernoyerkovskaya" as Rudneva recalled in her diary, on 27 March 1944. "The bodies were exhumed and brought back here in an ambulance aircraft." On 29 March 1944 entry, Rudneva wrote about Bondareva and Volodina: "Yesterday we had a weather appropriate for a funeral: it rained all day and in the evening. The girls were buried to the accompaniment of an orchestra and the salute of twenty rifles"[54]. (Archive of Anatoly Plyac)

Pilot Taisya Volodina. She lost her life on the night of 27-28 January 1944 when her aircraft crashed northeast of Novorossiysk, near the Russian port on the Black Sea.

"Night Witches" on the truck bringing them to their biplanes. Right to left: Nadezhda Studilina (navigator), Antonina Khudyakova (pilot), an unidentified air woman, Alexandra Akimova (squadron's navigator), and Yelena Nikitina (navigator). On 15 May 1944[55], the "Night Witches" were transferred to Belarus, under the command of Marshal Konstantin Rokossovsky, who was commanding the Central Front (renamed 1st Belorussian Front), during the Soviet advance through Belarus and into Poland. In that theater the 46th was tasked several times to strafe Axis troops in daylight. "On the Belorussian Front along the Neman River (also known as Nyoman, Niemen, or Nemunas - is a major Eastern European river rising in Belarus and flowing through Lithuania before draining into the Baltic Sea at Klaipėda – Edit.), there was a brisk advance of our troops," recalled Akimova. Suddenly at night she and the other "Witches" were ordered to get into the *Polikarpovs* and train the machineguns in the direction of the front line. "Some of the Germans had broken through. We were to shoot at the Germans from the aircraft on the ground. We stayed in our planes all night and fired at the enemy. The next day at dawn we could plainly see the Germans who had broken through. They were nearby, behind the house where our aircraft were stationed"[56].

Alexandra Fedorovna Akimova, in a typical over-sized male flight suit delivered to the Soviet air-women. During their stay in Belarus, the "Night Witches" were sometimes ordered to fly daylight missions. "In Belarus we were stationed in one of the villages," recalled Akimova. "The commander of the front called our unit because one small German group had broken out, and we were to look for them." The girls soon took off for a reconnaissance mission and then, after they located the enemy, they were ordered to attack them. "I fired at them with my machinegun... We did not want to kill, but we were in the regiment to fight and free our motherland... When we saw the captured Germans... we couldn't look at them without a throbbing of the heart. They were miserable figures in shabby clothes, absolutely starving, thin and weak, and we experienced a kind of pity even for the enemy." After the war, Akimova admitted feeling uncomfortable in killing young men, even if they were the enemy. "The very nature of a woman rejects the idea of fighting. A woman is born to give birth to children, to nurture. Flying combat missions is against our nature, only the tragedy of our country made us join the army, to help our country, to help our people... to be in the military is not quite natural for a woman"[57]. (Archive of A. Plyac)

Standing, left to right: Yelena Salikova, navigator; Olga Klyueva, navigator. Sitting, M. Olkhovskaya, technician; Anna Visotskaya, pilot, and Irina Kashirina, navigator, both killed on 31 July 1943; Marina Chechneva, pilot, Hero of the Soviet Union. Discouraged from becoming a professional pilot while still at the flying club before the war, Chechneva persevered and became one of the most skilled and bravest "Night Witches." She was assigned the most difficult and demanding missions. While in Belarus, Chechneva flew up to 18 sorties, amassing, at the end of the war, 1,000 flying hours and 810 combat missions. She was awarded the Gold Star and title of Hero of the Soviet Union on 15 August 1946.

★

Captain Klavdiya Ilyushina, engineer of aircraft equipment. Born in Moscow in 1916, she starved often during her youth. After secondary school, she entered a technical college, studying engineering and electronics. Afterwards, she worked in an electrical station but kept studying, joining the aviation department of a military engineering academy. She got married and graduated in 1941. When she volunteered for the front, she was posted to the 122 Air Group. Her husband was enrolled in the army and was killed in action. "In the Crimea we were advancing," she recalled, "and we moved into an Ukrainian settlement, a village; we were billeted in their houses... The housewife cooked special cakes and eggs and other good things to eat. We were so excited and happy that we at last were going to have substantial meals and a good sleep. By then all I could think about and dream about was a full night's sleep." Ilyushina dreamed that their aircraft were being bombed, when the housewife woke her up: Germans were bombing the airfield. She rushed to the airfield but "a German plane came down the road, following me with tracer bullets. He was flying at such a low altitude that I could see his face. I threw myself flat on the ground, and he flew over me"[58]. Ilyushina survived the war and remained in the military. She retired at 45 with the rank of lieutenant colonel.

Yevgeniya Maksimovna Rudneva, regiment's navigator. On 9 April 1944, while *46 GvNBAP* was back in the Crimea, she was given the assignment to bomb a German airfield at Bulganak, near Kerch. It was Rudneva's 645th mission. Her aircraft was clearly visible at an altitude of 600 m (1967 ft), against a thin layer of clouds lit by the moon above. "I watched them approach the target and drop their bombs," recalled Popova, "and then the searchlights were switched on and caught the plane in their web. A burst of fire shelled their aircraft, and it was immediately put on fire". The plane took fire near Bagerovo. "The flares that they carried began exploding". Rudneva chose not to burn alive and jumped from the aircraft, dying on the impact with the ground, as she did not wear – like all the other "Night Witches" – a parachute. "The burning plane crashed while the searchlight continued to hold it in their lights." She was the only daughter of her family, and reportedly had never been kissed even if she was engaged to Captain Ivan Slavik, since November 1943. Rudneva was awarded the Gold Star and title of Hero of the Soviet Union posthumously on 26 October 1944. A main belt asteroid, discovered on 11 September 1972 by Nikolai Chernykh at the Crimean Astrophysical Observatory (CrAO), in Nauchnyi, Ukraine, was named after her. (Archive of A. Plyac)

Polina "Panna" Prokopyeva. She was the pilot of Yevgheniya Rudneva, on the fatal night of 9 April 1944. A native of Irkutsk, one of the largest Russian cities in Siberia, Prokopyeva was a fellow countrywoman of pilot Kaleriya Rylskaya-Tsiss. She was a new, inexperienced pilot. "Calm and composed, all she lacked was sufficient combat experience," recalled Rylskaya[59]. Nadezhda Popova recalled, referring to Rudneva: "That night she was to fly with me, but she said that it was the first night flight of a new pilot (Prokopyeva – Edit.), and she would like to bomb with her. The assignment was very dangerous, and there were lots of fascist troops concentrated near the target"[60]. "When I was approaching my aircraft that night before take off, I tripped and I thought it was bad that Yevgeniya was flying with the new pilot - something would happen. I felt this in my heart, and when I looked into the face of that young pilot I saw something unusual, a disturbance"[61].

Nadya Popova, extreme right, witnessed the death of Yevgeniya Rudneva. The other "Night Witches" are, left to right: pilot Tatyana Makarova, with her navigator Vera Lukyanovna Belik, Polina Gelman, Katya Ryabova and pilot Dina Nikulina. Makarova and Belik were two of the most skilful "Night Witches". They escaped death many times, before finally being shot down on 25 August 1944. They had flown many dangerous missions over the Ukrainian steppe, the foothills of the Caucasus, the Kuban, Novorossiysk, the Taman and Crimean peninsulas, Belarus, and Poland. Belik, born on 5 August 1921, was the first daughter of a master electrician of the Voykov Plant Workers' Settlement near Kerch, in the Crimea. She was studying at the "Karl Liebknecht" Pedagogical Institute in Moscow when the German invaded the Soviet Union.

Tanya Makarova, at the beginning of her career as a "Night Witch". She is wearing, on her left chest, the first Order of the Red Banner which was awarded to her on September 1942. Makarova was a fearless pilot. To bomb more accurately, she often flew her biplane as low as 100-150 meters, breaking the rules that they fly at a safe height. She was regarded as a first class pilot, always cool and well coordinated. On the night of 25 August 1944, she took off with her navigator Vera Belik. They successfully bombed German tanks near Zambrów, in northeastern Poland. German anti-aircraft artillery reacted very violently, but thanks to her skill, Makarova managed to escape enemy fire. But during the return flight, when they were near the base, they were attacked by a German night fighter. The *Polikarpov* was set on fire and Makarova, notwithstanding all her attempts, could not manage to extinguish the flames. The aircraft crashed, killing the two "Night Witches." It was Makarova's 628th sortie and Belik's 813th. The two girls were buried in Ostrołęka, a town situated in northeastern Poland, on the Narew River, about 120 km (75 miles) northeast of the Polish capital, Warsaw. They were both awarded the Gold Star and title of Hero of Soviet Union, posthumously, on 23 February 1945.

Tanya Makarova and Vera Belik in front of their *Polikarpov*, divided by the wooden propeller of the biplane. "With her narrow and slightly rounded shoulders and a gentle oval face, Tanya Makarova resembled a flower on a long stern," recalled Natalya Meklin after the war. "Always a little ashamed of looking too feminine and not at all like a pilot, Tanya, to make up for it, strove to put on a reckless and merry air, and purposely spoke in a somewhat rude tone, but she never succeeded in fooling anyone." The night she was shot down, chief navigator Lara Rozanova, who flew with all the pilots by turns, had planned to fly with Tanya,

while Belik had been assigned to another pilot. "However they both objected. They prevailed and flew their last mission together… At dawn friendly ground troops told us they had found, in the battle zone, the remains of our aircraft with two scorched corpses in it. Apparently, it was shot down by one of the enemy fighters which for several days had been operating in our sector, hunting for our Po-2"[62].

After the death of Belik and Makarova, their girlfriends inscribed on this *Polikarpov*, just like they did after the death of Dusya Nosal: "To avenge our comrades Tanya Makarova and Vera Belik!" The two "Night Witches" were shot down by a *Luftwaffe* night fighter ace from *4./NJG 100*. That unit, equipped with *Junkers Ju 88*, was based just southwest of Zambrów, their target. The *NJG 100* was actually the only German air regiment that claimed any air victory against a *Polikarpov* during the night of 24-25 August 1944. *Leutenant* Richter shot down a *Polikarpov* at 22.52 of 24 August, recording his victory number seven. Another pilot from the same unit, *Leutenant* Klaus Scheer, shot down a second *Polikarpov* biplane at 01.35 of 25 August, his victory number 17.

"Night Witches" pushing a truck stuck in the mud. "When we advanced into Poland it became extremely difficult because the fields were so muddy, our aircraft, the Po-2, could not take off - the wheels stuck in the mud," Irina Rakobolskaya recalled. "The fuel trucks could not move in the mud either. We took apart long fences and laid them down to make runways. The crew would seize the wings of the plane and hold on while the pilot revved up the engine; then, when she signaled, they would let go, and the plane took off. When they landed, it was in the mud where the crew again seized the wings and pushed the plane back to the log runway. It was then refueled by carrying the fuel in jerry cans to the plane. Trucks couldn't come to the aircraft, so everything had to be carried to it"[63].

"Night Witches" armorers loading bombs on a *Polikarpov*. While in Poland, because of the thick mud that hampered truck on the airfield, everything had to be transported by hand. Each night the ground crews hand-carried three tons of bombs to the planes. As the lower wing was close to the ground, it was extremely difficult for the armorers to lift the bombs and fix them to the plane. "They crawled on their knees with the bombs in their arms," recalled Rakobolskaya[64].

Armorer Alexandra Akimova, fixing the under-wing bomb rack. "The biggest compilation to our duty was that we had to work at night loading the bombs," recalled Olga Yerokhina-Averyanova, "and we used torches. If the batteries gave out, we were forced to load the bombs by feeling with our hands where to attach then to the aircraft"[65]. Yerokhina survived the war and become a doctor after the war.

"Night Witches" checking maps on their "planchettes" before their combat sorties. Left to right: Aleksandra Akimova (pilot), Rufa Gasheva (navigator), Maguba Syrtlanova, unidentified, and Tatyana Kostina. Gasheva was regarded as one of the best navigators. She was born on 14 October 1921 in Verkhne-Chusovkiye Gorodki (today Chusovsk). Gasheva was the daughter of a schoolteacher. She was in the third year of the faculty of Mechanics and Mathematics at Moscow State University when she joined Raskova's Air Group. Gasheva bombed with precision and could navigate precisely, even in absolute darkness or when her plane was caught by the beams of blinding searchlights. She even assisted her pilot in evading enemy fire. However, once, returning from the Crimea, she almost fell out of the aircraft. Gasheva asked her pilot to execute two loops, but she had forgotten to wear her safety harness. During the second loop, she had to grab the sides of the cockpit in order to save herself from falling. Gasheva fought on the Southern Front, Trans and North Caucasus Fronts, 4th Ukrainian, and 2nd Belorussian Fronts. She took part in the liberation of Ukraine, the Caucasus, the Kuban, Taman and Crimea peninsulas, and Belarus. Finally, she flew in Poland and Germany, amassing 848 combat missions.

Rufina Sergeyevna Gasheva. In this picture she is holding the rank of *Leytenant*. On 13 December 1944, she took off with her pilot Olga Sanfirova for her 813rd mission. For a strange twist of fate, they had to bomb the station of Nasielsk, the same village that Makarova and Belik had attacked before being shot down. "We were approaching the front line when I noticed that the starboard wing had caught fire," recalled Gasheva later. Sanfirova tried to reach the Soviet-held territory, but at last they were forced to bail out on neutral territory. They were the first two "Night Witches" ever to use a parachute. "I pulled the rip cord. For some reason, the parachute failed to open, and I kept falling into the dark abyss like a stone. I was horror struck. Then I summoned my final strength and pulled the rip cord again. The parachute opened above me with a strong jerk." Gasheva landed in a mine field. "My hand came across something cold, metallic. The object was cylindrical in shape... it was a mine!" She had landed in a field of anti-tank mines. Avoiding the mines, she carefully crawled toward the Soviet trenches. The soldiers took care of her: "Only then I

sensed how tired I was. My leg were frozen - I had lost my flying boots. I was wearing a fur sock on one foot; the other was missing... I didn't dare to ask about Lelya"[66]. (Archive of A. Plyac)

Olga Sanfirova touched down about 500 meters (1,640 feet) to the north of Gasheva, when she baled out of her burning aircraft, on 13 December 1944. Unfortunately, she landed on a field with anti-personnel mines. A Soviet officer – recalled pilot Raisa Zhitova-Yushina – called to her and told her to go to the right. "But he meant to *his* right, and they went to their right, and Olga stepped on a mine. It exploded and tore off her leg and she was screaming, and the Soviet officer ran out to help her and stepped on a mine." Sanfirova, notwithstanding her severe mutilation, kept on crawling desperately toward Soviet lines, but in doing so, she pressed the fuse of another mine with her chest. The explosion tore her apart. When Gasheva was told that Sanfirova had been blown up by a mine, fell in utter shock. At dawn, Sanfirova was removed from the minefield. "I came out of the dugout to take a look at her. She was lying in a two-wheeled cart, her head inclined toward one shoulder. I saw her face only; the rest of her body was covered with tarpaulin"[67]. When at last she saw Sanfirova in the coffin for the last goodbye, she fainted. (Archive of A. Plyac)

Olga Sanfirova held the rank of guards *Kapitan* and she had flown 630 combat missions. Her awards included the Orders of Lenin, the Red Banner (two), the Patriotic War (first class), and – not common even for the "Night Witches" – the Aleksander Nevskiy. She was born on 2 May 1917, and was of Tatar origin. When she was an adolescent, she moved with her family in Uzbekistan, where she graduated from high school. She worked as a laboratory technician at the locomotive plant in Kolomna (*Коломна*), a city 114 kilometers (71 mi) southeast of Moscow, at the confluence of the Moskva and Oka Rivers, and where she joined an air club. Subsequently she enrolled at the Bataysk Flying School of Civil Aviation. She soon became the best student of the group. "Sanfirova flew with ease, like a bird, for she had an innate flying talent." When the war started, she was a flying instructor in a training air squadron near Novosibirsk, but in December 1941 she joined the 122 Air Group[68]. She graduated in 1940. Sanfirova was buried in Grodno (now Hrodna in Belarus, located on the Neman River, about 20 km from the Polish border) then in Soviet territory. Streets in Grodno and in her home town – that reverted to its ancient name of Samara – were named after her. (Archive of A. Plyac)

Rufina Gasheva (second from the right) among her girlfriends. Left to right: Natalya Meklin, Khivaz Dospanova, Katya Ryabova, Tatyana Sumarokhova and Nina Ulyanenko.

Vera Bondarenko, aircraft mechanic. The night support personnel of the "Night Witches" had to become accustomed to very uncomfortable conditions. "There were no hangars or stationary repair workshops," recalled squadron mechanic Antonina Vakhromeyeva. "Our Po-2s were based on random, unprepared airstrips, where we thoroughly camouflaged them and carried out field repairs, all on our own." At night, the mechanics had to meet the aircraft, inspect them, top off their tanks with fuel and lubricant, and repair defects and damages. All works had to be done in the dark by flashlights, and sometimes in the moonlight, as not to reveal the airfield location[69].

"Night Witches" in the typical oversized winter flying suits. Left to right: Tatyana Sumarokhova (navigator), Yekaterina Olcinik (pilot), Aleksandra Akimova (navigator), Yekaterina Ryabova (navigator), Mariya Smirnova (pilot), Anna Yelenina (Deputy chief of staff) and Marina Chechneva (pilot).

★

Right to left: Polina Petkelyova, navigator; pilot Raisa Zhitova-Yushina, flight commander; Mariya Pinchuk, navigator. Zhitova-Yushina was born in 1921. When she was assigned to the "Night Witches" on 13 July 1943, she had more than a thousand flying hours as a flying instructor. In Poland she experienced one of the most trying combat sorties of the "Night Witches." "In Poland in 1945 we were bombing Königsberg (now Kaliningrad, included in Russia – Edit.) as a snowstorm was approaching, but we persuaded Commander Bershanskaya to let us make one flight. We bombed successfully and then started to return home, but the ground was covered with heavy, heavy snow, and we were flying just above the trees. When we arrived at the area of the airdrome we couldn't find it, because we were flying in a milk of heavy snow. The stress was so intense my legs began to shake, and I knew the plane was turning yet I couldn't do anything to make it fly straight." At last, she managed to land and to take off and return to the airfield when the weather improved. But other crews were not so lucky: "Eight of our planes didn't return that night to their home field, one crew crashed, and one lost its landing gear while landing"[70].

Yevdokiya Bershanksya (center), evaluating the flight performance of an unknown *46 GvNBAP*'s crew. The "Night Witches" developed, sortie after sortie, an astonishing skill to fly and locate the target – most of the times – even in the utter darkness, without the need to illuminate the area with flares. "We used no illumination in our bombing because dropping flares by parachute lit up everything," recalled pilot Raisa Zhitova-Yushina, "and the enemy could see our planes and shoot us down. So no lights, no navigation lights. When a new pilot arrived at the regimental airdrome she had orientation flights with an instructor, and… after three or four flights she would start to see the small differences in the shadings of the terrain and adjust to seeing at night. When we went on bombing missions we were told only the approximate locations of the target, and it was our responsibility to find the target, bomb it, and return to our airdrome. I flew about eighteen hundred hours during the war from 1943 and 1945"[71].

Still Yevdokiya Bershanskaya, giving the last instructions to Larisa Rozanova (holding the map for the mission in her "planchette") and her pilot. Natalya Meklin, Hero of Soviet Union, recalled her commander: "During operational flying, she was always present at the take-off strip and, if necessary, flew missions herself… Invariably Bershanskaya would approach the aircraft awaiting the clearance to take off, to give the pilot her final instructions. Only a few parting words. For example: "Be careful." She really didn't have to say anything: the pilot already knew all there was to know about the mission and the air situation. However, Bershanskaya persisted in her habit. She did not smile and her voice sounded a bit cold. Nevertheless, behind her severe look we always detected warmth, trust, and something else which made us eager not merely to execute a most difficult mission, but also fly to the ends of the earth to accomplish the impossible"[72]. (Archive of A. Plyac)

Natalya Meklin with her awards. On 8 March 1945, in the Polish town of Tuchola, she was awarded with the Gold Star of Hero of Soviet Union and the Order of Lenin (along with eight other "Night Witches") by Marshal K. K. Rokossovskiy, Commander of the Second Belarussian Front. Her decorations included the Order of the Red Star, three Orders of the Red Banner, two Orders of Patriotic War and several campaign medals (bottom, left, the Medal for the Defence of Caucasus). With her regiment, Meklin fought along the Southern, Trans-Caucasian, North-Caucasian, 4th Ukrainian and second Belorussian fronts. She bombed *Wehrmacht* troops in North Caucasus, Kuban, Taman and Crimean peninsulas, Belarus, Poland and Germany.

Left, Colonel-General K. A. Vershinin, Commander of the 4th Air Army in which the *46 GvNBAP* was included. In the background, Natalya Meklin. Vershinin described her as: "a confident, fearless pilot. Neither anti-aircraft artillery nor enemy searchlights could prevent her from reaching her assigned target. She devotes all of her energy and applies all of her combat skill in executing the sorties that her commander have assigned to her. Her performance are a model for the entire personnel"[73].

Aleksandra Popova

Left to right: pilot Nina Altsibeyeva, navigator Aleksandra Popova, pilot Antonina Khudyakova e technic Aleksandra Radko. On the night of 9 March 1945, the *Polikarpovs*, armed with four explosive bombs and one flare bomb to illuminate the target, took off to bomb Danzig. Popova's aircraft never returned from that sortie. "To break through the menacing curtain of fire and light, we overflew the north-western district of Danzig," recalled Squadron Navigator Tatyana Sumarokhova. The aircraft piloted by Klava Serebryakova and navigator Aleksandra Popova also headed in that direction. "After we returned in the morning, we waited for them at the airfield, peering into the cloudy sky until our eyes hurt. We waited until there was no longer any hope." Serebryakova had 550 mission to her credit. She was found, unconscious and wounded, under the debris of her aircraft by Soviet soldiers, on the eastern bank of the Vistula River. Popova was unhurt and went back to her regiment, while Serebryakova was hospitalized in Tambov. "Her limbs suspended, motionless, Klava was bedridden for eighteen endless months... many times the bones had to be skillfully re-broken so that they could grow together correctly." Against all odds, thanks to her will to live, she walked again. After the war she married, had two daughters and worked as a high school history teacher and in Oktyabrsk, in Bashkiria, teaching to the children of oilmen[74].

Tatyana Nikokayevna Sumarokhova, navigator of *46 GvNBAP*.

On 3 May 1945, the day after Berlin fell, Irina Sebrova and Natalya Meklin flew at a height of under two hundred feet over the Third Reich capital in daytime. Berlin, all ruined and swathed with smoke, was burning. "The city was devastated," recalled Meklin. "But I felt no pity – not a trace. I thought, as I flew over this place where so much misery had been planned, that the Germans had got exactly what they deserved. It was not so much a feeling of hatred – that was already beginning to go. I just felt satisfaction"[75]. Sebrova and Meklin descended to a hundred feet along *Unter den Linden* ("under the linden trees"), the boulevard in the *Mitte* district of Berlin. They circled around the Brandeburg Gate (in the picture). Soon after they climbed to four hundred feet and wheeled slowly over the Reichstag (*Reichstagsgebäude)*, turning over the red banner that had been posted on the roof of the building that had housed the Parliament of the German Empire. (Archive of A. Plyac)

Record-woman: senior lieutenant Irina "Ira" Fedorovna Sebrova with her awards. Sebrova – a former locksmith and a repairer of sewing machines at a cardboard manufacturing plant – was the most successful "Night Witch". Bombing on the Southern, TransCaucasus, North Caucasus, 4th Ukrainian and 2nd Belorussian Fronts, on Poland and Germany, she scored the highest number of missions and flying hours ever reached in the *46 GvNBAP*: 1,100, of which 1,008 were combat sorties! She was awarded the Gold Star – and title of Hero of the Soviet Union – on 23 February 1945, the Order of Lenin, the Order of the Red Banner (thrice), the Order of the Patriotic War and the Order of the Red Banner. Recommending her, in October 1944, for the title of Hero of the Soviet Union, her commander, Yevdokiya Bershanskaya, reported: "Sebrova… is a very competent bomber pilot; she is brave, confident and persistent."

Yevdokiya Bershanskaya, commander of the "Night Witches", in front of the Brandenburg Gate (*Brandenburger Tor*) in the Pariser Platz ruins. When the Nazis ascended to power, they used the gate as a party symbol. The picture, as can be seen, was taken on 7 May 1943, the last day of combat for the "Night Witches." Bershanskaya's air regiment boasted eighteen pilots and six navigators who became Heroes of the Soviet Union, a much greater proportion than in the other women's regiments. The *125 GvBAP* had five Heroes of the Soviet Union, while the *586 IAP*, the fighter regiment, none. (Archive of A. Plyac)

Left to right, Guards majors and Heroes of the Soviet Union, on the Red Square, after the war: pilot Marina Chechneva, navigator Polina Gelman and pilot Raisa Aronova. Altogether they amassed 2,630 combat sorties.

Polina Gelman, with all her orders and campaign medals. May the 8th was the last day of the *46 GvNBAP* as an operational unit. "We were assigned a combat mission on May 8," recalled Gelman, "one day before the victory. Everything was ready, the bombs loaded and the crews on their way to the aircraft, when suddenly we saw the mechanics run to the aircraft, and do something. What they were doing was deactivating the bombs. The Germans had surrendered, the war was over. I burst out crying. Everybody cried that day"[76].

Raisa Aronova (center), with Natalya Meklin (left) and Katya Ryabova, right, in their typical oversized winter flying suite. Aronova was born on 10 February 1920, in Saratov, an industrial city on the Volga, in front of Engels. Her father, a railroad worker, abandoned her and his wife, a washerwoman, in 1936. She was raised by her mother, who found a job as a painter in a railway repair center. Aronova, still in high school, earned the Voroshilov Sharpshooter Badge and in 1938 she joined a flying club of paramilitary *Osoavyakhim*. She got her wings in 1939 and in 1940 she joined the Moscow Aviation Institute, to study aircraft design. She was enrolled in Raskova's Air Group were she was appointed navigator of the night bomber regiment. On 23 March 1943, she was wounded during a bombing mission on the Cossack village of Kievskaya. While recovering in the hospital in Essentuki, she learned that there was the chance to retrain as a pilot. She participated in this training and soon become a pilot. At the end of the war, she had flown 960 sorties and spent in the air, by night, 1,148 hours. Aronova was awarded the Gold Star and title of Hero of Soviet Union, plus the Order of Lenin (on 15 May 1946); moreover she was decorated with the Order of the Red Banner (twice), the Order of the Patriotic War 1st class, the Order of the Red Star, the Medal for the Defense of Caucasus and other several campaign medals.

Victory Parade. Some of the most succesful "Night Witches" walking the hall of fame in front of their old *Polikarpovs*. Left to right: navigator Rufa Gasheva, Hero of Soviet Union; pilot Ira Sebrova, Hero of the Soviet Union; pilot Natalya Meklin, Hero of Soviet Union; pilot Marina Chechneva, Hero of the Soviet Union; pilot Nadya Popova, Hero of the Soviet Union; deputy commander Serafima Amosova; pilot Yevdokiya Nikulina, Hero of the Soviet Union; Yevdokiya Bershanskaya, "Night Witches" only commander; pilot Mariya Smirnova, Hero of the Soviet Union; pilot Yevdokiya Zhigulenko, Hero of the Soviet Union. In August 1945, ten crews from *46 GvNBAP* took part in the victory parade in Moscow. The *46 GvNBAP* was reportedly the most successful *Polikarpov* unit. "Our regiment firmly held first place among all in the air forces for the number of flights," Polina Gelman stated[77]. The 46th boasted the largest number of Heroes of Soviet Union among all the Soviet *Polikarpov* regiments, even if that honorary title was awarded to a woman only after she had accomplished a number of sorties much more higher than that of a male pilot.

Bottom row, left to right, Yevdokiya Rachkevich, political commissar, and Yevdokiya Bershanskaya. Standing, Dina Nikulina and Serafima Amosova, deputy commander of the regiment. "Major Rachkevich, our deputy commander for political affairs, proved most helpful to me," recalled Amosova. "She made herself available at all times and always had the right thing to say, emboldening and cheering us up"[78]. According to several veterans of the Night Bomber Regiment, the large number of Heroes of the Soviet Union among the "Night Witches" was due to the political influence and the efforts of Rachkevich.

Yevdokiya Rachkevich (left) and Irina Rakobolskaya in front of the banner of the *46 GvNBAP*. "Our aircraft flew 1,100 nights of combat," Rakobolskaya recalled later. "There were 200 women in the regiment. We were the only regiment in the whole of the Red Army without any men serving in it… We started the war with two squadrons and finished the war with four. We trained our personnel at the front and had one auxiliary squadron used only for training"[79].

Navigator Yekaterina "Khivaz" Dospanova hugs another "Night Witch" who kisses her back. Relationships between the Soviet airwomen were sisterly and fraternal during all the conflict. Moreover the "Night Witches" never gave up their femininity even among the hardships of war. They usually regarded the war not as a "woman's business," something that they started just to defend their motherland. "There is an opinion about women in combat that a woman stops being a woman after bombing, destroying, and killing; that she becomes crude and tough," commented later Hero of Soviet Union, Mariya Smirnova. "This is not true; we all remained kind, compassionate, and loving. We became even more womanly, more caring of our children, our parents, and the land that has nourished us"[80].

"Khivaz" Dospanova, Hero of Kazakhstan. Dospanova was born in the village Ganushkino Guriev, now in Atyrau Region. In 1940, she finished school with a gold medal. Subsequently she joined an aeroclub. When she volunteered for the front, she was posted to the *588 NBAP* as a navigator-gunner. Khivaz flew more than 300 sorties over enemy lines. She was seriously injured when her aircraft collided with another *Polikarpov*. She lost the use of both legs, but wanted to go back to operations. For her bravery and courage Khivaz Dospanova was awarded the Order of the Red Star, the Order of the Red Banner, and many campaign medals. By decree of the President of Kazakhstan, on the eve of the 60th anniversary of the victory, Dospanova was awarded the title "Khalyk Kaharmany" (Халық қахарманы), People's Hero of Kazakhstan, the highest award conferred by the Republic of Kazakhstan, along with the Order of Golden Eagle. In 2010 a monument dedicated to her was unveiled. It is in the heart of the city of Atyrau, in the Asian part of the city on the avenue, near the Ural River. (Archive of A. Plyac)

NOTE

1   Kazimiera Cottam, *Women in War and Resistance*, p. 100

2   Anna Krylova, *Soviet Women in Combat*, p. 135

3   Anne Noggle, *A Dance with Death*, p. 30

4   Reina Pennington, *Wings, Women & War*, p. 84

5   Bruce Myles, *Night Witches,* p. 66

6   Pennington, p. 77

7   Noggle, p. 27

8   Noggle, p. 40

9   Bruce Myles, *Night Witches*, pp. 67-68

10   Myles, pp. 68-69

11   Myles, p. 69

12   Noggle, pp. 85-86

13   Noggle, pp. 58-59

14   Noggle, p. 96

15   Henry L. De Zeng IV and Douglas G. Stankey, *Bomber Units of the Luftwaffe 1933-1945 A Reference Source Volume,* p. 145

16   Noggle, p. 46

17   Christer Bergström, *Stalingrad – The Air Battle: 1942 through January 1943*, p. 69

18   Idem

19   Noggle, p. 26

20   Noggle, p. 68

21   Noggle p. 32

22   Noggle, p. 40

23   Cottam, *Women in Air War*, pp. 124-125

24   Noggle, p. 40

25   Noggle, pp. 23-24

26   Noggle, p. 36

27   Noggle, p. 55

28   Noggle, p. 55

29   Noggle, p. 86

30   Cottam, *Women in Air War*, pp.125-127

31   Rodric Braithwaite, *Moscow 1941*, p. 114

32   Noggle, pp. 74-75

33   *Plan Quadrat* 75 424, indicating a location immediately southwest of Novorissiysk

34   Cottam, *Women in Air war*, pp. 137-138; Cottam, *Women in War and Resistance*, pp. 74-75; Myles, *Night Witches*, pp.186-187-188; Pennington, p. 84

35   Franz Kurovski, *Wilhelm Batz*, p. 25

36   Cottam, *Women in Air War*, p. 183

37   Pennington, p. 84; Cottam, *Women in War and Resistance,* p. 65

38   Pennington, p. 84

39   Noggle p. 65

40   Cottam, *Woman in Air War*, p. 184

41   Idem

42   Cottam, *Women in Air War,* p. 183

43   Cottam, *Women in Air War*, p. 184

44   Cottam, *Women in Air War*, p. 185

45   Noggle, pp. 65-66

46   Cottam, *idem*

47   Foreman, Matthews, Parry, *Luftwaffe Night Fighter Combat Claims 1939-1945*, p. 100

48   Noggle, p. 46

49   Cottam, *Women in Air War*, pp. 142-143

50   Noggle, p. 82

51   Noggle, p. 82; Noggle, pp. 56-57

52   "Zvedy na kry'lyakh", Saratov, 1974, p. 11

53   Cottam, *Women in War and Resistance*, pp. 120-121

54   Cottam, *Women in Air War*, p. 191

55   Cottam, *Women in War and Resistance*, p. 79

56   Noggle, p. 93

57   Noggle, pp. 93-94

58   Noggle, p. 51

59   Cottam, *Women in Air War*, p. 145

60   Noggle, p. 84

61   Idem

62   Cottam, *Women in Air War*, pp. 160-161

63   Noggle, p. 28

64   Noggle, p. 29

65   Noggle, p. 59

66   Cottam, *Women in Air*, pp. 163-164

67   Noggle, p. 89

68   Cottam, *Women in War and Resistance*, pp. 52-55

69   Cottam, *Women in Air War*, p. 148

70   Noggle, pp. 89-90

71   Noggle, p. 90

72   Cottam, *Women in Air War*, p. 123

73   I. Ye. Gorobets et al. *Za muzhestvo I odvagu*, Kharkov, 1984, p. 224

74   Cottam, *Women in Air*, p. 194

75   Myles, p. 269

76   Noggle, p. 42

77   Pennington, p. 88

78   Cottam, *Women in Air War*, p. 142

79   Noggle, p. 30

80   Noggle, p. 37

SOVIET AIRWOMEN
OF THE GREAT PATRIOTIC WAR

586 IAP

Unit designations: 586th Fighter Aviation Regiment

Dates of service: 16 April 1942 - May 1945

Main operative areas: Saratov, Voronezh, Kostornaya, Kursk, Kiev, Zhitomir, Kotovsk, Beltsy, Debrecen and Budapest (Hungary)

Commanders: Tamara Kazarinova and Aleksandr Gridnev

Aircraft flown: *Yakovlev Yak-1, Yak-7 and Yak-9*

Female pilots: 37

Male pilots: 13

Female Staff and Political Officers: 20

Male Staff and Political Officers: 9

Female mechanics, armorers and engineers: 64

Male mechanics, armorers and engineers: 42

БОЕВОЙ ПУТЬ
586-го ИСТРЕБИТЕЛЬНОГО ПОЛКА

Map of *586 IAP* bases and movements during the Great Patriotic War. The Fighter Regiment was first based in Anisovka, near Saratov. Subsequently it moved to Voronezh, Kastornoe, Kursk, Zhitomir, Kotovsk, Beltsy, Debrecen, Tsinkot (Budapest), Vienna.

Valeriya Khomyakova, in front of the tail of her *Yakovlev Yak-1* fighter. Note the oversized flying suit that was issued to the women fighter regiment. "I remember when we received military clothing for the girls: jackets, overalls, boots, pants, all male clothing, everything was very large," recalled Yekaterina Polunina, *586 IAP* senior mechanic for armament. "We didn't receive any underwear for women… One of the girls received very, very large boots, and while she was checking the aircraft and getting it ready for a mission, she took off her boots and performed her job bare footed. At this moment the staff of the regiment was approaching. She realized that it was going to be a uniform violation and she would be punished, so she had to leave her job, jump into the boots, and stand straight in order to report to the staff"[1]. (Archive of Anatoly Plyac)

Mayor Tamara Aleksandrovna Kazarinova. The *586 IAP* started its active service on 16 April 1942 under her command. Tamara was one of two Kazarinova sisters that served in Soviet Air Force. She was the first

female cadet to get admission to the Military Theoretical School For Pilots in Leningrad, in 1929. Before, she had worked as a laboratory technician at the "Dinamo" Plant in Moscow. After graduating from the Military Theoretical School, she was sent to the Kacha Flying School and subsequently served in a ground attack *polk*. In 1937, she was awarded the Order of Lenin for her service. She was regarded as strict and severe. She rarely, if ever, flew after she took command of the Fighter Regiment, it seems because she had been wounded in the leg while servicing in the Caucasus. She is remembered to be merciless during post-flight debriefing. Reportedly, her squadron commanders and some of her most skilled pilots – Lidya Litvyak, Katya Budanova, Raysa Belyayeva and Klavdiya Nechayeva – were at odds with her right from the start, reportedly because they thought she was unable to fly the *Yak-1*. Kazarinova held command of 586th for just over six months.

Leytenant Aleksandra Aleksandrovna Makunina, chief of the staff. She was the second in command on the ground while Tamara Kazarinova was the regimental commander of *586 IAP* and she worked close with her. Before volunteering for Marina Raskova's air unit she was a postgraduate student of Physical Geography. She was a sports-woman: flew gliders, jumped with parachutes, and climbed mountains. Makunina was 24 when the war against Germany started. She was on an expedition to find minerals in the Urals. She came back to Moscow and, at first wanted to join the partisans on the ground. But she changed her mind and volunteered to Marina Raskova on 10 October 1941. She did want to become an aviator but Raskova

herself appointed her to be chief of staff. "In the regiments I've enough girls who can fly the planes, but to be chief of the staff I must be sure you are a person with brains," Raskova told her. "She would say that the staff was the brain of the regiment." She was also assigned the task to organize the work of the control post, responsible for the combat missions. "It was a strain for me to serve as a commander (of staff – Edit.), and as a consequence I began fainting. I never slept more than three hours a night, sometimes not at all... I asked to be appointed deputy commander because I couldn't physically stand the overstrain any longer"[2].

A *Yakovlev Yak-1* equipped with retractable skis. In January 1942, the 586th Regiment received 24 brand new *Yak-1s*[3]. Most of them had winter camouflage, made of washable white paint made of chalk and glue solution. Some others were painted khaki. The numbers on the fuselages all ended in zeroes: 10, 20, 30, etc. The landing gear had been replaced with retractable skis, 5 ft 5 ½ in long (165 cm) by 24 in (60 cm) wide for a total weight of 283 lbs (128 Kg). So equipped the *Yaks* could operate from snow-covered airstrips, and needed of just 820 ft (250 meters) to take off and 902 ft (275 m) to land. But the drag caused by the retracted skis slowed the *Yak-1* "winter version" down by 18.7/24.9 mph (30/40km/h). Future ace Boris Yeromin of *296 IAP*, the unit where Budanova and Litvyak were transferred in 1943, regarded it as a very unsatisfactory airplane, plagued with many maintenance problems. If a ski fell out of its lodgment, the aircraft would become uncontrollable. Pilots had to be very careful in landing and the skis proved too vulnerable. The *586 IAP's* fighters were part of the 830 *Yak-1s* ski-equipped built up to 25 February 1942. The *Yak-1* in the picture carries under the wing six rails for *RO-82* rockets.

A *Yak-1*, captured intact by the Germans (in the background, a *Junkers Ju 88*). The *Yak-1* was regarded as the best Soviet fighter in 1941. It was ideal for novice pilots with short training (like the *586IAP's* women pilots). It was stable and easy to land and take-off. The aircraft had light controls and was

very maneuverable. But every one of its variants was under-armed and the model of 1941 that was provided to the *586 IAP* was heavier than its main opponent, the *Messerschmitt Bf 109*. Having a weaker engine (*M-105P* with a power of 1,100 hp at 6,560 ft/2,000 mt), it was even slower in rate of climb at all altitudes. The *Messerschmitt,* thanks to its automatics flaps, was more stable in tight turns and in diving and climbing aerobatics. Moreover, being raw in construction, the *Yak-1* suffered from shortcomings like the ejection of oil from the gear valve.

The first base of the female fighter regiment was – for nine and a half months (24 April 1942 – 10 February 1943) - in Anisovka, a small settlement, southwest of Saratov outskirt. Here, the pilots from *586 IAP*

had the task to protect the *Yak-1* Factory Nr. 292, bridges, and railways. While in Anisovka, the 586th flew 509 sorties, 32 of them at night. In the picture, *586 IAP's* women, are getting out of a dugout in Anisovka airfield. Left to right, Mariya Batrakova, Aleksandra Akimova, Zinaida Solomatina, and Olga Shakova. Batrakova was credited with at least one kill (shared) of a reconnaissance twin-engine aircraft. She was awarded the Order of the Red Star for displaying competence on air mission defense and "boldness and bravery in strafing the encircled German troops near Korsun-Shevchenkovskiy."

◀◀ *Yak-1* with retractable skis. Note that the aircraft had no radio mast. Approximately 1,000 of the first *Yak-1s* produced in Saratov Plant Nr. 292 (where the 586th fighters had been produced), did not have even the simplest radio receiver. Subsequently by the end of 1941, for several months, only one *Yak-1* out of ten was installed with a radio. Among the *Yaks* delivered to the fighter regiment, only the squadron commander's aircraft had a *RSI-4* "Malyusha" two-way transmitting radio. The other *Yaks* only had receivers. But "our girls refused to fly without transmitters," remembered Irina Yemelianova, engineer for special equipment, "and they won." Raskova managed to acquire radios for the *Yaks*. However, in other regiments, many pilots removed them to save weight. The *RSI-4*'s range was inadequate and the quality of the radio link was scarce.

Two members of *586 IAP's* staff at work: *Adyutant* V. M. Eldakova and Lydia Aleksandrovna Bystrova, lieutenant of aviation (лейтенант авиации): note the two stars on the epaulet. There were about 20 girls servicing in 586th as staff members, political officers, or something similar.

Left to right, ground controller Nina Arkadevna Slovokhotova and pilot Zuleikha Gabibovna Seid-Mamedova. Slovokhotova helped pilots to plan the routes, explained how to avoid flak, and trained novice pilots in navigation. Her main task was, however, to work with the radar location station. The first radars were delivered in 1942 but the Soviets learned how to operate them effectively only the following year. In every base, the fighter regiment was given a certain area where to operate. The area was

divided into squares and Slovokhotova had the task to identify enemy aircraft on the radar screen and to direct the fighters to intercept them. "The radar was set up far from the runways and airdrome, usually three to five kilometers, and it was camouflaged so we were not bombed," she recalled later. She became one of the first radar navigation officers in the USSR.

Technicians of 586th Fighter Regiment servicing a *Yak-1*. Left to right: Antonina Yaroslavna Pyatrovskaya (armorer), Yekaterina Pavlovna Kirillova (engine mechanic), Valentina Ivanovna Abankina (armorer), Polina Gerasimovna Starova (instrument mechanic), Olga Afanasyevna Golubeva (engine mechanic). Armorers and motorists experienced extremely difficult conditions. During the winter, "when we touched the metal of the engine," remembered Senior Sergeant Galina Dobrovich, regimental mechanic of the aircraft, "our skin would stick to it and some of it came off on the metal. Our cheeks and foreheads were frozen too. On returning to the barracks our hands would be a deep blue color."

Female and male personnel of *586 IAP*. Originally in the 586th there were two squadrons of ten fighters each. The pilots were only women. Later, an additional squadron of male pilots joined the regiment. Many of the ground personnel were also men because the *Yaks* were quite sophisticated and the female mechanics had received only minimal training before moving to the front. "In our regiment the girls were attractive," remembered Senior Sergeant Yekaterina Polunina, mechanic of the aircraft. "They were very young and fresh, and nearby there was a male regiment. Well, they got acquainted and romance blossomed. Once, the commander of that male regiment came to our commander and said, 'I can give you as many aircraft as you want if you give me five girls (at this point he gave their names), let's make an exchange!'"[4].

Aircraft mechanic Yevgeniya Dmitryevna Borok, refuelling a *Yak* of *586 IAP* ready for take off. As the *Messerschmitt Bf 109*'s main advantage lay in vertical maneuverability, the Soviet designers in March 1942 lightened the *Yak-1* airframe. Of the 25 principle changes, one was the removal of the fuel tank's self-sealing feature. According to statistics, the production *Yak-1* managed to shoot down a German aircraft every 26 missions. The lightened *Yak* scored a kill every 18 sorties. It out-turned the *Bf 109*[5] but it easily burned when hit by enemy fire.

Klavdiya Ivanovna Kasatkina, regiment political organizer (*partorg*) wearing her Order of Red Star. "Captain Klavdiya Kasatkina, our party organizer," recalled Vera Tikhomirova, deputy political commander of the regiment, "was the life and the soul of our group. Always amongst our girls, she knew their needs and shared their joys and misfortunes. She was in demand everywhere: on the hardstands, on the take off strip, in the mess, in the workshops, and in the living quarters. The girls liked her and confided in her – whether they were happy or sad. Kasatkina went from one team to another; she would read a communiqué from the Soviet Information Bureau, hand out letters received from home for the girls, talk to the editor of the operational news bulletin, and sometimes would roll up her sleeves to assist those replacing a propeller"[6].

Senior Lieutenant (*Starshiy Leytenant*) Valentina Mikhailovna Lisitsina - assistant regimental commander, *586 IAP*, is at the combat simulator. The model she is aiming at is a *Yak-1*. The gun-sight appears to be a *PBP* reflector sight that had been installed on a *Yak-1*. It was unable to give an effective degree of deflection. Moreover, quality of the lenses was poor, compared to German devices, and it was replaced by the earlier and more primitive *VV* ring sight. Some Soviet aircraft had no gunsight at all. "We often ex-

amined the crashed remains and looked at MIGs, Yaks, LaGs, and other aircraft," recalled *Luftwaffe* ace Walter Krupisnki. "They often did not use any modern aiming or gunsight technology. It is true that many of the planes we found actually had hand-painted circles on the windscreen, which formed an estimated aiming point"[7]. But not all Soviet pilots complained about their gunsights. "We had good sights," recalled pilot Vitaly I. Klimenko, "but there was no time to use them in a dogfight – you'd use tracers from your own machinegun burst for aiming"[8].

586 IAP's armament mechanic, Liza Terekhova. She was a subordinate of Mariya Shcherbatyuk, chief of armament mechanics of Olga Yamshikova's aircraft. In the picture, Terekhova is taking out 12.7 x 108 mm ammo for the *Berezin UBS* (*Universalniy Berezina Sinkhronniy*) machinegun placed under the engine hood of the *Yaks*, equipping her regiment. The rate of fire for the *UBS* was 800 rounds per minute. Compared with the American Browning, the Soviet cartridge was slightly more powerful. The *Berezin* replaced the two rifle caliber *ShKAS* machineguns, scarcely effective against German aircraft that equipped the *Yaks* first delivered to the 586th. It weighed 25 kgs, compared to the 7.1 kgs of the 7.62 mm *Shkas*, but proved much more effective. However this gun had its shortcomings: "BS machineguns," recalled Hero of the Soviet Union Alexander E. Shvarev, "where prone to jamming. Bang, bang, and that was it"[9].

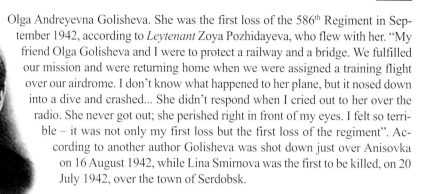

Olga Andreyevna Golisheva. She was the first loss of the 586th Regiment in September 1942, according to *Leytenant* Zoya Pozhidayeva, who flew with her. "My friend Olga Golisheva and I were to protect a railway and a bridge. We fulfilled our mission and were returning home when we were assigned a training flight over our airdrome. I don't know what happened to her plane, but it nosed down into a dive and crashed... She didn't respond when I cried out to her over the radio. She never got out; she perished right in front of my eyes. I felt so terrible – it was not only my first loss but the first loss of the regiment". According to another author Golisheva was shot down just over Anisovka on 16 August 1942, while Lina Smirnova was the first to be killed, on 20 July 1942, over the town of Serdobsk.

Leytenant Inna Kalinovskaya-Kalaceva, squadron *adjutant* and duty operations officer. The captions reads: "One more day of war left behind." Kalinovskaya is one of the very last veterans still alive, and one of the very few to have seen Katya Budanova and Lydia Litvyak. About the two future female "aces" she recalled: "They were not afraid of anything. But the best pilot between them was Budanova." Kalaceva recalled the hardships that the airwomen were compelled to face during the war. "Living conditions were extremely hard. For instance, there were no toilets, at least how we expected them to be. When there was snow, we used a shovel to make a small cabin in the snow. When it was too cold to go outside, we just made a hole in the wooden floor, and that was the toilet!"

Inna Nikolayevna Kalinovskaya-Kalaceva, with her future husband. He holds the rank of *Starshiy Leytenant*, is wearing the Guards Badge and the Order of the Red Star, the same decoration she was awarded. Born in 1921, she joined the 122 Air Group with no former military training in October 1941. She started her service with *586 IAP* in February 1942. Commander Gridnev regarded her as "persistent and energetic" and stressed "her ability to learn, work hard, plan operational training, and organizing her staff." Reportedly, she helped her commander in organizing 925 operational flights. Among them: 74 escorts of *Lisunov Li 2*; 38 missions to cover ground troops near Stalingrad; 32 low-flying air attacks. As a result of her work, six enemy planes were shot down. In 1943 she joined the Communist Party. After the war she went to live in the town of Bezhetsk, Kalininskaya Oblast, before moving to Moscow where she still lives.

"Party meeting" on the airfield for the *586 IAP* airwomen. An important part of the life in the regiment was the periodic meeting held by the Communist party organizer. Behind the group, the *Yak-1* "White 20". The canopy of that version was of the improved type introduced in 1942. To improve the rear view, the fuselage top decking was cut down and a teardrop canopy was installed. A bullet-proof windshield and a three-panel unit replaced the former curved windshield. The view that resulted was the best in Soviet fighters at the time[10]. However, the sliding hood had the unpleasant tendency to stick when the aircraft was in a dive, rendering it difficult to bail out. Moreover, the quality of Soviet glass was poor. Most Soviet pilots – even if it was forbidden – flew with their canopies open, which resulted in aircraft drag and reduced speed.

Parachute packer Zinaida Ermolaevna Butkareva. She was born on 22 October 1915 in a village of a peasant family. In 1931 her relatives brought her to Moscow. She went to work in a textile factory and slept in a dormitory. When the war broke out, she joined Marina Raskova's group and went to Engels to the flying school. At the end of six months of training the airwomen were assigned a speciality. "I was appointed parachute packer, and I was very disappointed because I wanted to work on the aircraft... I started crying. We had a field tent with a long table of fifty square meters where I could pack the parachutes… The minimum altitude for jumping was about two hundred to three hundred meters... The mechanic and the sergeants had a salary of seventy rubles a month, very good money at that time, and parachute packers and mechanics of armament and avionics got less. To bathe, we were carried in trucks to a nearby town bathhouse once every two weeks or even three weeks; it depended on the situation"[11].

Novice armorers of *586 IAP*, learning about *Yak* armament. "Early in the war our regiment had the *Yak-1* fighter with two machineguns of 7.62 mm caliber, the same as rifle bullets – very small caliber," recalled Yekaterina Polunina, aircraft mechanic. They had a high rate of fire, but in combat, the Soviet pilots discovered that the two *ShKAS* lacked penetrating power. "It was necessary to attack about three times to shoot down a plane," continued Polunina. Moreover, the *ShKAS* jammed easily. "It also had 48 ways of jamming," recalled pilot Viktor M. Sinaisky. "Some of them could be fixed immediately, some could not"[12]. In 1942, they replaced them with a 12.7 machinegun and a 20 mm cannon that shot through the gearbox shaft[13]. That improved model, according to statistic, achieved an air victory every 26 missions[14].

Olga Ivanovna Shakova reading a book on the airstrip, in front of her *Yak-1*. During summer of 1942 she escorted the *Lisunov Li-2* aircraft - with three other pilots - of General-Major Gromadin. Afterwards she

was promoted to officer rank. On 10 September 1942, she was temporarily sent (with pilots Lebedeva, Blinova, and Nechayeva) to *434 IAP* in Stalingrad. After she came back to her *586 IAP*, she flew a mission on 21 July 1944, escorting the Marshal of Artillery Forces, Nikolai Nikolaevich Boronov, with her commander Gridnev, Burdina, and Batrakova. Shakova flew 144 sorties but did not achieve a single air victory[15].

Pilots of 586th Fighter Regiment. The recruitment of women in the air force could be, according to Sergeant Zoya Malkova, mechanic of aircraft, to some extent "a kind of propagandistic action, but still and all we were mostly happy that we joined the army. We were elitist because students from aviation and pedagogical institutions and universi-

ties joined the army and that is why the atmosphere in our detachments was intellectually high. We had serious discussion, we took a record player with us and listened to classical music..."

The original caption of this photo reads: "Picture shows Litvyak (first from left) with Lieutenant Ekaterina Budanova, (center), her best friend and splendid fighter pilot, and Vera Kusnetsova. This is Lily Litvyak's plane. The three fighter pilots have just received a new battle order and are studying the map before carrying it out."

According to the regiment second commander, Aleksander Gridnev, Budanova and Litvyak were among the pilots who were opposed to their first commander, *Mayor* Tamara Kazarinova. Reportedly, the airwomen did not want to be commanded by someone who could not fly aircraft used in their unit. Some of the pilots requested the removal of Kazarinova. Actually, it was the *586 IAP's* commander, who, on 10 September 1942, transferred Budanova, Litvyak, Kuznetsova, and Belyayeva, and four more pilots, in male fighter regiments, to the Stalingrad Front. (Courtesy of Soviet Ministry of Information, December 1943)

Klavdiya Nechayeva. On 10 September 1942, Nechayeva was transferred to Stalingrad – together with Blinova, Lebedeva, and Shakhova – as replacements to the *434 Independent Fighter Aviation Regiment*, commanded by *Mayor* I. I. Kleschev. "When the girls from my regiment were going to fly to Stalingrad," remembered Nina Slovokhotova, deputy regimental navigator of *586 IAP*, "everyone realized that they could meet their death there. I remember their faces at that time, beaming with happiness. They were at last to fly to the front to fight the hated enemy, and they were saying, 'At last our dream came true.' I will remember that forever!"[16]. Nechayeva was commander of the women's flight in the 434th Fighter Regiment (renamed 32nd Guards Fighter Regiment in November 1942)[17].

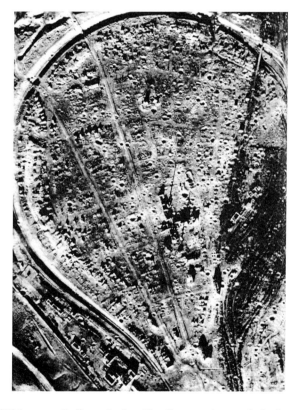

North Stalingrad. The so-called "tennis racket," riddled with bomb craters. The "racket" was actually the train yards of Chemical "Lazur" Factory. This famous railway track is south of the well known Red October Factory. The *586 IAP's* female pilots arrived at Stalingrad, while German *General* Friedrich von Paulus's Sixth Army was launching its offensive to fulfil Hitler's order to capture Stalingrad before 15 September 1942. The Germans were opposed by the Soviet 62nd Army, commanded by *General-Leytenant* Vasily Chuykov.

The wreckage of a shot-down *Messerschmitt Bf 109* among Stalingrad ruins. The Germans lost a relatively low number of these aircraft, compared to Soviets fighter losses. Between 5 – 12 September, the *Luftwaffe* flew 7,507 sorties, losing 36 aircraft in the Stalingrad area. During the same period according to German sources, Soviet aviation carried out 2,834 sorties, losing a number of aircraft six times higher. The eight female pilots arrived on 10 September 1942. On that day, *Feldwebel* Wihlelm Crinius of *I./JG 53*, who a week later shot down Klava Nechayeva, claimed three victories. *JG 53* lost three of its best pilots, among them 85 victory ace Walter Zellot, who was shot down right over Stalingrad.

Another *Messerschmitt Bf 109* wreck among the ruins of Stalingrad.
The *Luftwaffe* lost thirty *Bf 109s* (and 10 twin-engine *Bf 110s*) in combat,
during September 1942, an average of one aircraft per day.
In the same period, the Soviets lost 341 fighters (*Yak-1s*, *Yak-7s*,
La-5s, *LaGG 3s*, American *P-40s*) plus 179 bombers, ground
attack, and reconnaissance aircraft.

A *Messerschmitt Bf 109G-2* of *JG 53*, the same unit of Crinius and Erwin Meyer. Meyer was reportedly shot down by Litvyak on 13 September. In Mid-1942, the *Bf 109* was unquestionably superior to
any fighter the Soviets could afford. "The *109*? That was a dream, the *non plus ultra,*" recalled Gun-
ther Rall, the 275 kill *Luftwaffe* ace. "Of course, everyone wanted to fly one as soon as possible"[18]. "The
Bf 109 was a powerful aircraft, fast and very good in vertical maneuver," recalled Soviet ace N. G.
Golodnikov. It "carried very powerful weapons, with five firing points, for the most part cannon", he
added. "This was a very strong aspect of German aircraft"[19]. Equipped with a 1,475 hp DB 605-A engine, the *Bf 109G* was armed with two *MG 17* and three 20 mm *MG 151s*. The 20 mm cannons were
so effective to allow *Messerschmitt* pilots 75% chance to shoot down even the heavily armoured "Shturmovik" in one single attack from the rear[20].

Stalingrad: a German *Junkers Ju 87 Stuka* pulling out of its dive. The elite fighter *434 IAP* was one of the Soviet units which, through September 1942, almost daily faced the *Stuka* formations that relentlessly attacked Soviet strongholds in the eastern parts of Stalingrad. Klava Nechayeva was posted to this unit since the start of her replacement assignment on the Stalingrad Front. (Picture Bundes Archives - Bild 183-J20511)

Left to right: Yekaterina Budanova, Mariya Kuznetsova and Lidya Litvyak, beaming with happiness for being transferred to Stalingrad. They were posted along with Raysa Belyayeva, to Srednyaya Akhtuba Base, on the eastern bank of the Volga. In summer-autumn 1942, flying sorties over Stalingrad were extremely dangerous and demanding. Soviet sources indicate that from August through October 1942, the *Luftwaffe* flew 600-800 combat sorties per day within the Stalingrad Air Defense Region[21]. And for every *Messerschmitt* lost, the *Luftwaffe* shot down ten Soviet fighters.

Klavdiya Nechayeva. The 434th - the new Nechayeva Regiment - had its first combat assignment in Stalingrad on 16 September. On the following day, she flew her first mission, as wingman of *Kapitan* I. I. Izbinskii[22]. She was credited with one of the seven kills claimed by the 434th, four of them *Bf 109s* (actually, that day total *Luftwaffe* losses over Stalingrad were just four aircraft, including only one *Bf 109*). Then, on her fifth mission, returning from escorting *Petlyakov P-2s*, she was covering Izbinskii, landing with undercarriage lowered. Suddenly, two German fighters dived on him. Nechayeva intervened but was probably too inexperienced to face two fighters at very low altitude[23]. Reportedly, she drew fire from one of the *Messerschmitt Bf 109s* and "the *Yak* fell down to the ground like a blazing meteorite"[24]. Nechayeva was shot down by one of the pilots of *I./JG 53*[25], the great *Luftwaffe* ace, *Feldwebel* Wilhelm Crinius, from *3./JG 53*. Nechayeva was awarded posthumously the Order of the Patriotic War and her name was engraved in golden characters in the Hall of Soldier's Glory in Stalingrad (now Volgograd)[26].

Wilhelm Crinius, on 9 September 1942. In mid September, when he downed and killed Nechayeva, Crinius had a continuous high fever, was completely exhausted, and weighed just 53 kgs (118 pounds). The smell of gunpowder made him sick and in combat he frequently had to vomit. Notwithstanding his poor health, he was probably one of the most lethal fighter pilots in the sky over Stalingrad. On 17 September, Crinius was the only pilot to shoot down (at 09.51) a *Yak-1* at an altitude compatible to that of a landing aircraft (100 meters), in the Stalingrad area (*Planquadrat 40760, Film C. 2032/II Anerk: Nr. 410*). Nechayeva was Crinius' third of four aerial victories against a *Yak-1* that day (all in Stalingrad area), number 86 of his top ace career. In four months from the end of May to the beginning of October 1942, Crinius' unit – *I./JG 53* - had claimed an unprecedented number of kills (918) and Crinius was the top scoring *Experte* of the 1st *Gruppe* with 100 air victories.

Adolf Hitler is presenting the *Knight's Cross with Oak Leaves* to Wilhelm Crinius (first from right), in October 1942. On 23 September 1942, six days after he had shot down Nechayeva over Stalingrad, Crinius had been promoted to the rank of *Leutnant*, becoming the only German fighter pilot to be awarded the *Ritterkreuz des Eisernen Kreuzes* and, simultaneously, the *Ritterkreuz des Eisernen Kreuzes mit Eichenlaub*. Born on 1 December 1920 at Hohenhausen, in Lipper Bergland, he joined the *Luftwaffe* in January 1940. In February 1942, Crinius was posted, as a *Gefreiter* (it was the lowest rank to which an ordinary German aviator could be promoted), to *3./JG 53* based in Sicily. His unit in May 1942, was relocated to the Eastern Front. Here he achieved his two first victories on 9 June. In the following three months, he amassed 65 air victories. In November 1942, few weeks after meeting Hitler, Crinius and his *I./JG 53* were posted to Tunisia. Here, on 13 January 1943, Crinius was hit and wounded by *RAF Spitfires*. He force-landed on the sea, was rescued, and imprisoned. His score was 114 kills (100 in Russia) in about 400 sorties. He died on 26 April 1997.

Leytenant Mariya Kuznetsova in the cockpit of her *Yakovlev Yak-1* fighter (note the gunsight in front of her), in Stalingrad. "We met the enemy at every mission," recalled Kuznetsova. "I shot down three enemy aircraft... I shot down a *Ju-87* and a *Ju-88*, German bombers." Kuznetsova was herself shot down several times. "God saved me," she recalled. "My mother was a believer, and she prayed to God for my safety... Once my propeller blades were hit by bullets, and they skimmed down the fuselage, just missing the fuel tank. Another day I was fighting with a German aircraft and didn't notice that I was out of fuel. The engine stopped... so I decided to belly-land, and... it stopped just short of a very deep trench." Rumors reached her parents that she had been killed so, figuratively, they buried her twice. At last, Kuznetsova fell ill and when she recovered, she was repatriated to the *586 IAP*, along with Raysa Belyayeva. Only Litvyak and Budanova requested to stay in Stalingrad[27].

Valeriya Khomyakova. Born on 3 August 1914, she was the daughter of a chemical engineer. She studied engineering too, getting the diploma of chemical engineering from the Mendelev Institute. She started working in a plant but – dreaming to become a pilot – at the same time trained at a flying club. After one year she stopped working as an engineer to became a flying instructor. She joined the *Pyaterka*, a female aerobatic team, based at Tushino Airfield in Moscow, and performed in many air shows in front of thousands of spectators. When the war started, she volunteered for combat and was posted to Marina Raskova's air group.

Anisovka, 25 September 1942. *586 IAP* fighter pilots (left to right: Galina Burdina, Tamara Pamyatnyk, Valeriya Khomyakova, and Valentina Lisitsina). They are gathered around *Leytenant* Khomyakova to hear how she achieved her victory against a *Junkers Ju 88*. Piloting the *Yak-1* in the background, on the night of 24 September, she was alerted to an impending *Luftwaffe* attack on Saratov. When the searchlights illuminated a group of *Junkers Ju 88*, Khomyakova attacked them. She dispersed the formation and put some German *Junkers* on fire. One bomber dived steeply to extinguish the fire. *Oberleutnant* Gerhard Maak of the *7 Staffel* of *Kampfgeschwader 76* was piloting this *Ju 88* F1+HR. Khomyakova hit it repeatedly until the bomber exploded. Maak and his crew were reported as "missing in action". Actually, the *Ju 88* crashed just outside Saratov, near the bridge across the Volga, in a willow thicket on the river bank. Maak had been ejected by the explosion and the other crew member had bailed out but the parachutes had failed to open.

Vera Stepanovna Shcherbakova, aircraft engineer. "In the winter, we had to fix instruments on the aircraft with our bare hands, our skin stuck to the metal, and our hands bled," recalled later, Irina Lunyova-Favorskaya, mechanic of armament, another colleague of Shcherbakova. "I wrote to my mother saying that it was unbearable to work with bare hands and she sent a parcel to the front with a pair of pink silk ladies' gloves! I wore them and all the girls laughed and made fun of me"[28].

A crashed *Junkers Ju 88 A-4* of *K.G.76,* the same bomber unit of the plane shot down by Khomyakova on the night of 24-25 September 1942. Below the cockpit the "wasp badge" of the bomber unit. The unit had taken part in the campaign in Poland (September 1939), the attack on France and the Low Countries, and the Battle of Britain. It took part in Operation Barbarossa, carried on bombing sorties in Southern Russia, Crimea, North Caucasia, and Stalingrad. After the bombing of Saratov, it still conducted sorties against Stalingrad. On 24 October 1942, it was transferred to Armavir/North Caucasus, and subsequently, to Crete.

Valeriya Khomyakova (center) is being congratulated by *Mayor* Tamara Kazarinova (far right), regimental commander, for having shot down a *Junkers Ju 88* over Saratov, on the night of 24 September 1942. Reportedly, Kazarinova is telling her: "Your very first kill - that's good. But it wouldn't be easy to keep up the good work. From now on, you should demand even more that before from yourself and your subordinates. You'll be expected to perform even better, as befits a true combat pilot." The magazine *Ogonyok* printed a full page article about Khomyakova's victory. But on the night of 5 October, Kazarinova ordered her to wake up and take off immediately. In the absolute darkness, Khomyakova – who had just returned from a journey to Moscow and was exhausted – hit an obstacle, crashing to her death. Her girlfriend Prokhorova blamed Kazarinova for the accident. General Gromadin removed Kazarinova from her command and ordered General A. S. Osipenko to bring her to an investigation, but Osipenko took her to his staff in the headquarter of the Air Defense Force (*IA/PVO*).

Mayor Aleksandr Vasilyevich Gridnev. Actually he was the third commander of 586th. After Tamara Kazarinova, a *Mayor* Belyakov replaced her holding command for just few days. Gridnev arrived in Anisovka on 14 October 1942. He was the former commander of the 82nd Fighter Aviation Regiment. Gridnev had a troubled past, including two arrests by the Secret Police and a term of imprisonment in a *gulag* during the 1930s. He was remembered by women veterans as "the real commander of the regiment". The women called him affectionately "Batya", which means "dad" in Russian. "He was only ordinary-looking," recalled Aleksandra Makunina, *586 IAP* chief of staff, "but he was very funny… he's an excellent story teller, with a great sense of humor. It was very pleasant to be in his company... I have only good memories of Gridnev." Gridnev was the only pilot to be qualified as an ace with the *586 IAP*. He was credited with five individual and two group air victories. No woman of his regiment shot down five aircraft.

Mayor Aleksandr Gridnev, regimental commander of *586 IAP*, explaining the forthcoming mission to four female pilots. Gridnev soon started a training program for the regiment – through October and November 1942 – which included formation flying, navigation, and radar guided scrambles. At this time of the war, the *586 IAP* was often tasked to escort high ranking officers. In December 1942, Gridnev, with pilots Belyayeva, Burdina, and Mordosevich (male), escorted Nikita Krushchev (future USSR president) near Stalingrad. Gridnev held command of *586 IAP* till the end of the war.

Kommissar polk (Regimental Commissar) Olga Kulikova (second from right) with 586th female personnel. According to Nina Slovokhotova, Chief of Chemical Services, Kulikova, as political commissar, hated Tamara Kazarinova, first *586 IAP* commander, as she (Kazarinova) was not a member of Communist Party. "Kazarinova and Kulikova," recalled Yekaterina Polunina, "were both punished after the death of Khomyakova, but Kazarinova was removed and Kulikova was not."

Commander Gridnev arrival in the 586th marked the end of the fighter regiment as an all-female unit. A third squadron of male pilots was added in the fall of 1942, even because the 586th was still short of the squadron sent to Stalingrad in September 1942. Men became even deputy commanders, but they drew little attention and little is known about *586 IAP's* men. "They failed to mention the men's squadron," noted commander Gridnev. "It is as though they were never in the regiment at all."[29] In this photo group, female and male pilots and technicians. Sitting, left to right: engineer Lev Ilich Kurapeyev, engineer

Pavel Ivanovich Morshnev, pilot Vasiliy Ivanovich Malakhov, Commander Aleksander Gridnev, Stepan Aleksandrovich Podruzhko (staff), pilot Agnya Polyantseva, mechanic Aleksandr Naumovich Polyakov, engineer Anatoly Sergeevich Reutskiy. Standing, left to right: mechanic Nikolai Stepanovich Kurdin, Aleksandra Makunina, Zoya Vasilyevna Prokhoda (staff), armorer Klavdiya Terekhova-Kasatkina, pilot Mariya Kuznetsova, engineer Irina Ivanovna Yemelianova-Danilova, Lapteva, Yuriy Grigoryevich Reznik (staff), I. Ermolayev, Aleksei Timofeyevich Baurin (staff), and mechanic Yekaterina Polunina.

Yevgeniya Filipovna Prokhorova. She was one of the most skilful pilots of *586 IAP*. She held two world records in gliders. Before the war, she was the leader of the *Pyaterka*, the women's aerobatic team based in Tushino Airfield. The *Pyaterka* performed in many air shows and parades[30]. Appointed squadron commander of *583 IAP*, Prokhorova flew 12-14 hours per day, training the less experienced pilots. "She was the idol of all the women pilots, the technicians, in fact, the entire personnel of the regiment," remembered Gridnev. Of average height, with athletic build, "she had a big feature, a chin that was rather heavy, and a neck that didn't go well with her delicate figure," Gridnev added. "Maybe you could not call her a beauty, but she was 'a perfect shot' when shooting both towed and ground targets." She died in a flying accident in December 1942, while escorting a transport aircraft with other pilots in a snow storm. She made a forced landing, but the plane overturned, trapping her. During the night she froze to death[31].

Fighter regiment technicians enjoying a well deserved rest, while "their" aircraft are airborne. "In between flights, when we were waiting for our aircraft to return," recalled Inna Nikolayevna Shebalina, aircraft mechanic, "we had a little time to sit on the grass to talk and laugh"[32]. From 13 February until 16 August 1943, the 586th was based at Voronezh and the regiment had some of the most intense air battles. "During that time at Voronezh, every pilot had about three times the

usual work," recalled commander Gridnev. Moreover, "the food was terrible." Nevertheless, during these six months, the regiment performed 934 flights, flying for 901 hours and 31 minutes. It claimed seven *Junkers Ju 88s* and three *Focke-Wulf Fw 190s* shot down[33].

Tamara Yustinovna Pamyatnykh, pilot of *586 IAP*. Born in September 1919, she attended glider school when she was 16. Then went on the aviation school at Uliganovsk to become a flight instructor. After the German invasion, she became a military officer and taught cadets. On 10 October 1941 Raskova invited her to join her regiment and after training she assigned her to the fighter regiment. *Leytenant* Pamyatnykh flew her first combat mission in July 1942, escorting the aircraft carrying a member of the Politburo, Kliment Yefremovich Voroshilov, to Stalingrad. On her chest she wears what seems to be the Order of the Red Banner. On 19 March 1943 she received that award with her wingman Raya Surnachevskaya for attacking 42 German *Dornier Do 215s* and *Junkers Ju 88s* (on their way to bomb a railroad station crowded with Soviet troops and fuel supplies) and shooting down four of them (two each). Pamyatnykh was awarded an Order of the Red Star and received a gold watch sent by English King George VI. "Mine is inscribed," she remembered, "From the Minister of Foreign Affairs to the brave and gallant pilot Lieutenant Tamara Pamyatnikh, from the King of England, George VI" with her name engraved in it[34].

☆

Raysa Surnachevskaya in front of her *Yak-1*. She was born in Moscow on 8 August 1922. When she was 15 she enrolled in a technical school and joined the aeroclub across the road. She graduated two years later from both. When the war started, she volunteered for Raskova's regiment and started flying combat missions over the sky of Voronezh. "At the front we flew in pairs, and Tamara Pamyatnykh and I flew together. Our mission was air defense and we were sent up when there were Germans in our area," Surnachevskaya remembered. On 19 March 1943, they placed themselves with the sun behind and dived on the enemy bombers. "On this attack we each shot down a German aircraft, and then we quickly made another pass, and again each of us shot down another." However Pamyatnykh's aircraft was hit and fell spinning on fire. Surnachevskaya felt desperate about her friend, but continued to attack the bombers, setting several of them on fire. But she was in turn hit and had to make an emergency landing. "Later, in another battle, I shot down another German plane. It was a reconnaissance aircraft, and I was flying with the commander of the regiment," the old veteran recounted[35].

Pilot Tamara Pamyatnykh (left) being congratulated by three of her ground crew, 1943. They are, from left to right: armorer Margarita Vasilevna Kokina, aircraft mechanic Yevgeniya "Zhenya" Borak, and engine and armament mechanic Irina "Ira" Favorskaya-Luneva. Favorskaya was born in Moscow in 1921. She finished secondary school in 1940. When the Germans invaded her country, she was a second-year student of Geology Institute in Moscow. She volunteered for the front and was accepted in Raskova's air group. Transferred to Engels, she was assigned to armaments. "It was very hard for me," she later recalled. "The Yak fighters were new and intricate, and our education was limited... When we were stationed on the Volga River... we experienced shortages of everything: food, bread, soap, we suffered great hardships"[36]. Then, when the regiment was based in Voronezh, "suddenly they overloaded us with American food,"recalled their commander, Mayor Gridnev. "It was a feast: canned meat, dried eggs, canned milk"[37].

In spring 1943, the *586 IAP* was equipped with new, more powerful, *Yak-7Bs*. This fighter was a later development of the *UTI-26* trainer, substantially a two-seat *Yak-1*. The rear cockpit was retained as it could be used to carry technical personnel or cargo during redeployments, for rescuing shot-down pilots, for additional tanks, bombs or photographic equipment. Late in 1942 it became one of the best fighters of the time, especially regarding stability and handling[38]. "The aircraft enters a spin only in the case of considerable loss of speed and recovers easily," stated a report about the *Yak-7*. "It forgives even grave piloting errors with no serious consequences. The aircraft possessed a very broad range of safe speeds"[39].

Another picture of the *Yakovlev Yak-7*. To reduce vulnerability to fire of previous *Yak* models, the fuel tanks were provide with self-sealing coating and an inert gas pressurization system employing a bottle with carbon dioxide[40]. The two rifle caliber *ShKAS* machineguns of the first version were replaced with two *UBS* 12.7 mm. So equipped (including the 20 mm *ShVAK* cannon), it had a rate of fire 3.5 greater than that of the *Bf 109F* and 1.5 greater than that of the *Yak-1*. So improved, the *Yak-7* was one of the best fighters on the Eastern Front. But the heavier armament in the nose shifted the CG forward, and as a result, the aircraft had a tendency to nose over, especially if using the brakes on landing. Moreover, most pilots flew with their cockpit canopy open for fear of the hood jamming in an emergency, and the speed was reduced by 40-50 km/h (24.8-31 mph).

Mariya Dmetryevna Shcherbatyuk, chief of armorers of the *Yak-1* of Olga Yamshikova. Shcherbatyuk was "... a short, stocky, black-eyed girl," remembered Sofya Osipova, mechanic of the same aircraft[41]. In the picture, she is servicing the 20 mm *ShVAK* cannon of a *Yak* fighter. The *ShVAK* was a larger caliber version of the 12,7 mm *ShKAS* machinegun; it was one of the first 20 mm cannons to be used in the conflict. The *ShVAK* had a high rate of fire of 700-800 rounds per minute. As the *Yak-1* carried a reserve of 120 rounds, pilots were allowed just about 9 seconds of fire, statistically not enough to destroy an enemy aircraft. Actually it was necessary to expend an average of 147 rounds to down it[42]. By 1944, the *ShVAK* was replaced by the *Berezin B-20* auto-cannon that had the advantage of being 25 kg lighter[43].

Left to right, 586th pilots Olga Yakovleva, Tamara Voronova, and Klavdiya Terekhova-Kasatkina. Yakovleva was flight instructor at the Chelyabinsk Flying Club. When the war broke out, she volunteered to go to the front, "but instead my superiors assigned a group of girls to me to be trained as replacements for male flying instructors who had been conscripted," she later recalled. "But eventually I was assigned to Marina Raskova's air group"[44]. She was posted to the fighter regiment. She was credited with the destruction of at least one enemy aircraft. "With Ira Ol'kova we waited in our cockpits on a scramble alert," she wrote recalling her kill. "Suddenly, a reconnaissance plane emerged between the clouds. We started our engines in unison. A green flare shot up! In an instant, we were airborne, but the Nazi had disappeared... We turned and flew in the direction in which we had just seen him. Here he was! We approached him, but he kept disappearing in the clouds. Finally we caught up with him. Ira approached him from the port side and I from starboard. (His rear gunner kept firing at Ol'kova.) I approached him closer and fired at his wing and cockpit. His starboard engine began to smoke. The Nazi made another attempt to get away and hide, but suddenly he fell out of the clouds and plunged to the ground"[45].

Portrait of Olga Yakovleva. She is wearing a Parachute Jump Badge. On 14 May 1943, with Tamara Pamyatnykh, she intercepted a German aircraft. "After approaching him to a distance of 100 meters, we fired at his gunner and engines," she later wrote. "Suddenly, my machine-guns became silent. Now, to reload them quickly and again attack! Tamara approached the enemy from the port side and fired several bursts at the gunner, trying to draw his fire to herself, but the shining "stitches" stubbornly stretched toward my aircraft... Then I felt a jolt... A sharp, penetrating pain in my left arm made me screw up my eyes involuntarily..." Yakovleva made an emergency landing. She had to undergo eight months of rehabilitation. Nevertheless, she wanted to get back into combat but was only allowed to fly the *Polikarpov Po-2* in a communication squadron. After the war, she was permanently grounded.

Tamara Voronova was one of the reinforcement pilots of *586 IAP*. She was born in 1922, in the town of Yaroslavl, in the Volga region. She learned to fly when she was in the last grade of high school. Then she became a flight instructor. She graduated three groups of pilots before the German invasion. She volunteered for military aviation but was enrolled as a dispatcher in a fighter regiment. Subsequently was allowed to fly liason aircraft. "I flew in that section one year and was given the rank of junior lieutenant. I carried messages from one unit to another." Subsequently she was retrained to fly *Yak-3* and *Yak-7*. At last, in June 1944 she was posted to *586 IAP*. She stayed with the fighter regiment until the end of the war. Then she was one of the pilots chosen to ferry aircraft to Vienna, Austria, and from there to Ploesti, in Romania. Voronova survived the war, married, and had four children.

586th ground personnel. Left to the right. Standing: armorer Nina Karasyeva-Karasiova, Zinayda Alekseyevna Yermolayeva (staff), engine mechanic Antonina Fedorovna Kachurina, Valentina Ivanovna Abankina, engine mechanic Olga Afanasyevna Golubieva, mechanic Sofia Vladirovna Osipova, Nina Nikolaevna Shebalina, Polina Vasilyevna Sokolova. Sitting: P. Karyuchin, mechanic Lyublina Arkadyevna Bratsilova, mechanic of the aircraft Yekaterina Kuzminichna Polunina, Klavdiya I. Terekhova-Kasatkina, Anastasya Nikolayevna

Goryelova (staff), armorer Mariya Kapitovna Konkina. Yekaterina Polunina was the unofficial historian of *586 IAP*. Before enrolling, she worked at an aviation test factory. In the 586th Regiment she was at first chosen by deputy commander Olga Studenetskaya (that was credited with the kill of a *Junkers Ju 88*) to be the mechanic of her aircraft. Once, she was arrested and given 10 days in the guardhouse because, during "some technical work that took some fifty hours," she went to the mess to have a bowl of soup "and was not found on duty during a lineup." In 2004, she published a reference book about *586 IAP* airwomen: *Devchonki,Podruzhki, Letchitsy (Girls, Girlfriends, Pilots)*.

Left to right: pilot Galina Burdina (note the Order of the Red Star on her right chest); Captain R. Bengus, probably serving in staff (please note the four stars indicating her rank on the shoulder boards), and deputy commander and chief of staff Aleksandra Aleksandrovna Makunina, wearing the Order of the Great Patriotic War. "When I became the deputy commander," recalled A. Makunina, "my duties were to plan combat missions and training flights - schedule everything. My profession and training as a physical geographer helped me a lot. For example, when the regiment started for another airfield I had all the maps, and I explained to the girls the terrain and topography of the new area"[46].

Senior Lieutenant Valentina Mikhaylovna Lisitsina, pilot of *586 IAP*. She was born on 16 February 1921 in a family of Moscow weavers. She studied at school Nr. 555. In 1939 she joined the *Komsomol*. During the day she studied at school, and, three times a week, she studied flight theory and air navigation at the flying club. Here, later, she was hired as an instructor. On 5 May 1941, the magazine "Plane" included her in the list of the best flying instructors in Moscow. She was given the rank of junior sergeant and the task of teaching commanders of the Red Army to fly. In October 1941, Lisitsina voluntarily joined Raskova's unit and was posted to the 586th. She fought at Voronezh, Kursk, Kiev, and Kostornaya, flying *Yak-1*, *Yak-7*, and *Yak 9*. During 6 air battles in 1943 she claimed one *Ju-88* individually and three *Fw 190s* shared. Still in 1943 she trained a whole squadron to fly the new fighter *Yak-7*. She was awarded the Order of the Red Star and the Order of the Glory III. She amassed 1,025 flying hours on the *Polikarpovs U-2*, *UT-2* and *UTI-4* and on the *Yak-1*, *Yak-7* and *Yak-9* fighters. She flew 235 hours on *Yak-1* and 18 hours 25 minutes by night. Since April 1943 through 29 October 1944, she served as deputy commander of *586 IAP*. From 29 October 1944 to 30 October 1945, she was assistant regimental commander. After the war, in the period 30 October 1945 – 19 January 1946, she served in *39 GvIAP*. From 19 January 1946, she was transferred to the reserve, declared invalid of 2nd degree. She lived at 17, Pyatnitskaya Street, in Moscow. She died on 22 June 1989.

Commander Gridnev and Lisitsina. She was credited with the destruction of at least one enemy aircraft, on 14 June 1943[47]. Flying as wingman to *Lieutenant Colonel* Aleksandr Gridnev (in the picture), Valentina Lisitsina fought an air battle that was reported by *Pravda*. It happened near Voronezh, east of Kursk. They intercepted a twin-engine *Ju 88*, escorted by a *Fw 190*. Lisitsina and Gridnev attacked the bomber but in turn they were jumped by the fighter. While Lisitsina hit the *Ju 88* (she was credited with its kill) Gridnev claimed the fighter. But he was then chased by two more *Fw 190s*. Gridnev escaped into a cloud where the two German aircraft collided and fell in flames. The German fighters were most probably from *II./JG 51* or *II./JG 54* which were at that time equipped with the *Focke-Wulf Fw 190A*s, and based in Orel, north-west of Voronezh. However, German sources do not confirm the loss of any *Fw 190* by *JG 51* that day.

Looking at *586 IAP* airwomen flying, left to right, Mariya Shcherbatyuk, Mariya Konkina, *Leytenant* Nina Endakova, Laktaev (?) and *Leytenant* Aleksandra Makunina. In the background, a *Yak-1*. In this model, the upper fuselage behind the cockpit has been cut down to improve rearward visibility. In this way the canopy cockpit is given a streamlined teardrop shape. However the molded visor distorted pilots' vision of objects and enemy aircraft.

Galina Burdina in the cockpit of her *Yak*. During the Battle of Kursk (July-August 1943), when air combat involving up to 150 aircraft were commonplace, Burdina claimed a *Bf 109*. "The sky was so full of aircraft

in such a small area of airspace that it was terrifying," she recalled. "I broke out of the fight to gain height and look for a target. I dived down and pulled up underneath a *Messerschmitt Bf 109* and raked it with machinegun and cannon fire. It fell away immediately, burning. I had shot down two other Germans before that – a bomber and a transport – but that was my first fighter. I didn't feel any pity for the man I had killed. When it's kill or be killed, you don't feel that sort of thing"[48].

Mladishiy Leytenant Antonina V. Lebedeva. Her loss, during the summer of 1943 is still surrounded by mystery. On 10 September 1942 she was posted to *437 IAP*, along with Shakova, Nechayeva, and Blinova. Subsequently she was transferred to *653 IAP* (renamed *65GvIAP* on 18 March 1943), with Blinova and Shakova. While serving with that regiment, Lebedeva claimed three kills. She was MIA in July 1943. Her father, Vasiliy Pavlovich Lebedev, requested information from Yegeniy Ivanovich of Pestryakov. He answered in field mail Nr. 35428: "After the liberation of Orel, I found out that Tonya had been in a hospital there, but following its evacuation she was removed by the Germans… she was interrogated by German officers (*and*) she spat on their faces. No one knows what became of her after that." However, according to Yekaterina K. Polunina, veteran and unofficial historian of the *586 IAP*, Lebedeva was killed in combat on 17 July 1943. Her remains were found many years later and she was buried on 17 August 1983 at Vyazovaya, in Bolkhovskiy Disctrict, Orel Region[49].

Focke-Wulf Fw 190A "Red 9" of *JG 51*, on Eastern Front, July 1943. According to *Luftwaffe* historian Christer Bergström, Lebedeva was part of a formation of four Soviet *Yak-1s* of *65 GvIAP* that were all shot down by *Focke-Wulf Fw 190s*, on 17 July 1943, about 60 km east of Orel. In what was one of the few air combats between the *Luftwaffe* and Soviet 15th Air Army, she was flying along with *St.Lt.* Gavril Guskov, a 15 victories ace. The *Focke-Wulfs* that shot them down were probably of *Gruppe I* or *Gruppe IV* of *JG 51*, the same unit as in this picture, or of *I./JG 54*, both based in Orel.

Henschel Hs 129 ground attack aircraft. According to some sources, Lebedeva was pursuing a *Hs 129* when she crashed to her death. During the Battle of Kursk, *Oberleutnant* Bruno Meyer, commander of *4(Pz.)/Sch.G2* and pilot of a *Henschel,* was attacked by a Soviet pilot who flew his *Yak-9* skillfully and fired accurately. The *Hs 129* was hit and Meyer released his canopy to bail out. The canopy flew straight into the engine of the *Yak,* which caught fire and crash-landed. Meyer found a dead woman in the cockpit. According to Soviet documents, she was Junior Leitenant Antoniya V. Lebedeva[50].

Henschel Hs 129 - The *Hs 129* was equipped with two relatively low-powered French engines. The only crewman – the pilot – sat in the extreme nose behind a 7.5 cm (3 in) thick windscreen. The armored cockpit was so small that the reflector gunsight was mounted on the plane's nose. The *Hs 129* was (at least initially) scarcely appreciated for its flying qualities and engine reliability. But its armament was highly effective: it could carry a wide range of arms (four 7.92 mm *MG 17s*, or two *MG 17s* plus two 20 mm *MG 151s*, or a 30 mm cannon, *MK 101* or *MK 103*). *Hs 129* proved highly effective as a tank buster. For instance, ten days before Lebedeva was lost, the *Henschels* destroyed fifty tanks during the Battle of Kursk.

Guards *Leytenant* Klavdiya Mikhailovna Blinova-Kudlenko. She was born on 24 December 1922 in Mescersky Village, Moscow Region (now a capital's quarter). In 1939 she graduated from aeronautical school Zerginsky and became a trainer for flight personnel, getting mentioned in the May 1941 edition of the magazine "The Plane." She was serving with *586 IAP* when she was downed. "On 4 August 1943, while flying my second sortie," she later recalled, "I heard a loud crack in my cockpit and the aircraft began to break up in small pieces. I was falling with my cockpit, out of control, and in my hand I squeezed the now useless control stick. It took me a while to realize that I had been shot down"[51]. Blinova was captured by the Germans and taken to a POW camp but managed to escape while on a train to another camp. After wandering for two weeks in Bryansk Forest, she returned to her regiment. Subsequently she was sent to the Higher Air Tactics Officers' School in Lyubertsy, near Moscow. Then she took part in the fighting for the Baltic regions and Belarus, and for the capture of Berlin. She died in a *sanatorium*, a vacation resort, near Kiev on 23 September 1988.

Luftwaffe Expert Karl-Heinz Weber. Blinova fell victim to this superb pilot. Weber was the only pilot over Kursk-Orel region to claim a *Yak-7*, the type of aircraft flown by Blinova, the day she was shot down. Karl-Heinz "Benjamin" Weber was born on 30 January 1922 in Heringsdorf, Pommern. A glider pilot, he volunteered for the *Luftwaffe* in the autumn 1939. Weber joined *7./JG 51* on 1 October 1940 as a *Leutnant*. He claimed his first victory on 24 June 1941 and his 20th on 9 August. On 3 September his *Bf 109 F-2* "White 0" was damaged in combat with Russian bombers and he bailed out but was wounded by a German sentry. While still in the hospital, he was awarded the *Ehrenpokal* on 30 September. He returned to combat and was decorated with the *Deutsches Kreuz* in Gold on 16 March 1943. He was one of the top aces of the Battle of Kursk, claiming five victories on 5 July (his victories 41 to 45) and six on 7 July (46-51). *Oberleutnant* Weber recorded his 100th victory on 10 October and received the *Ritterkreuz* on 12 November 1943. By now serving as *Staffelkapitän* of *7./JG 51*, he was promoted to *Hauptmann* on 25 May 1944. On 29 May, *7./JG 51* was transferred to the Western Front for the defense of the Reich. On 3 June 1944, Weber was appointed *Gruppenkommandeur* of *III./JG 1*. Four days later, in his *Bf 109 G-6/AS* "White 20," he led *III./JG 1* against Allied fighters south of Rouen. It was his first mission over the invasion front. Weber never came back and was never found. He could have fallen fighting against *RAF P-51 Mustangs*. He was posthumously awarded the *Eichenlaub* (Nr. 529) on 20 July 1944. Karl-Heinz Weber is credited with 136 victories on over 500 missions.

Raisa Belyayeva. Regarded as one of the most capable and skilled pilots of *586 IAP*, her death as well is still surrounded in mystery. Born on 25 December 1912, before the war, Belyayeva had 1,000 flying hours and had parachuted more than 100 times, training hundreds of parachutists and parachute instructors. She joined the *Pyaterka*, the female acrobatic team. She volunteered for Raskova's 122 Air Group and was posted to *586 IAP*. On 10 September she was transferred to *437 IAP* in Stalingrad, before being sent to *9 GvIAP*. On 13 September, reportedly, a *Bf 109G* was going to shoot her down and Litvyak saved her. Afterwards she was shot down while apparently on a training mission[52]. She was credited with a kill over a *Bf 109* shared with Litvyak on 27 September. She returned to *586 IAP* in December 1942. Subsequently she flew many escort missions for Soviet VIPs. On 19 July 1943 she crashed to death on her airfield in Voronezh. Polunina and Anatoly Plyac stated that she had been shot while returning from a mission. As there are no known claims in the Voronezh area by German fighter pilots[53] she may have been hit before returning, in combat with fighters from *I.* or *II./JG 52* or *I./JG 51* (the nearest *Luftwaffe* units), then located in Orel, about 160 km (100 miles) N-N/W of Voronezh, only about 15 minute of flight on a *Bf 109* or a *Fw 190*.

A female technician from *586 IAP* is learning how to use a *ShKAS* 7.62 mm. Note the gunsight mounted on the barrel of the machine gun. When placed on the *Yaks*, these "machineguns, started with compressed air, with a very long tube to the compressor, and if the tubes broke in the air, the pilots couldn't fire the guns," later recalled Yekaterina Polunina. "It was difficult to adjust these machineguns so they wouldn't hit the propeller. The guns were called 'kliks' because they made that kind of noise. Each gun weighed 20 kilos, and it was heavy to clean and oil in the winter"[54].

Original Soviet caption reads: "Male officers, technicians and engineers handing the girls their experience in operation of aircraft in combat." Left to right: Anatoliy Sergeyevich Reutsky, engineer of the 2nd squadron; Aleksandr Naumovich Polyakov, engineer of the 1st squadron; Irina Ivanovna Yemelianova-Danilova, electrical equipment engineer; Senior engineer Pavel Ivanovich Morshnev; technician of squadron Nikolai Stepanovich Kurdin; engineer of armaments Lev Ilich Kurapeyev.

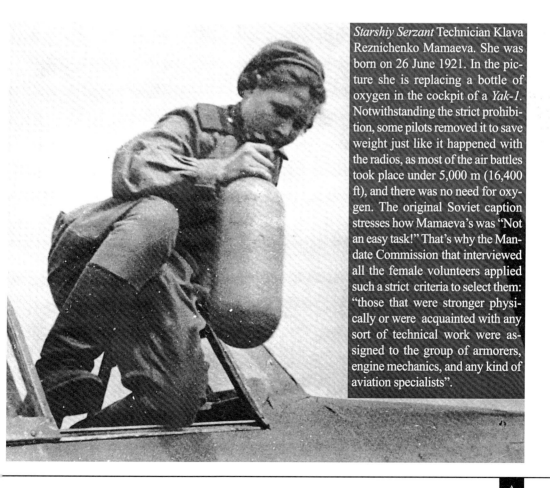

Starshiy Serzant Technician Klava Reznichenko Mamaeva. She was born on 26 June 1921. In the picture she is replacing a bottle of oxygen in the cockpit of a *Yak-1*. Notwithstanding the strict prohibition, some pilots removed it to save weight just like it happened with the radios, as most of the air battles took place under 5,000 m (16,400 ft), and there was no need for oxygen. The original Soviet caption stresses how Mamaeva's was "Not an easy task!" That's why the Mandate Commission that interviewed all the female volunteers applied such a strict criteria to select them: "those that were stronger physically or were acquainted with any sort of technical work were assigned to the group of armorers, engine mechanics, and any kind of aviation specialists".

Mariya Kuznetsova reading a book in front of her *Yak-1*. She was born in a city near Moscow, in a peasant family. She began flying in 1936 when she was eighteen. "I became a flight instructor in the *Po-2* at a military school and I taught there for five years, graduating about sixty pilots. In 1941 I joined the army and was assigned to the 586th Fighter Regiment as a pilot, guarding targets like bridges and such." When she was based near Stalingrad, she intercepted, along with Belyayeva, "a group of about 10 German bombers". "We started a dogfight" she wrote, later. "During the maneuvers Belyayeva's plane was shot down, and I kept on fighting... We shot down two fascist aircraft. The German bombers dropped their bombs in an open field and turned back." The date of the engagement, in this case too, remains unknown.

Tatyana Nikolaevna Khrulkova, from *586 IAP's* staff. Every volunteer that had even a few flying hours had asked Raskova to be assigned to the pilots' group. Many of the girls who had no flying experience preferred to be mechanics. Those selected to be clerks or staff workers were the most disappointed of all. Many cried when they learned that they had been assigned to offices. "It seemed to them," recalled Yekaterina Migunova, Raskova's deputy of staff in *587 BAP*, "that all their hopes had collapsed. 'My girlfriend will be fighting, but I will sit and pore over papers!'"

Azerbaijani pilot Zuleika Seid-Mamedova, regimental navigator, getting ready to take off. She had been a navigator before the war and the regimental navigator of the 586th Fighter Regiment. After the war she was demobilized and returned to Baku. She joined the Communist Party. At last, in 1952 she became Azerbaijan's Minister of Social Security.

Olga Yamshikova, with the map in her hands, and her wingman, Alexandra Akimova. Yamshikova was the protagonist of one of the biggest day of the 586th. On 19 December 1943 she led eight of her squadron to intercept three German formations of aircraft bound to bomb the crossing across the Dnieper, west of Kiev, Ukraine. Yamshikova and Akimova, together with other Soviet fighters from Brovary and Zhulyany airfields, attacked the *Luftwaffe* planes, seven of these being shot down in the Kiev area[55]. Yamshikova landed with almost no fuel and ammo. "Her machine was shot full of holes and Akimova lost one of her landing flaps," remembered Nina Slovokhotova, the chief of chemical service[56].

Olga Nikolaevna Yamshikova was 17 when, thanks to a Komsomol city committee pass, she enrolled at the Leningrad School for Aircraft Mechanics. In 1933 she graduated from an aeroclub and a higher parachuting school. She became a flying instructor and trained more than 100 pilots. In the same year, she set a glider record. When the Germans invaded the USSR in June 1941, she was in the last year at the "N. Y. Zhukovskiy" Air Force Engineering Academy. Marina Raskova tried to convince her to become an engineer of the future *586 IAP*. Yamshikova, who had more than 1,000 flying hours, preferred to be a fighter pilot. She was finally transferred to the 586th in the fall of 1942. During the conflict she flew about 200 sorties. One of these, flown on 14 July 1943, was to escort, with other five *Yaks,* the *Lisunov Li-2* transporting General Khodyakov from Voronezh to Kursk[57].

Fighter regiment pilots, Alexandra Akimova (left) and Mariya Batrakova, training with a *ShKAS* antiaircraft machinegun with a fighter gunsight. Before the war, Batrakova was a teacher in School Nr. 15 in Yenakiyev, Donetsk Region. She was credited with at least one air victory against a reconnaissance aircraft. Akimova is still a little known historical character.

Pilot Valentina Abramovna Petrochenkova. She joined the fighter regiment in November 1943, in Kiev. In autumn 1941 she had tried repeatedly to join Raskova's 122 Air Group but had been rejected. As a flying instructor, she was posted to Stalingrad to train pilots for *Voyenno-vozdushnyie Sily* (Air Force). Subsequently she was tasked to train airborne troops. After instructing 60 soldiers, she was sent to Penza Flying School. At the time she had 300 flying hours on training aircraft such as the *Ut-2*, but at first the commander refused to accept her. He had already in his school pilots like Aleksandra Akimova and Mariya Batrakova and was sick of female pilots. However, after Valentina had waited all night outside his door, he allowed her to show him how she could fly. The commander was amazed with her flying technique and enrolled her in his school. At last,

she was assigned to *586 IAP*, but commander Gridnev required her to train for another 20 days before declaring her combat ready. After the war, her husband, a test pilot, forced her to choose between family and aircraft, threatening divorce. She decided to hang up her aviation career.

Some of the less known 586th fighter pilots. Left to right: Zina Solomatina, Anya Demchenko, Masha Batrakova, Sasha Akimova, Galya Burdina, and Valya Petrochenkova. Solomatina flew 96 sorties and was involved in many air combats. However, she could not claim any victory. Senior Lieutenant Anya Nikolayevna Demchenko was commander of a *Zveno* (tactical Soviet formation composed of three or four aircraft) of 586th. "When she learned that we had fought severe dogfights with the enemy," recalled pilot Mariya Kuznetsova about Demchenko, "out of envy she escaped from the female regiment in the plane of a male pilot who had fallen ill and flew to the male regiment where we served... She did this without permission and was punished for it"[58]. Subsequently, Demchenko distinguished herself in the support operation to ground troops during the Korsun–Shevchenkovsky Offensive that led to the Battle of the Korsun-Cherkassy Pocket (24 January-16 February 1944). On that occasion, Demchenko led her fighter group in an attack to an airfield from where German bombers waited to take off.

(Right) Tamara Pamyatnykh helps *Leytenant* Galina "Galya" Burdina to fasten her parachute before ▸▸ a night sortie. Burdina was one of the "top guns" of the female fighter regiment. "All in all," she remembered, "I shot down four enemy aircraft." During the Battle of Kursk she flew as wingman to the regimental commander. She downed a *IV./JG 51 Bf 109* and a transport *Junkers Ju 52* on 9 February 1944. During the Battle of the Korsun-Cherkassy Pocket (fought in Central Ukraine, was hailed by Soviets as the "Stalingrad on the Dnieper"). Moreover, she shot down a *Ju 88* on 9 April 1944[59]. Burdina was shot down once: she force-landed and suffered injuries to her head, face, and mouth. She remarked: "After the war I returned to a pilot school and taught flying to cadets, and then I flew for fifteen years in civil aviation for *Aeroflot*."

Mechanic Valentina Vasilyevna Kovalyeva-Sergheicheva (left) and engine mechanic Nastya Fedosova. Kovalyeva was born in 1919. In 1933 she finished the secondary school of seven grades and enrolled in a technical school. After graduating, Valentina was sent to work in a military searchlights factory. She attended glider courses and became a flying instructor. When the war broke out, she volunteered for Raskova's regiment, requesting to be a pilot. "In the regiment I became a mechanic," she recalled. Full of grief, she wrote to authorities to let her be a pilot. "But they said then they would have to train another to be a mechanic," as there was need of mechanics. "We would warm the planes at night every two hours to keep them from freezing, and after warming them we covered them with special blankets, as if they were babies." She was first posted to ground crew of pilot Irina Olkova. Subsequently was assigned to one of the new pilots who came in as reinforcement, Tamara Voronova. This picture was taken in Kiev, in 1943.

Valya Vasilyevna Kovalyeva-Sergheicheva. She came from an illustrious family, the Popkovs. They were repressed during Stalinism. Her father perished during the Civil War. Her mother could not take care of her so they took "Valya" to an orphanage. When she was five, her aunt got married, took her from the orphanage, and brought her up. Meanwhile, all of her family's relatives were imprisoned because her uncle was pronounced to be "people's enemy". After the war, she was dismissed from the plant where she worked and all of her *586 IAP's* former colleagues were warned by the *NKVD* not to see or phone her, because she came from a family of an imprisoned enemy of the people. All her telephone calls were recorded. After the fall of the Soviet Union she could get in touch with her former colleagues and comrade in arms. In the 1990s she was appointed responsible for the work of the regimental council.

Evgeniya Dmitryevna Borak and Mariya Shcherbatyuk reading and studying in the regiment library. In the early spring of 1944 the regiment was transferred to Zhitomir. "Here we set up a reading room," recalled Vera Tikhomirova, Deputy Political Commander of the regiment, "where we displayed photographs, issued operational news bulletins, produced good quality wall newspapers, and organized evening amateur talent performances. Many of the girls were so talented! We had painters, poets, dancers and masters of all trades..."[60].

Pilot Zoya Pozhidayeva, extreme right, as a Communist party member, lectures male and female personnel on the airfield. She witnessed the first loss of the 586th when her friend Olga Golisheva nosed down into a dive and crashed. She flew mainly escorts of Soviet VIPs to Stalingrad. While the regiment was based in Voronezh, on an indeterminate day, she was scrambled to intercept an enemy plane. At an altitude of 8,000 meters (26,238 feet), a German reconnaissance aircraft, seemingly a *Junkers Ju 88*, was spotted. The aircraft dived to escape. Pozhidayeva pursued and fired as it pulled out of the dive. "I went on attacking him, and I could see the white trail of steam coming from his aircraft," she remembered. "But he crossed into German-held territory, and I ran out of fuel over the neutral ground between the Soviet and German lines and had to make an emergency landing." Pozhidayeva flew 237 missions without scoring, reportedly, any victory[61].

Junior Lieutenant pilot Zoya Pozhidayeva. "I lived and worked in Moscow after I graduated from trade school," she later recalled. "In the evening I attended a glider school. Then I was sent to pilot school to become a pilot instructor. When I graduated, I was sent to Moscow to instruct. We flew both the *Po-2* and *U-2* aircraft"[62]. She married a fighter pilot, a Hero of Soviet Union, during the war, and flew with his regiment until she had a child in 1946. Then she moved to the Urals where her husband was forming a fighter regiment. After his death in 1985, she came back to Moscow, helping her daughter to raise her two nieces.

Lyudmila Mikhailovna Bratsilova, aircraft mechanic, fitting the interior of the landing gear lodgement. Bratsilova is smiling, notwithstanding the extreme hardships that fighter regiment technicians had to face every day. "The living conditions were really very difficult for us," her colleague Shebalina Inna Nikolayevna recalled later. "We lived in trenches that we dug on the airfield at the tails of our airplanes. These

trenches were covered only with canvas, so we lived underground. First of all, there was no place to live; and second, there was no time to sleep. In daytime, pilots flew combat missions, and at night, we had to repair the aircraft. We worked at night with a cover over the engine and used torches for light. In some areas we lived in destroyed houses or in barracks if they were available"[63].

Senior Lieutenant Anya Nikolayevna Demchenko, surrounded by her ground crew, explains how the dog-fight went. Demchenko was born on 26 June 1920, in Kharkov, Ukraine. Her father was a laborer. After finishing the secondary school and a course in the Polygraphic Institute, she entered the Kherson Aviation School. After two years she went to Moscow were she kept flying and at the same time worked as chair-man of a community military court. She was one of the most experienced pilots to volunteer for Marina Raskova's 122 Air Group, in October 1941. She had amassed 1,150 hours of flying on biplanes like the *Polikarpov U-2* and *R-5* and on more advanced training aircraft like the *Yakovlev Ut-1* and *Ut-2*. With the 586th she fought on the Second Ukrainian and South-West Fronts. Overall, she flew 203 missions with 191 of these being operational flights: 16 escorts to *Lisunov Li 2* transporting VIP, 36 cover missions for troops near Stalingrad, and 15 for Stepnoi front troops, 11 protection sorties for Dnieper River crossing (in Ukraine) and 8 air combats against enemy fighters. Demchenko was awarded the Order of the Red Star and the Medal "For the Defense of Stalingrad" (Медаль «За оборону Сталинграда» Medal «Za oboronu Stalingrada»). After the war, she abandoned the military career, gave birth to a son and worked in the catering business. She died in 1969.

586 IAP's airwomen and aviators look in good humor, consulting a geographical chart. The fighter regiment was based in Zhitomir-Skomorokhi from 21 March to 2 September 1944. The pilots' task was to protect fixed targets and rail junctions. During those five months the 586th was involved in 15 air combats (seven in daytime). Commander Gridnev and Surnachevskaya shot down jointly a *Heinkel He 177*, while Nikolai Korolev and German Konstantinovich Tsokaev (both male) claimed a *Junkers Ju 88*. In one of the night interceptions Galya Burdina was credited with the kill of another *Ju 88*. While in Zhitomir, the fighter regiment flew 611 missions, including 274 sorties to cover ground targets, 237 interceptions of reconnaissance aircraft, 35 night missions, 49 escorts of transport aircraft (*Lisunov Li-2*) and 14 free-hunt sorties.

Heinkel He 177 of *Kampfgeschwader 50* on the Russian Front. The *He 177* was a long-range bomber, comparable to the American *Boeing B-29 Superfortress*. It flew exceptionally well during the Stalingrad campaign. *He 177s* flew transport missions and subsequently were equipped with an *MK 101* cannon in the nose for suppression of antiaircraft batteries. Raysa Surnachevskaya and *586 IAP's* commander, Aleksander Gridnev, claimed in spring-summer 1944, one such plane, mistaken for a reconnaissance aircraft. The Surnachevskaya and Gridnev victory is one of the very few achieved by the Soviet Air Force against this aircraft. Soviet pilots, trained and equipped mainly for low-level interception and ground-attack roles, were unable to hinder these bomber that flew at about 6,000 m (19,690 ft) to the relatively high speed of 565 km/h (351 mph). Moreover, Soviet aviators were not accustomed to engage such big aircraft. The *He 177* had a length of 22 meters (72 ft 2 in) and a wingspan of 31.44 m (103 ft 1¾ in). Russian pilots were even intimitadet by the powerful defensive armament and usually did not press home their attacks. The A-5 model had one 7.9 mm machine gun in the nose, one 20 mm *MG 151* in front ventral gondola; two 7.9 mm *MG 81* in rear ventral gondola; two 13 mm *MG 131* in remotely operated dorsal barbettes; one 13 mm *MG 131* in manned dorsal turret; another *MG 151* in tail[64].

Klavdiya Pankratova, left, planning a sortie with Tamara Pamyatnykh (right), with maps, using the tail of a *Yak* as a table. On 5 June 1944, Klavdiya Pankratova and her wingman, Kolya Korolev, were scrambled to intercept an enemy reconnaissance aircraft. "Maneuvering among the clouds," recalled Pankratova, "we quickly climbed to an altitude of 6,000 meters. Suddenly we saw an *Heinkel He 111* directly in front of us." In combat among the clouds they managed at first to put the engine of the *Heinkel* on fire and later to downing it. "… we dove after the falling enemy. I drew a cross on the map, near the (Ukrainian) town of Zhmerinka, to mark the site of Nazi pilot's crash. We flew home wing to wing tip, like in an air show." Korolev was mortally wounded a month later[65]. Pankratova was the daughter of a worker at the Kerch Metallurgical Plant. She graduated from the factory training school attached to the plant. "In 1935 I was given a Komsomol pass to study at a glider school... Then came the training in the flying club and in the Kherson Flying school. After graduation I was directed to the Magnitogorsk Flying Club as an instructor. By the beginning of the war, I had given a start, in their flying careers, to some fifty new pilots." The order to place herself at Raskova's disposal reached her at Saransk Military School, where she was employed as an instructor[66].

Heinkel He 111, the type of aircraft claimed by Pamyatnykh and Korolev. This twin-engine bomber first appeared to the public as a civil passenger transport. It made its first flight in 1935, an elegant streamlined aircraft with elliptical wings and outstanding handling characteristics[67]. Soviet pilots were intimidated by *Heinkel He 111s*. They were "fearsome war machines with strong defensive armament," recalled fighter pilot and Hero of Soviet Union Mayor General Alexander Shvarev. A *"Heinkel 111… capable of firing in almost any direction, was a hard nut to crack"*[68]. The *He 111H-3* was armed with a 20 mm *MG FF* cannon and an *MG 15* machine gun in the ventral gondola, plus two other *MG 15* in the nose, another dorsally mounted, and similar weapons in beam positions. However by the end of the war the *He 111* was becoming obsolete and was flown only in the transport role.

Flight Commander Valentina Ivanovna Gvozdikova. Not much is known of her. She is mentioned in a letter by Lidya Litvyak to her mother of 29 March 1942. Gvozdikova is regarded as a first class pilot and one of Lily's best friend. "I am friendly with Valya Gvozdikova, Anya Demchenko and Klava Pankratova. We all fly very competently"[69]. After the war she became an air traffic flight controller for *Aeroflot* in Adler-Sochi International Airport, along the Black Sea coast and near the southern Russian border with Abkhazia, Georgia. Her son Yevgeniy became a civil aviation pilot[70].

Sergeant mechanic Nina Niko-layevna Shebalina. She was born on 1 November 1920 in a family of a medical assistant in Lepsinsk, Alma-Ata region (Kazakhstan). In 1923 the whole family moved to Gia-rkent (now Panfilov), where she finished 8 grades of school. In 1936 she moved to her elder sister's house in Stalingrad where she continued studying and joined Komsomol. In 1938 she entered Kharkov Institute of Aviation, motor construction faculty. In 1940 she transferred to the Moscow Institute of Avi-ation Technologies. While studying, she attended the course for machinegunners. When the war began she was a third-year student at the Moscow Aviation Institute. She wanted to become an aircraft designer. She volunteered for the front and was allowed to join Raskova's group. At first she was a "mechanic of the reg-iment" and was assigned to pilot Raisa Belyayeva, the commander of a squadron. When Belyayeva was killed, she had already been assigned to the aircraft of Aleksander Gridnev, the regimental commander. "During the war my attitude toward my aircraft was really like it was a living creature, like a baby," she recalled later. "I cared for it every day and night and I had to go through lots of tears when I lost my plane… When I received a new plane, it took some patience and time for me to accustom myself to it. We all knew our own aircraft: you didn't have to see it, you just heard it and you knew"[71].

Mariya Batrakova, *586 IAP* pilot, is showing to her commander Agnya A. Polyantseva on the map the exact point where the claimed reconnaissance aircraft fell. The date of the kill is so far unknown. She was awarded the Order of the Red Star "for very competently carrying out air defense missions assigned to her" and "for displaying boldness and bravery in machinegunning the encircled German troops near Korsun'-Shevchenkovskiy."

Inna "Nina" Arkadevna Slovokhotova, chief of Chemical Services, deputy regimental navigator. She was a post-graduated student in chemistry in June 1941. Marina Raskova asked her to be Chief of Chemical Service, but as there was not chemical war, in 1943, at age of 24, she was trained as a navigator for the regiment. "I planned the routes for the pilots," she later recalled, "showed them how to escape the anti-aircraft fire, and trained pilots in navigation, but my major responsibility was to work with the radar location station." After the war she became a professor and doctor of science and chemistry, doing research in radiation physics and polymeric chemistry[72].

586 Fighter Regiment pilots and technicians. Since 2 September 1944, for two weeks, the 586th was based at Kotovsk, in Ukraine, and was subordinated to *141 IAD*. The regiment protected the railways of Kotovsk, Obhodnaya, Slobodka, Popeliukha, Gura-Kamenka, Zherebnovka, and the communication lines of the troops of the Second Ukrainian Front, also railways and river crossing above the Dniester River, in the areas of Ribnitsa and Kamenka. Actually in the last months of 1944 the fighter regiment saw little action. From 7 October to 20 December, it was rebased in Byeltsy (nowadays Bălți in Moldova).

Leytenant Pilot Agnya Alekseyevna Polyantseva, *586 IAP*'s squadron commander. Born on 2 February 1909, in Mamliutka Station, Omskaya Oblast (Omsk region), she was of petit bourgeois origins. Polyantseva graduated from Moscow Institute of Aviation in 1940 as an engineer. Her specialty was aircraft construction. Between 16 June 1941 and 5 November 1941, she worked as a test pilot. In the period 2 December 1941-30 April 1943, she was a test pilot at Factory Nr. 482 in Moscow. Between 7 May 1943 and July 1943 she worked at the Penza Center of Fighting Aviation. In July 1943 through October 1945, Polyantseva served as a commander of the 586th, holding the rank of *Leytenant*, on the South-West Front. After the war (May 1946-February 1953), she was hired by Factory Nr. 464 of Minaviaprom (Ministry of Aeronautical Industry of USSR). She stopped working as a test pilot on 31 January 1953. Subsequently, she trained Chinese pilots, worked for the Communist Party, and was active in Soviet Committee of Veterans. During her career she was awarded 11 orders and medals. Polyantseva died on 24 September 1988, leaving her husband and her son in Moscow.

Eskadriliya Commander Agnya Polyantseva, with her ground crew. Standing left to right: mechanic Valentina Ilinichna Skachkova, Agnya Polyantseva, armorer Sofya Sidorovna Tishurova. Sitting right to left: mechanics Tatyana Mikhailovna Ivanchuk and Semen Grigorevich Nizin. Nizin was a non commissioned officer (the highest ranking Soviet NCO)[73]. "Semen was a master of all trades and had a wonderful pair of hands," recalled Polyantseva. "He treated the motor mechanic Tanya Ivanchuk in a fatherly manner," she continued. "The enthusiasm with which she worked and her unusual skills inspired his respect. Master armorer Sonya Tishurova handled our 45 kilogram (the *ShVAK*, actually weighed 42 kgs/93 lbs – Ed.) cannon with ease, but the chief mechanic kept teasing her good-naturedly. The entire team functioned very well." After the war, Nizin returned to Odessa and married the girl that had waited for him for five years. He worked in the factory for some time and subsequently was elected secretary of the Communist Party.

Female and male personnel. Note that first and third pilots from the left wear the Order of the Red Star. Technical female personnel came from factories, university and technical institutes, and the *Komsomol*. Male technicians were necessary to keep the effectiveness of the *Yaks* (a *Yak-1* is on the background). "The *Yak* fighter was a sophisticated and difficult plane to maintain," recalled Yekaterina Polunina, mechanic of the aircraft, "so the senior engineer and squadron engineers were men. But the engineers in avionics and the engineers in armament were women"[75].

Left to right, fighter pilots Anya Demchenko, Mariya Kuznetsova, and Zoya Pozhidayeva at Byeltsy, 1944. While based in this Moldovian city, the 586th had the task to cover the fixed and floating bridges of the Dniester, a river that runs through Ukraine and Moldová. But few *Luftwaffe* planes tried to bomb or scout the targets that the Soviet airwomen were protecting. Subsequently, on 23 February 1945, the *586 IAP* was relocated to Hungary, at Debrecen. But in two months the fighter regiment flew only 12 combat sorties.

Leytenant pilot Valentina Volkova-Tikhonova. Born in 1915, she started flying when she was 23. She became first a glider and subsequently a *Polikarpov U-2* instructor. She amassed a great amount of flying hours before the war broke out. She joined the *586 IAP* in 1942. "I was considered to be a second-generation military pilot," she later recalled. "When I was young during the war, I was convinced it was a job for a woman to fly combat. In those times our only thought was to defend the Motherland, to save the country... Now I realize that the stress was very great and that it is not a female job. The task was even more aggravating because when you are the sole person in the plane, you have to be extremely alert and aware; you are the gunner, navigator, and pilot all in one person." Volkova-Tikhonova had 518 hours of combat flying during the war[74].

Radio-technician Klavdiya Semenovna Volkova

Another portrait of
Klavdiya Semenovna Volkova

Servicing of the *ShVAK* 20 mm cannon (firing through the propeller hub) of a *586 IAP*'s *Yak*. Actually this aircraft appears to be a *Yak-3*: note the lack of the oil-radiator, no longer placed under the chin (like in the *Yak-1* and in the *Yak-7B)* and the two oil coolers housed in the roots of the wings. Moreover, this type lacks of any aerial radio mast aft of the cockpit, has a lowered rear fuselage decking, and an all around glass canopy. The pilot remains unknown. One of the very few women to fly the *Yak-3* was Junior Lieutenant Tamara Voronova. Born in Yaroslavl in 1922, she became a flight instructor. Then she enrolled as a liaison pilot in a combat military regiment. Eager to fly fighters, she was allowed by the commander "to retrain to fly the *Yak-3* fighter, and I flew the *Yak-3* as the only woman pilot in that regiment. Later I was transferred to the 586th Fighter Regiment. I arrived in June, 1944"[76]. Note the compressed air bottle on the ground. "The brakes worked by air pressure," recalled Senior Sergeant mechanic Inna Pasportnikova, "and the compressor air container weighed sixty kilograms. In the summer I could roll it, but in the winter I had to carry it. I would put it on my shoulder and carry it from one plane to another, because the engines started with pressurized air"[77]. Moreover compressed air was required to retract the undercarriage and to reload and fire the guns.

A *Yakovlev Yak 9* during checkout tests. The *586 IAP* was equipped with this fighter in April 1945 when the fighter regiment was based in Vienna, Austria[78]. The type in the picture is the "U". Please note the one-piece molded windscreen. This type was equipped with the *Klimov VK-107A* engine. The report after tests stated: "The *Yak 9U*... is the best among the known Soviet and foreign fighters as regards basic performance characteristics in the range of altitudes from sea level to 6,000 m (19,680 ft)". It was an extremely versatile aircraft. It was, structurally, a development of the *Yak-7*, but more effective and more agile. The pilots who flew it regarded it comparable with the *Messerschmitt Bf 109G* and the *Focke-Wulf Fw 190A* . It was the first Soviet aircraft to shoot down a *Messerschmitt Me 262* jet. Production of 14,579 aircraft (in 15 versions) during the war made of the *Yak-9* the most widespread Soviet fighter in the Great Patriotic War. But the power plant was plagued by shortcomings. The main defect was the water and oil temperatures exceeding the specified limits during combats or at maximum speed. Other defects were vibrations, oil spilling, dropping of oil pressure.

Deputy political commander Vera Ivanovna Tikhomirova teaching politics to female personnel. "On 9 May 1945 our regiment formed up on the green expanse of our airfield," she later recalled. "Squadron commanders reported that their crews were combat ready. But there was no longer any need to fly operational missions. The war had ended and the enemy had been defeated. During our last meeting, at a solemn send-off ceremony, our personnel promised to pursue their peacetime endeavours just as conscientiously as they had fought, and to uphold the honour of our regiment. They swore to remain faithful to their wartime friendship, sealed with the blood of their fallen comrades, and they kept their word"[79].

Vera Tikhomirova had been an instructor pilot in civil aviation before the war. She joined Raskova's Air Group, but in late 1944 a serious illness put a stop to her military career. She came back to flying in *Aeroflot* five years later. For the successive 20 years she served in *Aeroflot*, flying the *Lisunov Li-2* and the *Ilyushin Il-14*, a twin-engine commercial and military personnel and cargo transport aircraft.

Mariya "Masha" Batrakova, ready to take off, protects herself by the darting sun with un umbrella. During summer 1945, when the war was already over, she did not come back from a routine operational flight. She took off for the last time on her *Yak-9* from Cinkota Airfield, northeast of Budapest, in Hungary. It was 12 July 1945[80]. Her name was engraved on the monument to commemorate the fallen Soviet soldiers in Gellert Mountain, in Budapest and a small museum was created in School Nr 15 of Yenakiyev in Donetsk Region (Ukraine) by the local Young Pioneers.

Military Merit Prizewinning Mechanics of regiment, left to right: Soniya Osipova, Masha Shcherbatyuk, Praskoviya Radko, and Tanya Ivanchuk. The aircraft technicians operated during the winter in extreme adverse weather conditions. So Osipova remembered a night of November 1942, when she was awakened to protect the aircraft engine from freezing: "As we were moving step by step toward the cowlings, along an icy crust, the wind keeps knocking us off the wings... Finally we opened the tank. We have to replace the cover to retain the rest of the heat in the engine. But... the wind grabs the heavy, iced-over covers out of our hands. You threw one end upward and the other one flew back with the wind, knocking you off your feet. Three times I was knocked down from the wing to the ground. Finally, with armorers Shcherbatyuk and Krasnoshchekova, we fasten the cover. The water bowser drives up. Streams of hot water grabbed by the wind splash on our faces and soak our clothing... My wet hand froze to the propeller blade onto which I was holding; the right hand, tensed, ached from holding the spray gun of the water bowser"[81].

Aircraft mechanic Tatyana Mikhailovna Ivanchuk at work. "This girl had a wonderful pair of hands," remembered Deputy Political Commander Vera Tikhomirova. "She was an electrician, a radio operator, a motor mechanic. She knew her aircraft inside out and looked after it with loving care. On her duty days, she was the first to arrive at the airfield. Strong and robust, she handled tools and carried the heavy airfield batteries as well as compressed air cylinder like a man. With her short hair and waddling walk, she resembled a young lad... Tanya was the editor of our wall newspaper, and an organizer of amateur talent performances"[82].

Regiment female first captains. Left to right, Aleksandra Makunina, Anastasya Aleksandrovna Kulvits (staff), R. Bentys (?), Nina Arkadyevna Slovokhotova (staff), Klava I. Kasatkina-Terekhova.

A pilot and her ground crew. Left to right: mechanic Marina Muzhykova, pilot Alexandra Akimova and armorer Anatoly Petrovich Kuzmin (?). In the back, Aki-mova's *Yak*.

Left, pilot Alexandra Yakovlevna Akimova. Before joining the fighter regiment she was sent to training at Penza Flying School. Penza is a city located 625 kilometers (388 miles), southeast of Moscow, on the Sura River.

Pilot Mariya Kuznetsova with ground crew.

Mariya Fedorovna Orlova, engineer.

Rolana Borisovna Kats, head special department.

Klavdiya Kasatkina-Terekhova (sitting, far left), the party bureau.

Left, squadron commissar E. Kurbakova and "partorg" Klava Kasatkina. Kasatkina was among those airwomen who pursued an interesting peacetime career. She graduated from a textile institute and became chief engineer of a textile factory.

Antonina Fedorovna Kachurina, motorist.

Female and male ground crews. Sitting, in the center: squadron engineer Anatoly Sergeyevich Reutskiy, mechanic Leontiy Ivanovich Klochkovskiy, engineer Viktor Nicholayevich Kazanin.

One of the nine male members of fighter regiment staff, Stepan Aleksandrovich Podrushko. On his right chest is wearing a Guards Badge. On his left chest is recognizable the medal "For the Victory over Germany in the Great Patriotic War 1941–1945" awarded to Soviet service personnel (approximately 14,933,000) who participated to the Great Patriotic War.

Elizaveta Abramovna Shur, military clerk.

Komsomol meeting of unidentified fighter regiment personnel.

586th second squadron.

Nina Alexandrovna Sokolova, armament mechanic.

Nina Nikolaevna Andreyeva, member of staff and chief of cipher code office.

★

Aleksandra Kostantinovna Muratova, navigator of regiment.

Galina Drobovich, mechanic. After the war she worked at a nuclear research institute and subsequently as a telephone station master.

Anastasya Nikolaevna Gorelova, member of 586th staff.

Antonina Konstantinova Skvortsova, engineer of regiment.

Another picture of Antonina Konstantinova Skvortsova, engineer of *polk*.

Original caption reads: "Day after the battle." On the left, the nose of a
Yak. The typical shape of the "mouth" of the oil-cooler under the nose
of the aircraft identifies it as a *Yak-9*.

Tatyana Sergeyevna Gu-
bareva, armorer.

Fedor Fedorovich Lunev, aircraft engineer.

Aircraft mechanic Lidya
Pavlovna Girich.

Left to right: armorer Vera Sergeyevna Gushina, pilot Anya Demchenko and A. Butuzova.

Klavdiya Ivanovna Yagodkina, squadron commissar.

Elizabetha Andreyevna Terekhova, technician

Vera Sergeyevna Gushina, armorer.

Zoya Vasilyevna Prokhoda, staff.

(Left) Ekaterina Nikolayevna Smykova, technician.

Anastasya Aleksandrovna Kulvits, staff.

Two unidentified 586th female members.

(Far right) *Starshiy Leytenant* (ста́рший лейтена́нт, Senior Lieutenant) Olga Yamshikova. Yamshikova was commander of an *eskadriliya* of *586 IAP*. In this group photo she poses with her pilots. When the war was over, Yamshikova, who had a degree in engineering, applied to realize her long-standing ambition to became a test pilot. During her career she would have amassed more than 3,000 flying hours in 45 types of aircraft and about 8,000 take off/landings.

586 IAP's technical staff with the division commanders, on Victory Day, in Budapest. The 586th was the first of Raskova's Regiments to be disbanded after the war. "Our colors were turned over to the Museum of Soviet Army and our HQ documents were transferred to military archives," recalled later Vera Tikhomirova. "The ordinal number of our regiment had been entered on the list of Soviet Air Force units in perpetuity"[83].

SCHEDULE OF COMBAT SORTIES OF 586 IAP

Intercept missions:	337
Escorts of bombers and ground attack aircraft:	49
Escorts of transport aircraft:	301
Cover flights for troops:	484
Reconnaissance flights:	16
Patrol over fixed targets:	1,159
Air battles fought:	125
Aircraft claimed:	38
TYPE OF AIRCRAFT SHOT DOWN:	
Fighters:	12
Bombers:	14
Transport:	1
Reconnaissance:	11
Ground targets destroyed:	two *Junkers Ju 52s*, four tanks, 30 vehicles, 20 horses killed
Losses:	approximately 10 pilots, 30% of flying personnel, including pilots lost in other regiments and a male one, Nikolai Korolev.
Undetermined sorties:	2,073
Total Combat sorties:	4,419
Number of female pilots:	37
Number of male pilots:	13

NOTE

1   Noggle, Anne *A Dance with Death: Soviet Airwomen in World War II*, p. 167

2   Noggle, pp. 165-166

3   Cottam, *Women in Air War*, p. 215

4   Noggle, p. 166

5   Yefim Gordon, *Soviet Airpower in World War II*, p. 149

6   Cottam, *Women in Air War,* pp. 297-300

7   Colin D. Heaton and Anne-Marie Lewis, *The German Aces speak*, pp. 46-47

8   Artem Drabkin, *Barbarossa & the Retreat to Moscow*, p. 15

9   Artem Drabkin, *Barbarossa & the Retreat to Moscow*, p. 24

10   Y. Gordon, *Soviet Air Power in World War 2*, pp. 146-148

11   Noggle, pp. 184-185-186

12   Artem Drabkin, *Barbarossa & the Retreat to Moscow*, p. 60

13   Noggle, p. 164

14   George Mellinger, *Yakovlev Aces of World War 2*, pp. 7-8

15   Y. Gordon, *Soviet Air Power*, p. 149

16   Noggle, p. 180 - Mellinger, p. 83

17   Colonel A. Khorobrykh, *Serdtse Gvardeytsa* (A Guardman's Heart) <Aviatsiya I Kosmonavtika> - Aviation and Cosmonautics - 1979, Nr. 6, p. 25

18   Jonathan Glancey, *Spitfire*, p. 152

19   A. Drabkin, *Barbarossa and the Retreat to Moscow*, pp. 135-136

20   Christer Bergström, Andrey Dikov and Vlad Antipov, *Black Cross Red Star – Everything for Stalingrad Vol. 3*, pp. 13-14

21   Pennington, p. 132

22   Pennington, p. 138

23   Pennington, p. 138

24   Cottam, *Women in Air War*, p. 249

25   Bergström, *Stalingrad The Air Battle,* p. 83

26   Cottam, *idem*, p. 249

27   Noggle, pp. 167-170

28   Noggle, pp. 208-210

29   Pennington, p. 111

30   Pennington, p. 33

31   Pennington, pp. 114-115

32   Noggle, p. 204

33   Pennington, pp. 118-119

34   Cottam, *Women in Air War*, pp. 217-219

35   Noggle, p. 187

36   Noggle, pp. 210-211

37   Pennington p. 119

38   Y. Gordon, *Soviet Airpower in World War II*, pp. 153-155, 158-159

39   Y. Gordon and D. Kazanov, *Yakovlev's Piston-Engined Fighters*, p. 42

40   Gordon and Kazanov, *idem,* p. 45

41   Noggle, p. 228

42   Y. Gordon, p. 167

43   Williams & Gustin, *Flying Guns World War II*, p. 26

44   Cottam, *Women in Air War*, p. 239

45   Cottam, *Women in Air War*, pp. 240-241

46   Noggle, pp. 165-166

47   Bergström-Antipov, p. 165. She achieved her victory on 26 June 1943, according to Pennington, p. 119

48   Bruce Myles, *Night Witches: The Amazing Story of Russia's Women Pilots in World War II,* p. 210

49   Cottam, *Women in Air*, pp. 248-302

50   Dmitry B. Khazanov, *Air War Over Kursk*, p. 83

51   Cottam, *Women in Air War*, p. 245

52   George Mellinger, *Yakovlev Aces of World War 2*, p. 84

53   O.K.L. Fighter Claims, July-December 1943, pp. 31-32

54   Noggle, p. 164

55   Seidl, *Stalin's Eagles,* p. 296

56   Cottam, *Women in Air War*, p. 22

57   Pennington, p. 119

58   Noggle, p. 170

59   Christer Bergström, Andrey Dikov and Vlad Antipov, *Black Cross Red Star – Air War over the Eastern Front, Volume 3, Everything for Stalingrad,* p. 165

60   Cottam, *Women in air War*, p. 298

61   Noggle, pp. 216-217

62   Noggle, p. 215

63   Noggle, p. 203

64   Donald David, *German Aircraft of World War II*, pp. 47-54

65   Cottam, *Women in Air War*, pp. 235-236

66   Cottam, *Women in Air*, p. 282

67   Walter J. Boyne, *Clash of Wings*, pp. 31-32

68   Artem Drabkin, *Barbarossa & the Retreat to Moscow*, pp. 24-28

69   Cottam, *Women In Air War*, p. 257

70   Cottam, *ibidem*, pp. 284-285

71   Noggle, pp. 202-204

72   Noggle, p. 178

73   Cottam, *Women in Air War*, pp. 280-281

74   Noggle, pp. 201-202

75   Noggle, p. 163

76   Noggle, p. 212

77   Noggle, p. 197

78   Noggle, p. 164 – Belyakov, p. 40

79   Cottam, *Women in Air War*, p. 299

80   Belyakov, p. 40

81   Cottam, *Women in Air War*, p. 229

82   Cottam, *Women in Air War*, p. 298

83   Cottam, *Women in Air War*, p. 300

SOVIET AIRWOMEN
OF THE GREAT PATRIOTIC WAR

587 BAP/125 GvBAP

Unit designations: 587th Bomber Aviation Regiment – 125 Guards Bomber Aviation Regiment
Dates of service: January 1943 – May 1945 (disbanded)
Main Operative Areas: Stalingrad, Tambov, Vysedki, Borisoglebsk, Yezovnya, Orsha, Grislinen (Poland)
Commanders: Marina Rasova and Valentin Markov
Aircraft flown: *Petlyakov Pe-2*
Combat missions: 1,134
Bombs dropped: 980 tons
Heroes of the Soviet Union: 5 (all female)
Female pilots: 30
Male pilots: 3
Female navigators: 28
Male navigators: 3
Female gunners: 11
Male gunners: 30
Female mechanics, armorers and engineers: 67
Male mechanics, armorers and engineers: 101

Arguably the most representative airwoman of the female day bomber air regiment, *Guards Major* Mariya Ivanovna Dolina pilot and flight commander of the *125 GvBAP* poses in front of her *Petlyakov Pe-2*. Born on 18 December 1920 in the village of Sharovka, Poltava District, in the Omsk Region of Siberia. She was the eldest of ten children from a peasant family. She trained in a paramilitary *Osoavyakhim Aeroklub* and subsequently in the Kherson Flying School. At first, she flew the *Polikarpov U-2* to transport *VIPs* and wounded. She was recruited by Raskova and assigned to the 587th Dive Bomber Regiment. Dolina flew sorties on the North Caucasus, the Orel-Bryansk and Smolensk sectors, Belarus, Baltic Republics and East Prussia. She bombed German troops, artillery batteries, ammunition stores, trains and ships. Altogether she flew 72 missions and was awarded the Gold Star of Hero of the Soviet Union on 18 August 1945. (Archive of Anatoly Plyac)

The female dive bomber regiment was the last to enter action, on 28 January 1943. The main reason was that the crew had initially trained on the *Sukhoi Su-2* but then switched to new *Petlyakov Pe-2*. Because of this delay, the *587 BAP/ 125 GvBAP* flew 1,134 sorties compared to the 24,000 of the *46 GvNBAP* and of the 4,419 of the *586 IAP*. Moreover, the dive bomber regiment had the highest percentage of men in its ranks: one third of the flying crew were men (three pilots, two navigators and 30 gunners). However the five Heroes of the Soviet Union who came from this regiment were female[1].

A winter-camouflaged *Petlyakov Pe-2*, equipped with retractable sky, built by plant Nr. 22. This aircraft could operate even from an unprepared airstrip while the German aircraft could not move. But as an ex-fighter, its bomb load was small for a bomber: normal load was 600 kg (1,322 lb). Only experienced crews could load up to 1,000 kg (2,204 lb) of bombs. The first aircraft delivered to the *125 GvBAP* was armed with rifle-caliber *ShKAS* machineguns. The rear firing machinegun was clearly insufficient to repel fighter attacks, so it was replaced by a heavy machinegun: the *Berezin BT*, 12.7 mm. It had the advantage to be installed on the airfield in four to six hours by two specialists. But even a strong gunner was unable to swivel it more than 45°-50° because of the slipstream.

Another picture of the *Petlyakov Pe-2*. Extremely fast for a bomber (actually it was designed as a high al-titude fighter), it was difficult for German pilots to intercept. It could even chase and shoot down enemy aircraft. Nevertheless the *Pe-2* had several faults. It could stall suddenly and asymmetrically when the wings had an attack angle of just 11° in tight manoeuvres during air combats and landings, that occurred at a rather high speed (145 km/h-90 mph). Another dangerous shortcoming was the emergency airbrake mechanism similar to those of the German *Junkers Ju 88*. Other defects were insufficient defensive arma-ment, a great risk of fire, and insufficient armor protection.

Marina Raskova, first commander of *125 GvBAP*. Tragically, she was in command for only a few months and never went in combat. The 125th left Engels on 1 December 1942 to join the 8th Air Army on the Western Front, but it was delayed by bad weather. Subsequently the regiment was assigned to Stalingrad. Raskova was the last to leave for the future Volgograd. On 4 January 1943 she took off from Lopatino with two other *Petlyakovs* delayed by engine troubles, but the weather deteriorated. "The visibility was so bad," *Starshy Leytenant* Galina Tenuyeva-Lomanova recalled, "I could hardly see the wings of my own plane! We were descending and my navigator said, 'There is the earth!' As she said it, I pulled back on the stick, the aircraft bumped the ground, we crashed and the aircraft was destroyed. All three of our planes crashed. All three crew members (the regimental navigator Kirill Ilich Khil, the gunner N.N. Erofeyev and a mechanic, V.I. Kruglov – Edit.) perished in Raskova's plane, all of us survived in the other two planes"[2].

Marina Raskova's crypt in the Kremlin Wall and (on the next page) a memorial plaque. "When Raskova's plane crashed into the embankment her head hit against the gun sight," still recalled Galina Tenuyeva-Lomanova, "and it split her head in two. When her body was found - she was to be in an open casket - a doctor performed surgery on her and restored her head and face, using a picture"[3]. For ten days Soviet newspapers and magazines published articles about Raskova's tragic death and letters by Stalina and

Valentina Grizodubova. Hers was the first state funeral of the war time. Her remains were interred in the Kremlin Wall. Access to her tomb has been denied to foreigners till now.

Air women of the *587 BAP*. Front row, sitting, first from the right, Klavdiya Fomicheva (pilot). Beside her, Nadezhda Nikiforovna Fedutenko, wearing the Gold Star of Hero of the Soviet Union awarded to her on 18 August 1945. Far left, Tamara Ivanovna Rusakova (pilot, she disappeared with her crew while flying over the sea in bad weather after the war). Fedutenko and Fomicheva took part in the first combat sorties on 28 January 1943, which was limited to squadron commanders at Stalingrad. Two *Petlyakovs* of the 125th flew with seven aircraft of the *10 BAP*. The following day the *Pe-2s* that participated in the bombing sortie were augmented to three. On 30 January, the 125th started to fly missions independently. The targets of the regiment were enemy troops, firing points, and enemy defensive positions. (Courtesy of Valentin Rusakov)

Aviators and aviatrixes of the dive bombers regiment. A total of 75 women flew with the *587 BAP*, at the beginning. After the death of Raskova, Yevgeniya Timofeeva took temporary command of the regiment. On 2 February 1943, the new commander, Mayor Valentin Markov, arrived. Markov had been commander of a bomber regiment and was recovering from combat wounds when he was commissioned. He was bitterly disappointed about the assignment. He was sure he "would have to go through hell" in a female bomber regiment. "We will begin with discipline," he warned the airwomen. With his male navigator, Nikolai Nikitin, he conducted intensive training in formation flying with fighter escorts. Markov at first was very unpopular with the girls. "He was young, thin, and very stern in appearance," recalled Fedotova. And behind his back the girls called him "bayonet". Subsequently, the girls realized how Markov cared about their safety and welfare. "We survived the war because of our regimental commander," recalled gunner Antonina Khovkhlova-Dubkova. At last the women renamed him "Batya" (daddy)[4].

Mariya Ivanovna Dolina-Melknikova, deputy commander of the dive bomber regiment. With her navigator Galya Dzhunkovskaya, she was involved in what is remembered as the most important air battle of the regiment, that took place on 2 June 1943, in North Caucasus. Her port engine was hit by flak, but she kept on flying to the target. On the way back, her flight was attacked north of Krymskaya by *Messerschmitt Bf 109s* of *JG 52*, the top scoring wing in history. "We had to fly there and bomb without a fighter escort," Dolina recalled, "because our fighters had started a dogfight with enemy fighters. The German planes attacked us and we had to fight alone". Her crew claimed one *Focke Wulf Fw 190* and a *Bf 109* shot down, but "of our nine bombers, five were shot down"[5]. Dolina crash landed just after crossing the frontline. The whole aircraft went up in flames. Vanya, the male gunner, even though wounded in his leg, pulled the two wounded girls out. They were all on fire and had to roll on the ground to extinguish the flames. The battle was recorded in the history of Soviet Air Force as a model of flight personnels' skill and valor. Dolina spent over a month in the hospital with a spinal compression injury that plagued her until her death.

Oberfeldwebel Rudolf Trenkel, ace of the *Jagdgeschwader JG 52*, climbing out of his *Messerschmitt Bf 109*. He shot down two of the *587 BAP*'s *Petlyakovs* on 2 June 1943. The bombers where flying at an altitude of 400 - 600 meters because of a thick layer of clouds. They were on their way to bomb the Soviet village of Krymskaya in the Kuban, in southwest Russia. That day, Trenkel claimed his first air victory[7], at 1.27 pm (Berlin time) at an altitude of 600 meters, his kill number 74. A minute later, he scored a second air victory[8], at an altitude of 500 meters. His two victims were Sholokhova and Fedotova. "Eventually, the aircraft of Olga Sholokhova and Katya Fedotova were knocked out," recalled flight commander Antonina Skoblikova. "They broke away from the formation, descended to a lower level, and kept flying straight in an attempt to reach the front line." The two pilots survived the crash of their two bombers[9]. A third aircraft, probably the one flown by Dolina, was claimed by *Gefr.* Goöpfert at 1.29 pm and a fourth at 1.45 pm. The 587th lost five aircraft but, in turn, claimed four German aircraft[10]. Actually, German sources reported that day, that *JG 52* did not lose any aircraft, while *Luftwaffe* pilots claimed just four *Petlyakovs* shot down.

Oberfeldwebel Rudolf Trenkel with his awards. Bottom, on his right chest, he wears the *Deutsches Kreuz* in Gold. He was awarded the *Ritterkreuz* on 19 August for 76 victories. Trenkel was born on 17 January 1918 at Neudorf, in Sachsen. He joined the *Wehrmacht* in 1936 but transferred to the *Luftwaffe* in 1939. On 22 February 1942, with the rank of *Unteroffizier*, Trenkel was posted to *III./JG 77* on the Eastern Front. He claimed his first victory – a Soviet *Polikarpov I-153* biplane fighter – on 26 March. On 1 May, Trenkel was transferred to *JG 52*. He recorded his 20th victory on 2 November. On 17 December, Trenkel shot down six enemy aircraft. On 2 June 1943, besides the two *Petlyakovs*, he claimed two *Lavochkin La-5s*. He served as a flying instructor for four months in *Ergänzung-Jagdgruppe Ost*, then, claimed 18 victories in October. In November he was shot down and wounded by a *Yak-9*. He recovered and was promoted *Oberleutnant*. On 14 July 1944, Trenkel claimed his 100th victory. In October, downed 12 aircraft in 10 days but was shot down five times. On 15 March 1945, he was shot down again (by *flak*) and wounded. He surrendered to the Americans, but they handed him over to the Soviets. However, due to severe wounds, the Russians freed him. He died on 26 April 2001. Trenkel holds the 42nd place in the list of the most successful aces in history, with 138 air victories in over 500 missions.

Klavdiya "Klava" Yakovlevna Fomicheva-Lev-ashova. Born in Moscow on 25 December 1917. Her father, a white collar worker, died when she was a child. She spent her childhood in the village of Znamenka, in poverty. She graduated from a primary school and became a bookkeeper apprentice at the Moscow State Bank. She started flying gliders and became a flying instructor. She requested Raskova for assignment to the fighter regiment but, because of her expertise, she was tasked to pilot the very demanding *Petlyakov*. During the second Battle of Smolensk (7 August–2 October 1943), on 17 September 1943, while bombing near Yelnya, *flak* hit her *Pe-2*. Klava crash-landed on a bombed fighter airfield. Her aircraft flipped over and burst into flames. Fomicheva and her navigator, Galya Turabelidze, survived with serious wounds but the gunner was killed. Fomicheva was hospitalized and was grounded until 1944[11].

Flak 37 anti-aircraft 88 mm cannon batteries. The dive bomber regiment suffered heavy losses on account of the antiaircraft *Luftwaffe* defense. During the second Battle of Smolensk the regiment lost two crews (six aviators) to anti-aircraft fire, one on 28 August and one on 22 October 1943. The 88 mm gun was used by Germany in large numbers and on every front throughout the war. It was one of the most effective German weapons of the war. The original models were developed into a wide variety of guns. The *Flak 37* portrayed in the picture was an improved version with updated instrumentation. The parts of the various versions of the guns were interchangeable. Like all 88 mm type, the *Flak 37* as well could, if necessary, be used as anti-tank artillery[12].

Messerschmitt Bf 109 of the *JG 51* on the Soviet Front. In the central sector of the Eastern Front, the 125th had to face *Jagdgeschwader 51 Mölders,* another of the elite fighter wings of the *Luftwaffe.* Its pilots were awarded more *Ritterkreuz des Eisernen Kreuzes* than any other fighter units. The *JG 51,* when started to fight in the Battle of Smolensk, had already amassed more than 6,000 victories. Its *Experten* included outstanding aces like 'Toni' Hafner (204 victories), Günther Schack (174), Heinrich Hoffmann and Otto Gaiser. *JG 51* had been renamed by late 1942 by its legendary commander Werner Mölders. Note on the blade of the propeller of the aircraft, the writing *IV./JG 51* which indicates that this aircraft belonged to the fourth *Gruppe.*

JG 51's ace, *Unteroffizier* Otto Gaiser, sitting in his *Messerschmitt Bf 109* (note the writing "Annelie" that refers to Gaiser's girlfriend (Annelise). On 14 October 1943, Gaiser and his unit clashed with the 125th. That day, the regiment was tasked to bomb enemy artillery and mortars near Orsha (or Orscha) in Belarus. Orsha was then the base of the 1st, 3rd and 4th *Gruppen* of *JG 51*, equipped with *Focke Wulf Fw 190s* and *Messerschmitt Bf 109Gs.* Nadya Fedutenko lead the usual nine ship formation. Along the route, the *flak* hit the right engine of Lyubov Gubina. Her aircraft lagged behind. Her two wing-women, Anya Maksimovna Yazovskaya and Irina Osadze slowed down to protect her. But a formation of German fighters intercepted them. At 4,000 meters, east of Studenez, Otto Gaiser, at 11.33 (Berlin time), got on the tail of Osadze's *Petlyakov* and set it on fire, wounding the pilot and navigator Valya Volkova. It was Gaiser's 58th victory. Four minutes later, north of Rasdel, he shot up his second *Petlyakov*, most likely that of Yazovskaya. The pilot and the navigator, Yelena Ponomareva, were killed, while the male gunner, Valentin Kotov, parachuted to safety.

Otto Gaiser, showing the damage received by his *Messerschmitt Bf 109*. To his luck, the fighter was provided with a steel plate to protect the pilot seat. Otto Gaiser was born on 5 October 1919 at Reutlingen. With the rank of *Unteroffizier*, he was posted to *10./JG 51*, on the Eastern Front, at the end of 1942. He claimed his first victory on 16 March 1943 when he shot down a *LaGG-3* fighter near Vyazma. Gaiser claimed 17 victories in August, including five *Ilyushin Il-2 Sturmoviks* ground-attack aircraft. He downed 14 aircraft in September, including five *Yak-1s* on 26 September (his victories 38 to 42). In October 1943, Gaiser achieved 10 kills, including the two *Petlyakovs* of the 125th, destroyed on 14 October. He recorded his last four victories (63-66) on 15 January 1944. A week later, near Berditschew (Berdychiv or Berdichev) in northern Ukraine, Gaiser engaged combat with four *Il-2 Sturmoviks*. His *Bf 109 G-6* never came back to base. He has remained MIA to this day. Probably he was the victim of the Soviet anti-aircraft defenses. Gaiser was posthumously rewarded with the *Ritterkreuz* and the rank of *Leutnant*. He is credited with 66 victories (plus eight unconfirmed), during 380 missions, all achieved on the Eastern Front.

Navigator Galina Brok-Beltsova. Born in 1925, she was one of the very young replacements sent to the 125th after the heavy losses suffered from *flak* and air combats, during fall and winter of 1943-44. "On 6 April 1944," recalled Brok-Beltsova, "our nine new aircrews – of Tonya Spitsina, Lena Malyutina, Toma Maslova, Nina Malkova, Tamara Malashvili, Masha Tarasenko, Tamara Rusakova, Masha Pogorelova, and Anya Shishkova – arrived at our destination near Yel'nya. The 'veterans' received us warmly... At first we studied the operations area, took tests, and practiced flying – in brief, we were being put into action gradually". (Courtesy of G. Brok-Beltsova)

Another picture of Galina Brok-Beltsova. After two and a half months of training, she was sent into action with the other replacements on the first day of the Vitebsk-Orsha Offensive (23 June 1944 – 28 June 1944), part of Operation Bagration. "On 23 June 1944, the beginning of the Belarussian Operation," recalled Brok-Beltsova, "we flew our first operational sorties. Our regiment's mission was to destroy the artillery and mortar positions in a large center of enemy resistance in the Bogushev sector. The front line shown on the map, when viewed from the air, turned to be a broad strip of black anti-aircraft shell explosions. They distracted us, so we didn't see the ground at all. We dropped our bombs when we saw the leader doing so. Such was our baptism of fire"[13]. (Courtesy of G. Brok-Beltsova)

Squadron navigator Galina Ivanovna Dzhunkovskaya-Markova. Still on 23 June 1944, on her very first day of flying with Klava Fomicheva, the *flak* set fire to their *Pe-2* and they had to parachute at an altitude of 150-200 meters. "Klava was evacuated to a hospital in Moscow," recalled Dzhunkovskaya, "while I managed to persuade Mariya Ivanovna Ponomareva, our regimental doctor, to let me stay in our medical unit. And so I was hobbling on one leg in the ward, wearing a short soldier's night-shirt, tied with tape at the throat; my burnt black face was adorned with green ointment spots"[14]. Dzhunkovskaya flew 69 combat sorties. She was selected to take part in the Victory Parade on 24 June 1945 and was awarded the Gold Star of the Hero of the Soviet Union on 18 August 1945. She married the commander of her regiment, Valentin Markov, and become deputy chief navigator. She retired in 1950, graduated from the Kirovgrad Pedagogical Institute and worked as an English teacher until 1967.

Late July 1944, the *Yak-3*'s flight line of the Normandie-Niemen fighter regiment of the French Air Force, fighting with the Soviets on Eastern Front. That unit flew in conjunction with the 125th in several sorties during the latter part of the war. At first, the French airmen were unaware that the *Petlyakovs* they were protecting were flown by women. When they discovered it, were pleasingly surprised. "We were more than amazed, we were delighted," stated *Colonel* Leon Cuyaut, an ace credited with 15 victories, "when we learned that Soviet women were taking part in air battles on all fronts. We observed them in action and we just had to admire them"[15]. "We had very good air cover," recalled *Leytenant* Yevgeniya Gurulyeva-Smirnova, "not only Russian but also French fighters provided us with protection when on bombing missions"[16]. The Normandie-Niemen flew 5,240 missions, claiming 273 enemy aircraft destroyed during 869 aerial combats.

Didier Béguin, one of the representative aces of the Normandie-Niemen in front of his *Yak-9*. A collegue of Béguin, Jacques André, one of the four French pilots declared Hero of the Soviet Union (the other three were: Marcel Albert, Marcel Lefèvre, Roland de La Poype), on 11 March 1960, recalled how, during the war, the 125th aviatrixes "proved themselves men's equals in valor while fighting against the common enemy." Béguin, in the picture with Russian mechanics Nazine and Casimire, was credited with 6 to 8 air victories. He was awarded the prestigious Legion of Honour (*Ordre national de la Légion d'honneur*, the highest decoration in France), the Order of Liberation (*Ordre de la Libération*), the Orders of the Red Banner and of the Great Patriotic War 2nd Class. Eventually, Béguin transferred to the Western Front and was killed by *flak* near Arnhem, Holland, on 26 November 1944, while serving as head of the squadron "Strasbourg Group Alsace". Of the 95 pilot that flew with the "Normandie," 42 were killed.

Marcel Lefèvre, Lieutenant of the Normandie-Niemen, between his Russian mechanics. Behind him, his *Yak* with personal emblems and ten crosses, indicating his air victories. Altogether he was credited with 11 victories[17]. On 28 May 1944, he landed and his *Yak-9* caught on fire. Badly burned in the face, hands, and thighs, he was evacuated to a hospital in Moscow. Marcel Lefèvre died on 5 June 1944. He was awarded the Legion of Honour, the Order of Liberation, the *Croix de Guerre,* the Orders of the Red Banner and of the Patriotic War 2nd Class. He was posthumously declared Hero of the Soviet Union.

Navigator Galina Brok-Beltsova still keeps, after 70 years, a moving and grateful memory of the French airmen. "The pilots from the nearby-based 'brother' regiments treated us very well... Sometimes, we recognized the broken Russian of our neighbors, French pilots from the nearby 'Normandie-Niemen' Regiment. And when there were friends in the sky, the attacking enemy fighters seemed less terrible"[18]. But even the gallant escorting French airmen could not protect the 125th airwomen against the German antiaircraft artillery. The "replacements" experienced bitterly the effectiveness of the *flak* during the combat mission of 24 July 1944. "The enemy artillery was ready for us," recalled Yelena Malyutina, "they fired at us so much that many planes were set on fire, but there were no plane shot down"[19]. (Courtesy of G. Brok-Beltsova)

Yelena Yushina, navigator of the 125th. On 24 July 1944 she flew in the aircraft flown by pilot Yelena Malyutina, to bomb German tanks concentrations near Obeliai, just across the border with Lithuania. "Only a few seconds before reaching the target," recalled Galya Brok-Beltosva, "Malyutina was wounded in the abdomen by shrapnel... Soon after navigator Yushina had released her bomb load, the pilot slumped against the control wheel, unconscious... Yushina revived Malyutina with liquid ammonia". Malyutina summoning her remaining strength managed to land and fainted. The divisional commander, while visiting Malyutina in the hospital, took off his own Order of the Red Banner and pinned it on her chest. The same Order (in the picture) was awarded to navigator Yushina. (Courtesy of Y. Yushina's family)

Another shot of Yelena Yushina. Before enrolling in *125 GvBAP* as a navigator, she attended the Moscow Air Force School of Communications. She was among the students who volunteered to be trained as gunner-bombardier. Yushina was one of the seven girls who were found to be completely fit by several medical boards, along with Galina Brok, Lena Azarkina, Valya Konkina, Lyuda Popova, Tonya Pugacheva and Galya Vasilyeva. Subsequently she was sent to a reserve air regiment where she was trained in elementary air navigation, handling of weapons, and parachute jumping. (Courtesy of Y. Yushina's family)

Pilots and aviatrixes of *125 GvBAP* in front of one of their *Petlyakov Pe-2s*. Standing, first from right: Galina Brok-Beltsova (navigator); second from right: Yevgeniya Gurulyeva-Smirnova (navigator); third from right: Antonina Spitsina-Bondareva (pilot). Spitsina, a glider pilot at 16, became a flying instructor one year later. When at last was allowed to join the 587th, she already had 2,000 flying hours. At the end of the war she was one of the three women pilots who requested to remain in the air force and was retrained to fly the *Tupolev Tu-2* and flew until 1950. Gurulyeva (born on 24 December 1922) started flying gliders too, at 16. Before joining the 125[th,] she flew in an auxiliary medical regiment. She was one of the few aviatrixes of the regiment wounded. She was hit by *flak* while bombing German tanks in Lithuania. A shell splinter from a 25 cm gun struck her thigh. After the war she married and had a child.

Hero of the Soviet Union, Klavdiya Fomicheva. Shot down on 23 June 1943, she was back in action by 28 August 1944. Reportedly, she distinguished herself during the difficult air battles in the Baltic Region and in East Prussia during the winter of 1944-45. "On 29 December 1944," recalled her navigator Dzhunkovskaya, "we were to bomb enemy artillery and mortar positions near Auce (a town in southern Latvia near the Lithuanian border – Edit.)" Each aircraft was loaded with 1,000-1,300 kilograms of bombs. She completed 55 combat missions by December 1944. Fomicheva was the highest scoring female bomber ace of the Great Patriotic War. She was credited with 11 aerial victories (in group combat). After the war, Fomicheva became a flight instructor at the Air Force School for Pilots in Borisoglebsk. In 1956 she retired due to poor health and came back to Moscow. She died on 5 October 1958 from an undisclosed illness and was buried in the ancient Novodevichye Cemetery in Moscow.

Squadron Navigator Antonina "Tonya" Leontyevna Zubkova. Born on 12 October 1920 in the village of Semion, she was a brilliant student. Tonya was admitted to the Moscow State University's Faculty of Mechanic and Mathematics without entrance exams. On her first bomb training mission in Engels, she dropped her load in the center of the target. When, on 2 September 1943, the division commander was shot down, she lead the whole formation of 54 *Petlyakovs* to bomb the enemy fortifications near Yelnya. On 16 April 1945, Zubkova led the formation of all the division aircraft to the target: the East Prussian port of Fischhausen, located on the Vistula Lagoon, after 1945 known as Primorsk (in Russian, *Приморск*). Notwithstanding the poor weather, Antonina found the target and sixty tons of bombs fell on Nazi troops and their equipments. She flew altogether 56 missions and became Hero of the Soviet Union on 18 August 1945. After the war she went back to the university and became professor of mathematics at the "N. Ye. Zhukovskiy" Air Force Engineering Academy. She was killed in an accident on 13 November 1950, falling under a train. (Archive of A. Plyac)

◀◀ Galina Brok, navigator of 125th Regiment, with her husband, Beltsov. She was trained in a military school in 1941-42, after which she was assigned to the Emergency Aviation Regiment. She became a *Petlyakov Pe-2* navigator and was sent as a replacement to the *125 GvBAP*. "While I was awaiting assignment to the front I had met a male pilot," she recalled, "and we become engaged. After I went to the regiment at the front I received a letter from him every single day. The whole of my squadron read them, because very few of the other girls received letters. They used to say to me, 'Galina, it's true love.' Later I married him, and the whole squadron was present at our wedding. He came to our regiment to marry me, and it was the happiest episode of my life." After the war, Brok quit the Air Force and became an *NKVD* agent. Subsequently she got a doctor's degree and became head of the history department at the Moscow Engineering Institute[20]. In the picture, Galya wears (top, left) the Order of the Red Star, the Order of the Great Patriotic War and (bottom) the Guards Badge. On the right side, Beltsov wears the Order of the Red Banner and, just like his future wife – recognizable for the ribbon – the Medal "For Victory over Germany in the Great Patriotic War 1941-1945" Медаль «За Победу над Германией в Великой Отечественной войне 1941-1945 гг.» Medal «Za Pobedu nad Germaniej v Velikoj Otechestvennoj vojne 1941-1945 gg.» (Courtesy of G. Brok-Beltsova)

Male and female *125 GvBAP* personnel in front of a *Pe-2*. On 19 February, the regiment was awarded the coveted Order of Kutuzov 3rd Class. "The end of the war found us at the airfield of Grudziai (Lithuania)," recalled flight commander Yekaterina Fedotova, "That evening, the phone kept ringing and ringing, but we were all loath to get out of bed after flying several operational missions. Finally, Masha Kirillova could not stand the ringing any longer, so she got up and took the receiver off the hook. For an instant she froze, pressing the receiver to her chest. Then, turning to us – but still unbelieving – she said in a faltering voice: 'The war has ended!' We jumped out of our beds, screaming, hugging, and kissing one another. Then we ran out onto the street and opened fire with pistols"[21]. On 28 May, the 125th was decorated with the Order of Suvurov. Seventy-five women flew in the regiment. Five aircrews – a total of 14 aviatrixes – perished during the war and five airwomen became Heroes of the Soviet Union[22].

NOTE

1   R. Pennington, *Wings, Women & War,* pp. 183-185

2   Noggle, p. 153

3   *Idem*

4   Pennington, p. 97

5   Noggle, p. 120

6   H. Sakaida, *Heroines of the Soviet Union*, Osprey, p. 9

7   Koordinaten Planquadrat 85 112

8   Koordinaten Planquadrat 85 121

9   Cottam, *Women in Air War*, p. 36

10 Noggle, p. 120

11 H. Sakaida, *Heroines of the Soviet Union*, Osprey, pp. 11-12

12 Jean-Denis Lepage, *The Illustrated Handbook of FLAK German Anti-aircraft Defences* 1935-1945, pp. 105-106

13 Cottam, *Women in Air War,* pp. 93-94

14 Cottam, *Women in Air*, p. 88

15 Cottam, *Women in Air War*, p. 109

16 Noggle, p. 111

17 J. D. Clarke, *French Eagles Soviet Heroes The 'Normandie-Niemen' Squadrons on the Eastern Front*, p. 238

18 Cottam, *Women in Air War*, p. 96

19 Noggle, p. 130

20 Noggle, p. 134

21 Cottam, *Women in Air War*, p. 84

22 Noggle, pp. 104-105-106

Lydia Vladimirovna Litvyak

Name: Lidya
Patronimic: Vladimirovna
Surname: Lityvak
Born: 18 August 1921
Place of Birth: Moscow
Rank: Starshina (Master Sergeant/Flight Sergeant)/Mladshy Leytenant (Flight Officer/Junior Lieutenant)
Units: 586 IAP, 437 IAP, 9 GvIAP, 296 IAP (later renamed 73 GvIAP)
Air victories: 12 individuals and 2 (or 4) shared
Day of Death: (presumed) 1 August 1943
Place of Death: Dmitryevka (Ukraine)
Awards: Order of the Red Star, Order of the Red Banner, Order of the Great Patriotic War, Order of Lenin, Gold Star of Hero of the Soviet Union

Lydia Vladimirovna Litvyak, the most famous female fighter pilot in history. She is one of the only two female "aces" in history (the other is Katya Budanova). An ace is a pilot who has achieved at least five aerial victories. Litvyak is usually credited with 12 individual kills and two or four shared, plus an observation balloon during 168 sorties and 66 dogfights against the *Luftwaffe*. Her end is still surrounded in mystery after 70 years.

(Right) Anna Vasilyevna, Litvyak's mother. She worked as a shop assistant in Moscow.

Vladimir Leontevich Litvyak. Litvyak's father worked for the railway, as a railway-man, train driver and clerk. Declared "enemy of the people," he "disappeared" during Stalin's 1937 purges. But his charges were never specified nor proved. Litvyak was determined to become a fighter pilot. She was absolutely convinced of her father's innocence and believed that she could redeem her family name by gaining honour in combat.

Litvyak and her family lived on the first floor of *Novoslobodskaya Ulitsa 14/88*. They stayed in a typical two-room Moscow flat with a kitchen shared with other families. Now the building is divided into small flats and tourists are denied access.

Seventeen year old Lydia with her brother Yuri in 1938, while still a student of a technical-mechanic institute. As a student, Litvyak kept pictures of Marina Raskova, Polina Osipenko, Valentina Grizo-dubova and other famous female pilots in her notebook. Yuri was eight years younger than her famous sister. He survived the war but changed his surname to Kunavin; he was afraid of retaliations on account of her disappearance. He was presented with her sister's award after Soviet President Mikhail Gor-bachev approved it in May 1990. Kunavin died soon afterward. With his death, the Litvyak Family came to an end.

Lidya Litvyak as a teenager in Moscow. She trained in Engels with Marina Raskova and she appeared much too young for her age. "I looked at Litvyak then," remembered Inna Pasportnikova, her aircraft mechanic. "She was small, delicate and beautiful; still completely a little girl. How could she be a strong, courageous, tough-willed fighter pilot?... I never imagined... that she would become the only woman in the world to have 15 enemy aircraft to her credit-killed by her in difficult air battles"[1]. Her real name was Lidya, but many called her Lilya or even Lilii.

SOVIET AIRWOMEN OF THE GREAT PATRIOTIC WAR

A very young Litvyak (extreme left) with her colleagues (or trainees) at the aeroclub. Keen of aviation since she was a child, Litvyak enrolled at Kalinin *Aeroklub* when she was just 14.

Right, Litvyak in front of her *Polikarpov U-2* training aircraft, with her mechanic. Litvyak graduated from Kalinin *Aeroklub* in 1938 "cum laude". In the same year, she flew for the first time in the *Polikarpov U-2* while at Kherson Flying School. Later, she shifted to the *Yakovlev Ut-1* and trained intensively. Kherson (*Херсон*), in southern Ukraine, was an important port on the Black Sea and Dnieper River. There was an important ship-building industry there. Most aviatrixes went to Kherson to train in the local military flying school. Note how Litvyak, in opposition to what was reported by some veterans (probably to support the theory that the small skeleton found near the *Yak-1* wreck in Kozhevnya was hers), did not look at all to be too "tiny and petite".

Lidya Litvyak during her Kherson flying course. She is wearing a Parachute Jump Badge by *Osoavyakhim*. Her skill in parachuting would become extremely useful in a couple of situations. Litvyak parachuted for the first time on 20 July 1943 from her burning *Yak-1* after German *Messerschmitts* had shot down and killed her commander, Ivan Golyshev. She probably parachuted from her crippled *Yak-1* few days later, on 1 August 1943, after she flew into clouds to escape from pursuing *Luftwaffe Experten* from *JG 3* or *JG 52*.

Parachute Jump Badge by *Osoavyakhim* (Society to Support Aviation and Chemical Defense). This was Litvyak's first award.

Lidya Litvyak, in civilian clothes, as a flying instructor at the Moscow Aero-club in 1941. She trained 45 pilots before volunteering to the front. When the war broke, on 22 June of the same year, she was on Klyazminsky *aeroklub*. She was one of the first to volunteer but – reportedly – she was rejected because she had enough flying experience. The legend goes that she augmented of 100 the number of her flying hours to get enrolled. Eventually she was posted to Marina Raskova training regiment. Already during the training in Engels, she showed her flying capabilities. "I started to watch her", Inna Pasportnikova, her mechanic, wrote. "Litvyak was one of the best pilots."

Litvyak in front of her *Yakovlek UT-1*. The *UT-1* was a modern (it had entered service in 1937) but very small and simple aircraft for advanced training and aerobatics. It had wooden wings and a *Shvetsov M-11* radial engine (visible in the picture) of 115 hp. It was not easy to fly. It was an intermediate aircraft between basic trainers and the fighters. Actually it required careful piloting. During the war, was used as a liaison aircraft, for reconnaissance and even as improvised light fighter-bomber until it was totally supplanted by *Ilyushin Il-2 Shturmoviks*.

Lydia in winter flying coverall. In Engels, after the women were issued their winter gear, she spent a whole night to unstitch the white goatskin used to line their boots and sew it on the uniform collar. During the morning roll call, Marina Raskova asked her what she had on her shoulder and Litvyak candidly answered: "A goatskin collar. Why, does it not suit me?" Raskova agreed and asked Litvyak when she had had time to do that. "Last night", answered her, among the laughters of the other girls. "You'll have to spend one more night without sleeping, Litvyak", ordered her Raskova, "and sew back on the collar that is supposed to be on that uniform!"[2].

A fascinating pose of Lidya Litvyak. Her (presumed) liaison with Hero of Soviet Union, Aleksei Solomatin, is well known, but few knows that Litvyak had been in love before, while based in Anisovka, near Saratov. Actually, many airwomen took for granted that being in love was inevitable, given their age and the proximity with many young men. Near the *586 IAP*, actually, there was another male regiment. And many girls started to flirt with the boys of it. "I have just decided that I am in love with one boy (either a pilot or mechanic)", Lidya wrote in a letter to his mother in May 1942, after four months of service, defending Saratov factories and installations. "His name is Tolya... Unfortunately, I'm not counting on seeing him often but, at least, I do not feel like a nun... Am I worse than others? All our girls are in love"[3].

Left, to right, *586 IAP's* pilots: Valentina Guozdikova, Klavdiya Pankratova and Lidya Litvyak. According to Aleksander Gridnev, Fighter Regiment's second commander, Litvyak was one of the pilots (the other being Prokhorova, Belyayeva, Khomyakova, Budanova and Nechayeva) that from the start were at odds with the first, Tamara Kazarinova. Reportedly, these pilots became enemies with the commander, because she did not know how to fly a fighter and requested that the commander should be changed. But eventually it was

Mayor Kazarinova that on 10 September sent eight pilots to Stalingrad in two different air regiments. Litvyak was posted to *437 IAP* along with Katya Budanova, Raya Belyayeva and Mariya Kuznetsova. On 13 September they arrived to Srednyaya Akhtuba. The regiment commander, *Mayor* Khvostikov, was not exactly pleased to see them. "This is combat, not a flying club!", he commented. "There are air battles every day. We're waiting for real pilots, and they sent us a bunch of girls." As a result, no male pilot, for the first days, accepted to fly with one of the girls as his wingman.

Litvyak meets Erwin Mayer (or Meier or Meyer), the German ace from *Jagdeschwader JG 53*, that she is credited to have shot down in the sky of Stalingrad on 13 September 1943 (along with a *Ju 88*, not confirmed): the first air victory by a woman in history. Of this historical events, surprisingly, is not known to exist any photograph, but this painting, by Nikolay Ivanovich Chuprov, preserved in the Museum in School Nr. 1 in Krasnyi Luch. The German ace shot down by Litvyak was, reportedly[4], a three times winner of the Iron Cross or even a holder of the Knight's Cross. But scholarship proves that no German ace awarded the Knight's Cross was shot down on 13 September 1942 in Stalingrad[5]. Actually, when he was shot down, Meyer had approximately 11 air victories[6] and to deserve the *Ritterkreutz* on Eastern front initially were needed 25 air kills, raised by the end of 1941 to 40. By the end of 1942, the requirement to be awarded the Knight's Cross had raised to 40[7].

Litvyak in flying helmet, with an assertive fighter pilot expression. "Liliia Litvyak was a very aggressive person", remembered Boris Nikolaevich Yeremin, Hero of USSR, and *General Polkovnik* (Colonel General). When he refused to accept her and Budanova in his regiment (*273 IAP*, later renamed *31 GvIAP*) in Stalingrad[8], his divisional commander asked him the reason of that refusal. "I was ashamed to answer, because the girls were right there." He held at the time the rank of *Mayor*, while Litvyak was still a *Starshina* (the top non-commissioned officer), but Litvyak said with contempt: "He is afraid of us, that's all. He's young, a regimental commander, a bachelor – he's afraid." On 14 September Litvyak was credited with the kill of a second *Bf 109*, shared with Katya Budanova, but *Luftwaffe* that day lost only a *Bf 110*, a *Fw 189* and a *Ju 88*.

Litvyak in combat gear, between sorties. Stalingrad front. She achieved her first confirmed air victory on 27 September 1943 on Stalingrad. That day Soviet Lieutenant General, Vasily Ivanovich Chuikov (Василий Иванович Чуйков), launched a counterattack against the *Wehrmacht* in Stalingrad, but his troops were soon smashed by waves of howling *Stuka* dive bombers. Then two German division advanced to seize the *Krasnyy Oktyabr* settlement and *Mamayev Kurgan* hill. Among the few Soviet fighters that took off that day there was Litvyak's *Yak-1*. She was flying as a wingman of *437 IAP's* commander, *Mayor* A.V. Khvostikov, when they intercepted a formations of five bombers *Junkers Ju 88* escorted by *Bf 109s*, bound to bomb *Stalingradskiy Traktornyy Zavod*, the famous tractor factory. They soon attacked the German aircraft, but Khvostikov was hit by *Lutwaffe* gunners while Lidya was attacked and hit by a *Bf 109*. She managed to out-turn the *Messerschmitt* and from 30 yards shot down the bomber, a *Ju 88* of second *Gruppe* of *KG 76*, the only loss of *Luftwaffe* on Stalingrad that day. Then, she teamed with *Starshiy Leytenant* Raisa Belyayeva and attacked a *Bf 109*, claiming her second (not confirmed) shared kill of the day.

Soviet ace Amet-Khan Sultan, in front of his fighter. He was just one of the several *9 GIAP* pilots that courted Litvyak while she was posted in this elite unit in late 1942. When he was himself assigned to *9 GIAP*, along with his fellow ace Vladimir Lavrinenkov, he first met Litvyak and Budanova in the dormitory. They stopped at the door, surprised to found some girls there, but

Litvyak welcomed them: "Come on in! Don't be embarrassed... Have you only just arrived?" One of the pilots confirmed it and Lidia added: "Us, too. Let's get acquainted. Liliia Litvyak, and this is Katya Budanova." When the famous ace, Mikhail Dmitrievich Baranov, deputy commander of the regiment, told the pilots to choose their place in the dormitory, Amet-Khan put his suitcase on a bed near the one where the two girls were staying. "I have already chosen!", he stated, but Baranov told him that the women should have moved in other billets[9]. Amet-Khan was awarded twice the Gold Star of Hero of Soviet Union. He was credited with 30 individual air-victories and 19 shared. In the picture he is wearing just the Order of the Red Banner and the Order of the Red Star.

Lidya Litvyak in a portrait. She was regarded as a real beauty, pretty, thin and feminine. "Lilya bleached her hair white", later recalled Senior Sergeant Inna Pasportnikova, "and she would send me to hospital to get hydrogen peroxide liquid to do it. She took pieces of parachute, sewed them together, painted it different colors, and wrapped it around her neck"[10]. The famous Soviet ace Vladimir Lavrinenkov, Hero of Soviet Union, that met her in late 1942, while they were both in *9 GIAP*, was struck by her radiant beauty. "Litvyak was a model of femininity and charm", he later remembered and looked "thoughtful and quiet"[11]. She still had very short hair. At first she opposed to the order of Marina Raskova, to have them cut in the military style. *Kapitan* Klavdiya Terekhova-Kasatkina, secretary of the party organization of the regiment, remembered: "When the girls were ordered to cut their hair very short, only one girl, Litvyak, refused to do it." Terekhova reported it to Raskova, that ordered to go back and fulfill her order. "I came to Lilya with tears in my eyes and asked her to please do it, and at last she agreed"[12].

The actress Valentina Vasilyevna Polovikova-Serova (Валенти́на Васи́льевна Половикова-Серо́ва). Born in Kharkov, on 23 December 1917, she married Anatoli Serov in 1938, a test and fighter pilot that died the following year in an air crash. She was one of the biggest Soviet movie stars, envied and imitated. According to Litvyak mechanic, Pasportnikova, "she was pretty and thin an looked like the actress Serova."

Vladimir Dmitriyevich Lavrinenkov in Stalingrad, in front of a *Yak-7*. During the fight on the future Volgograd, he amassed nine individual air victories and seven shared during 40 air combats. In late 1942 he was posted to *9 GIAP* as a leader of second *Eskadriliya*. Here he first saw Litvyak. Many pilots were infatuated with her but – he recalled – she "reacted extremely reservedly to the rapturous glances... she showed no preference to anyone. And this was especially impressive to us."

Litvyak's *Yak-1* fighter beeing refuelled, before another sortie. On 11 February, flying as wingman of commander of third *eskadriliya*, Aleksey Solomatin, in a formation with Regimental Commander, Nikolay Baranov and a fourth pilot, intercepted 16 *Stukas* escorted by 13 *Focke-Wulf Fw 190s*, bound to bomb Rostov on Don. Reportedly, she attacked and hit the leading German bomber, that exploded. Soon after she teamed with Solomatin to shoot down one of the *Focke-Wulfs*.

Litvyak and her best friend, Katya Budanova. At the beginning of January 1943, while based in Kutelnikov, the *9 GIAP* was reequipped with American built fighter *Bell P-39 Airacobra*. So, on 8 January, they were transferred to *296 IAP* (later renamed *73 GIAP*), on the same airport, so that they still could fly their *Yak-1s*. Litvyak was then credited with four single and two shared air victories. But – according to her mechanic Polunina – when Litvyak and Budanova went to report to the command post, a *296 IAP's* technician heard them to declare, respectively, one and two air victories.

Litvyak's painting, in Krasnyi Luch Museum. Here Lidya is portrayed as a *Leytenant Aviatsiy* (лейтена́нт авиа́ции), Lieutenant of aviation (note the two silver stars on the epaluette), wearing the Order of the Red Star. After her double victory of 11 February, on 19 February, *Serzhant* Litvyak was commissioned *Mladshiy Leytenant* (Junior Lieutenant) and was awarded the Order of the Red Star. Moreover, she was selected to fly as *Svobodny okhotniki*, or "free hunter". In this new role, she was allowed to fly in pair with another experienced pilot, to search and destroy enemy targets on their own initiative, on imitation of the *Luftwaffe Rotte,* the basic fighting *Luftwaffe* unit.

Lidya Litvyak posing in front of her *Yak-1.* On 1 March 1943 she was credited with the destruction of another *Fw 190*, while flying as wingman of *Mayor* Baranov. On 22 March she was scrambled with six other *73 GIAP* pilots to intercept a dozen *Ju 88* bombers approaching Rostov On Don. Litvyak claimed a *Ju 88* but she was immediately attacked by six escorting *Bf 109s*. She claimed one of the attackers but was herself hit and wounded. She had to force-land her crippled aircraft and was picked up by a *Shturmovik* pilot that landed near the wreck of her *Yak-1* and took her to an hospital[13]. According to other sources, Litvyak shot down two *Bf 109s* from *JG 3*, those flown by *Leutnant* Franz Müller and Karl-Otto Harloff.

Feldwebel Josef Schütte, one of the most effective ace of *II./JG 3*. Most probably he was the pilot that hit and forced Litvyak to crash-land on 22 March 1943. Actually, Schütte was the only pilot to have claimed a *Yak-1* in the Southern Front, on that day. Moreover, the location fits perfectly the area of the air combat. In his report he indicated the *Planquadrat Koordinaten* 98 812, that localize a place about 12 km South-West of Rostov, halfway between Rostov and Asow. Litvyak had been his kill number 26. Schütte was killed in action on 4 December 1943, during aerial combat with *P-47 Thunderbolts* in his *Bf 109G-5*, crashing at Achterveld, 7 km West of Barneveld Holland. At the time of his death he had amassed 41 air victories.

Unteroffizier Karl-Otto Harloff (right) of *9 Staffel* of *JG 3*, in front of his *Bf 109G-4*, illustrating his last dogfight. He was – according to some sources – shot down by Litvyak on 22 March 1943 (but according to historians Joachen Prien and Gerhard Stemmer, Harloff was shot down on 16 March, not on 22). On that day, two *eskadriliy* of *296 IAP* intercepted 12 *Junkers Ju 88* bound to bomb Rostov on Don. Litvyak was credited with two air victories. One of his victims was Harloff, who was flying the *Bf 109G-2* "Gelb 2". Harloff was a rather inexperienced fighter pilot. He had to his credit only two kills: an unknown aircraft on 26 February 1943 and a *Petlyakov Pe-2* on 15 of March. According to other sources he scored his first victory, a Soviet *LaGG-3,* near Belojorowka, on 21 May 1943. Subsequently he shot down a *LaGG-5* 2 km East of Malaya-Ivanovka on 21 July 1943. After *JG 3* was moved West for the Defence of the Reich, he was credited with a victory against a *B-17* bomber, NW of Sindelfingen on 6 September. He downed a *B-24* at Penz, near Steyr Austria on 23 February 1944 and, again, a *B-17* SW of Magdeburg on 3 March 1944. But he was killed in a dogfight with *P-38 Lightnings* on Grosskitzighofen (Großkitzighofen) west of München.

On 20 April 1943, the weekly illustrated magazine "Ogonyok" (*Огонёк,* in Russian) published on the cover this photo of Litvyak (on the left) and Katya Budanova. The caption reads: *Vozdushnych Pobed* (About air victories). The article inside celebrates the achievements of the two girls, giving a combined number of their sorties and kills. Three weeks before, on 31 March, the "Komsomolskaya Pravda" had published on front page the picture of the two female "free hunters", commenting: "They have shot down 11 enemy aircraft, Budanova six and Litvyak five."

Lydia at home in Moscow during her leave, after she was wounded in combat on 22 March 1943. Anna Vasilyevna was shocked by the changes in her daughter. "Lily's mother said that her daughter no longer seemed able to relax", recalled Natalya Meklin. "She was obviously still in pain from her leg wound..." but, nevertheless, "... so anxious to get back to the front line where she had so recently avoided death... She was a very different person from the carefree girl who had gone to the war." The dress that Litvyak is wearing in the picture, tailored by her mother, is preserved in Krasnyi Luch's museum.

Litvyak, displaying her Order of the Red Star. On the left side, the Guards Badge. May-June 1943. She was regarded – whatever her number of victories was – as a very skilful pilot. *General Polkovnik* Boris Niko-laevich Yeremin, that had not accepted her in his regiment in Stalingrad, stated that the girls were out-standing air women, especially Litvyak was an exceptional aviatrix, "a born fighter pilot". Yeremin recalled how Aleksei Solomatin, that was regarded himself as an excellent fighter, "had a very high opinion of (Litvyak) as a pilot". Marshal of Aviation, Konstantin Andreevich Vershinin, commander of the 4th Air Army, as well, rated Litvyak performance quite highly.

Litvyak's Guards Badge, preserved in Krasnyi Luch Museum, Ukraine. Litvyak was awarded it when her regiment, *296 IAP*, was renamed *73 GvIAP*, on 1 May 1943.

Aviators of *73GvIAP* pilots, soon after having been awarded the honorary title of Guards, Pavlovka, May 1943. Third from left, regimental commander, *Mayor* Nikolay Baranov wearing an Order of the Red Banner. Litvyak (wearing just the Order of the Red Star) sits, smiling. Baranov would have been killed few days later, on 5 May 1943. His plane was hit and he bailed out, but his parachute was already on fire and he died when he hit the ground. Just before and soon after his death, Litvyak claimed two *Messerschmitt Bf 109s*, one on 5 and one on 7 May, but these two victories are not confirmed by German sources. Aleksei Solomatin is bent on the car's hood.

Right, Aleksei Solomatin, May 1943. Reportedly, it was him that persuaded commander Nikolay Baranov to permit Litvyak (and Budanova) to stay in the *296 IAP*. Subsequently, Solomatin allowed Lydia to fly as his wingman and – according to some historians[14] "Litvyak soon became his fiancée." Subsequently he started to fly sorties with her photo in his cockpit. According to someone they even got secretly married. After his death Lydia wrote to her mother: "You see, he was a fellow not my taste, but his persistence and his love for me compelled me to love him, and now... it seems to me that I shall never again meet such a person"[15]. However, according to historian Kazimiera Cottam, author of several books about Soviet airwomen, there was no evidence that Litvyak and Solomatin had something more sentimental than a professional relationship.

Drawing of Aleksei Solomatin in dress uniform. Born of a peasant family, on 12 February 1921, in Bunakovo-2 Ferzikovskogo, a small settlement in Kaluga region (about 150 km/93 miles South-West of Moscow), in 1939, he attended the Kacha Military Air College. He served first with 160th reserve AP near Odessa in June 1941, as an instructor. In July 1941 he was posted to *296 IAP*. On 9 March 1942, Solomatin was involved in the air combat dubbed the "Battle of seven versus 25" (seven *Yak-1s* versus 18 *Luftwaffe*'s fighters and seven bombers). The Soviets claimed seven kills (one – a Bf 109 – by Solomatin) for no losses. From August 1942 his unit operated over Stalingrad. There he was promoted Senior Lieutenant (стáрший лейтенáнт авиáции, *Starshiy Leytenant)* and made leader of an *eskadrilya.* And it was in this unit that he first met Litvyak, when she was transferred there with Katya Budanova, at the beginning of January 1943, in Kotelnikov. In the picture, he wears: (left to right) Guards Badge, Order of Lenin (two), Order of the Red Banner and (top) the Golden Star of Hero of the Soviet Union.

Aleksei Solomatin. By February 1943 he had been credited with 12 individual and 15 shared victories during 266 missions and 108 air combats. On 1st of May he was awarded the Golden Star of Hero of USSR and promoted *Kapitan*. Three weeks later, on 21 of May 1943, he was killed on Pavlovka airfield. Some author's[16] states that he crashed while training a new pilot in a mock dogfight over the airfield. But Russian historian Anatoly Plyac and Natalya Meklin-Kratsova reveal that he was shot down by a German aircraft. As the only two *Jagdgeschwaders* that operated in the area were *JG 3* and *JG 52,* he was most probably killed by one of the pilots of these air regiments. Actually, there are no known kills claimed on Pavlovka area, so Solomatin probably crashed before the German pilot could record the kill. Solomatin final score was of 17 individual and 22 shared kills.

A German observation balloon. On the basket, usually took place a crew equipped with radio, parachute and binoculars to spot Soviet troops movement and direct artillery fire.

On 31 May 1943, Litvyak volunteered to destroy a *Wehrmacht* ballon near the village of Troitskoe, ten miles behind enemy lines. The balloon was protected by a strong screen of antiaircraft guns and could be promptly lowered. Several male pilots had failed in destroying it. Litvyak decided to surprise the enemy with a new tactic. She flew along the front North and then turned West and crossed the German lines where the anti aircraft defense were weak and she penetrated into enemy territory before turning again to attack the balloon from the rear. The Germans, surprised by her brave attack, had not time to lower the balloon and Litvyak destroyed it during her first pass.

Litvyak standing on the wing of her *Yak-1*. On 13 June she was appointed flight commander of the third squadron of *73 GvIAP*. Few days later, she was flying as wingman to the new regimental commander, I. V. Golyshev. Trying to intercept a reconnaissance aircraft they were attacked by the four escorting *Messerschmitt Bf 109s*. Golyshev was wounded and Litvyak's *Yak-1* was heavily damaged by the German fighters. She managed to land but her aircraft had 10 bullet holes. In the picture, Litvyak wears on the sleeve the badge of Air Force pilots, renamed "chicken" by Soviet pilots. It was intended for middle-level and juniors commanders (pilots, flight observers, navigators, flight bombardiers, flight radio-operator, gunners, flight engine operators). This badge was declared obsolete by Order N°25 of 15 January 1943, of the People's Commissar of Defense.

Oberleutenant Emil Bitsch, from *8./JG 3*, one of the most successful *Luftwaffe*'s "top gun" active on Ukrainian front. Behind him, his *Bf 109 G* "Schwarze 7". Most probably, Bitsch was Litvyak's victor, during the air battle of 16 July 1943, near the front. On that day Lidya was escorting *Il-2s* with six other pilots when they intercepted a *Luftwaffe* formation of 30 *Junkers Ju 88* bombers and six escorting *Bf 109* fighters. Litvyak claimed a *Ju 88* and a *Bf 109* (shared) but was in turn attacked, by a German pilot that hit her *Yak-1*, and wounded her, forcing her to crash-land her aircraft. The German pilot was – with any evidence – Emil Bitsch, who claimed an air victory against a *Yak-1*, flying at 3,000 meters (10,000 feet) at 18.25. For a simple twist of fate, the location of this kill that he indicated (Grid Square 98 142) is extremely near to Novokrasnovka (actually very close to the Mius front-line) where, three days later, still Bitsch would have downed and killed Litvyak's best friend, Katya Budanova. (Elke Bitsch photo-album, by Thijs Hellings)

Right, Ivan Golyshev, the new regimental commander, that replaced Baranov. On 20 July 1943 Litvyak was flying as his wingman, while escorting *Petlyakov Pe-2* bombers. While returning, they were attacked by ten *Bf 109s*. Golyshev was immediately hit and killed. Litvyak's *Yak* was put on fire and she had to parachute. Shooting them down were probably two *JG 3* pilots: *Ltn.* Hermann Schuster and *Hptm.* Paul Stolte, that claimed two *Yak-1s,* respectively at 10.05 and 10.07 on the Mius front area.

Left, *Ltn.* Herman Schuster of *4/JG 3.* Schuster was – along with *Hptm.* Paul Stolte – most probably one of the two pilots that shot down Litvyak and her commander Golyshev, on 20 July 1943. He claimed a *Yak-1* at 1,000 meters (3,280 feet), at 10.05 on Mius Front – his 31st kill – 3 minutes after Stolte had shot down another *Yak-1*. Schuster was one of the most promising replacement officer, but the following day he failed to return after an air combat with *Il-2s* in the Permovaysk area and was reported as MIA. The picture was taken on a forward airfield in the East less than two months before his disappearance.

Lydia Litvyak, July 1943, Mius front. Notwithstanding the low quality of this picture, it is still possible to identify her awards. Left to right: Guards Badge, Order of the Red Star, Order of the Red Banner and the Medal for the Defense of Stalingrad. Litvyak, not yet 22 years old, looks much older, due to the strain of continuous combats.

The author on the site of the Kalininskiy airstrip, from where Litvyak took off on 1 August 1943. At his back, where sunflowers grow, there was the dispersal area. On the site of the airstrip, there is now a village and a school with a small museum dedicated to Litvyak and Budanova. On the memorial stone, the writing says: *To the fighters of the Eight Air Army from the Sverdlovsk citizens. 9 May 1985.*

Dmitrovka's sign, Eastern Ukraine. Nearby flows the river Mius, along which stretched the Mius front. In that sky, on 1 August 1943, Lidya Litvyak fought her last battle. Her base was Sovkhos Kalinin aerodrome, in Kalininskiy, in the area of Krasnyi Luch, Southern jointly with fellow pilots from *73 GIAP*. On a fourth mission (in the afternoon according to some source) she was flying one of the six *Yaks* that attacked 30 bombers *Ju 88* and 12 escort fighters in the sky of Dmitryevka. She reportedly shot down another *Bf 109* (unconfirmed) but was in turn attacked and hit. She was last seen diving into a cloud, trailing smoke, pursued by a *Rotte* of two German fighters, over enemy territory. Her combat record was of 12 personal victories (including an observations balloon) and four shared, during 168 sorties. But several of her victories do not appear to be supported by German sources. For instance, on 1 August, *Luftwaffe* lost only two fighters but none of them fits Litvyak claims. *JG 3* lost just one *Bf 109*, over Marinovka, but in air combat against ground attack aircraft (*Il-2s*) and *JG 52* lost another exactly in the sky of Dmitryevka, but rammed by un unknown *Yak-1*.

Soviet ace, Ivan Ivanovich Borisenko, the last to see Litvyak on 1 August 1943 in action. Borisenko flew 245 sorties, claiming 25 victories in 63 combats, during the Great Patriotic War. Hero of USSR (15 May 1946), awarded three times with the Order of Red Banner and two with that of Red Star, one with that of Lenin. Of Litvyak's last combat, he later recalled: "Lily just didn't see the *Messerschmitt 109s* flying cover for the German bombers. A pair of them dived on her and when she did see them she turned to meet them. Then they all disappeared behind a cloud"[17]. With any evidence, Lidya was shot down by a German *Experte*'s *Messerschitt Bf 109* (her victor was Hans Schleef, from *JG 3* or Hans-Jörg Merkle, from *JG 52*).

Oberleutnant Hans Schleef, from *JG 3*, probable victor of Lidya Litvyak, wearing his awards. Actually he claimed, at 5.25, the kill of a *LaGG-3* (a type of aircraft often confused by German pilots with the *Yak-1s*) South-East of Stepanovka, exactly in the spot where Litvyak was downed. Schleef was born on 19 July 1920 at Groß-Börnecke near Magdeburg, in Germany. He held the rank of *Unteroffizier* and was serving in *7./JG 3*, when, on 5 February 1941, he achieved his first air victory (a *RAF Hawker Hurricane* fighter near St. Omer). His second victim was a *RAF Blenheim* twin-engine bomber, downed on 31 May. He was awarded the *Ehrenpokal* on 23 September 1941, the *Ritterkreuz* on 9 May 1942 for 41 victories, the *Deutsches Kreuz in gold,* on 14 May 1942 and, just five days later, the coveted *Ritterkreuz des Eisernen Kreuze*, an award that recognized extreme battlefield bravery or successful leadership. On the same month, he was transferred to *Ergänzung-Jagdgruppe Ost* for a spell of instructing. Schleef returned as a *Leutnant* to front line duty in January 1943 with *7./JG 3*, still based on the Eastern front and soon started to amass an impressing *crescendo* of air victories. On 6 July, Schleef claimed his 80th victory. At dawn 1 August, when he took off for Mius front, on his *Messerschmitt* tail there were 79 (or even 90) markings, one for every air-to-air victory.

Oberleutnant Hans Schleef, in winter flying suite. Soon after the probable air-victory against Litvyak, he was relocated with his unit to the Western front for *Reich* defense. In Germany there was desperate needing of expert pilots to face the massive USAAF bombing of the Third Reich. But in the new war theater, Schleef was not able to replicate the outstanding successes achieved on the Eastern Front. The tactics, the type of aircraft and the training of enemy pilots were all too different. In the following 17 months he managed to destroy just six enemy aircraft (two bombers and four fighters). Eventually, Schleef was shot down and killed in aerial combat with British *Spitfires* near Bad Durkheim in his *Bf 109 G*-10 (W.Nr. 490 758) "Blue 4". It was 31 December 1944. At the time, Hans Schleef was credited with 99 confirmed kills and at least two unconfirmed, during more than 500 missions. He recorded 91 victories over the Eastern front, including fifteen *Il-2 Shturmoviks*. Of his eight victories recorded over the Western front, two were four-engine bombers.

The author on the official crash-site of the *Yak-1* of Lydia Litvyak. The place is located south of Dmitryevka (Dimitrovka, in Ukrainian). But this is not the real one. That spot was chosen as it is easier to get to for the students of Ukrainian schools. Actually her aircraft fell in a nearby place, on the outskirts of Kozhevnya settlement, about 500 feet far from the last village houses.

Fragments of Litvyak's *Yak-1* aircraft found at the outskirt of Kozhevnya, preserved in Krasnyi Luch Museum of School Nr. 1. Some of these fragments were sent to Moscow where, by serial numbers, they were identified as those of Litvyak.

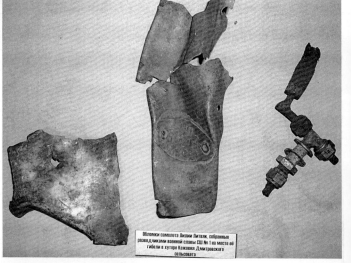

Other fragments of Litvyak's *Yak-1*. Those are parts of the feed-belt ammunitions of one of the two engine mounted *ShKAS* machine-guns. Krasnyi Luch Museum of School Nr. 1.

Hero of Soviet Vladimir Dmitriyevich Lavrinenkov getting out of his fighter. Awarded his first Gold Star of Union on 1 May 1943, on 23 August of the same year, while flying a *P-39 Airacobra*, he rammed a *Focke Wulf 189* on the Mius river, exactly the area where Litvyak was shot down, and was captured by Germans and taken in a prisoner camp. Subsequently while they were moving him to another camp in Odessa, he managed to evade and to return to Soviet territory. He later revealed to *586 IAP's* pilot Klava Pankratova Tubalova that he had read the name of Litvyak on the prisoners list affixed in the *Kamp* where he had been first taken.

Litvyak's monument, unveiled on 1 September 1977, in front of the School Nr. 1 in Krasnyi Luch where is located the museum dedicated to her, created by teacher Valentina Vashchenko. In 1968 the *Komsomolskaya Pravda*, that in Spring 1943 had published a picture of her and Budanova with a blurb, requested that Litvyak was awarded the title of Hero of the Soviet Union posthumously and, in 1971, Vashchenko, and a group of Pathfinders, started to look for Litvyak's aircraft.

The actual point where Litvyak's *Yak-1* crash-landed, on 1 August 1943, 500 feet off Kozhevnya. Signs of the excavation to recover the wreck are still evident. According to the official truth, on 23 July 1979, student pathfinders, researching for Litvyak aircraft, learned from Dmitryevka resident F. M. Mikhailov that 10 years before, near Kozhevnya, the brothers Fedor and Nikolay Sachki and their friend Sergey Sapitskiy, pursuing a little snake, discovered, under the wing of an aircraft, a skeleton of small size. The official version says that doctors examined the bones and found that the skull, still covered by a flying helmet, had a small round hole in the front and that the pelvis bones were female, moreover a silk bra underwear was discovered. As there was only a female fighter pilot in Southern front still MIA (Litvyak), those bones where identified as hers. Afterwards the bones had been reburied in the Brotherhood tomb Nr. 19, in the centre of Dmitryevka.

Inna Pasportikova (extreme left) and the two Sachki brothers that discovered the presumed body of a pilot of small size, beside the wreck of her *Yak-1*. Pasportnikova had searched for three years, after the war, helped by her husband and three nephews, Litvyak relic. They found the wrecks of 30 aircraft but not Litvyak's. She was sure that the skeleton found by the Kozhevnhya children, was Litvyak's: "They found a body – her body… – it was the body of a woman pilot, very small, and they found hair, her flying suit, and a gold tooth"[18]. But Nikolay Sachki revealed to the

Author in July 2011 that they knew – as everybody in Kozhevnya – that there was an aircraft there, and that they had declared to have found it by chance, pursuing a small snake, because were afraid that the Soviet authorities could punish them, as they were unearthing a relic without permission. Moreover he denies that they ever found any blonde hair or golden tooth, and that they had never been told afterwards that the bones were of a female.

The Author pays homage to Litvyak, in front of her tombstone, on the wall surrounding the "Brotherhood Tomb" Nr. 19, Dmitrovka, Ukraine (July 2011). Actually, there is more than one doubt that Litvyak's remains were ever buried there. Historian Kazimiera Cottam, reports how "for many years a rumor persisted that Litvyak had run off with several German officers." Someone think that she managed to escape from the POW camp, where her presence was observed by Vladimir Lavrinenkov, a fellow prisoner, and there is speculation that she availed herself of that opportunity to leave the Soviet Union[19].

Litvyak's tombstone at the extreme right end of the long honorary wall that frames the brotherhood tomb Nr. 19. Ekaterina Polunina, aircraft mechanic, regimental archivist of *586 IAP*, after the war, recalled how she had given a bottle of vodka to the gravedigger of the cemetery in Dmitryevka to have him writing with yellow paint, the name of Lidya Litvyak on an unknown tomb. That was necessary, as Soviet authorities could not declare anyone missing as an Hero of the Soviet Union. Actually, any MIA or PoW was suspected to be a traitor. Stalin declared that every Soviet soldier captured by Germans was not less than a traitor. So to have Litvyak declared as an Hero she and Pasportnikova needed a tomb and remains that could be regarded as hers.

Inna Pasportnikova speaks in front of the Monument of Litvyak, in Krasnyi Luch, 1 September 1988. She holds in her hand the model of the *Yak-1* Nr. 23 of Lydia she was flying on 13 September 1942 when, reportedly, she shot down the German ace Erwin Meyer. Please, note the clear color of the aircraft. Who saw the relic of the aircraft near Kozhevnya remembered how the tail, that rose out of the ground, was of a clear color, almost white.

The Author with Alexandra Ivanovna, director of the Museum of Lydia Litvyak in Dmitrovka, Ukraine. In the center of the village, in the "Brotherhood Grave Nr. 19" are buried the presumed remains of Litvyak and those of more than 2,000 identified and unknown soldier. How was it possible to find them to examine them and why, after they discovered that they were Livtyak's, they did not bury them in an individual grave? "Actually they were never exumed", answers Mrs Ivanovna to the Author in July 2011. "They were of small size and she was notoriously petit. Moreover, the fragments of the aircraft found beside the body had the serial numbers of Litvyak's *Yak-1*. So it was decided that those bones were Litvyak's". On these basis, on 31 March 1986, the Ministry of Defense acknowledged that the remains were Litvyak's and on 5 May 1990 she was at last awarded the title of Hero of the Soviet Union.

Yuri Vladimirovn Litvyak, brother of Lydia, speaking during the ceremony of inauguration of her sister monument, in Krasnyi Luch, on 1 September 1988. Yuri, that changed his surname in Kunavin, after the war, was presented the Gold Star of Hero of USSR of her sister after Soviet President Mikhail Gorbachev signed it in May 1990. Kunavin died soon afterwards. With his death, Litvyak family extinguished. Prabably his wife still preserves the Gold Star of Lidya Litvyak.

Міністерство освіти і науки України

**КРАСНОЛУЦЬКА ГІМНАЗІЯ №1
ІМЕНІ Л. ЛІТВЯК**

Луганська область

School sign of high school intitled to Lydia Litviak, in Krasnyi Luch. The writing says "Ukranian Education and Science Ministry – Krasnyi Luch Gymnasium Nr. 1 named to L. Litvyak – Lughansk Province".

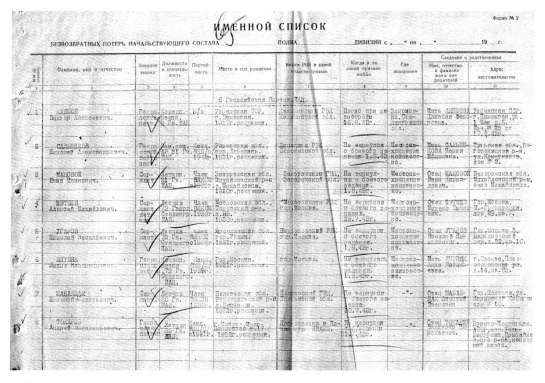

Millitary record in which is written about the disappearance of Lidya Litvyak and her home address in Moscow, *Novoslobodskaya Ulitsa 88/14.*

Original document by Central archives (Tsamo) listing Litvyak awards (Order of the Red Star, Order of the Red Banner, Order of the Great Patriotic War and Golden Star of Hero of USSR), kept in Dmitryevka Museum.

Junior High school Nr. 1 named to Litvyak, Krasnyi Luch, Ukraine. Inside there is the Museum of War and Glory created by Valentina Vashchenko, dedicated to Lidya Litvyak.

Left, cover of the book by Valeri A. Agranovsky, *Белая лилия (Человек среди людей) - The White Lily,* Москва, 1979.

Yekaterina Kuzminichna Polunina, *586 IAP* aircraft technician. In her book[20] Polunina writes how during the 55th anniversary of VE-Day, Russian television correspondent from Switzerland introduced a former Soviet female pilot of Great Patriotic War, mother of three children who had been twice wounded during the war and was living abroad since the war. Nina Raspopova, a veteran of the *46 GvNBAP*, declared to be sure that she was Lidya Litvyak. Still Polunina writes how Aleksandr Gridnev, commander of 586th fighter regiment heard Litvyak speaking to the German radio, after her capture.

The author with an old Dmitryevka resident (we keep his name reserved). He remembers how a friend of his used to repeat how during the war a pilot girl parachuted from about 7,000-10,000 feet over Kozhevnya. The only female pilot that could ever bail out on that area, from that height, is Lidya Litvyak. Aviation historian Anatoly Plyac told the Author: "Litvyak survived and was taken prisoner, I can't tell you anything more." And Galina Brok-Beltsova, veteran of *125 GvBAP* and former *NKVD*'s agent, revealed to the Author, in May 2010: "Litvyak survived and went to Switzerland, where she got married and had sons."

Lidya with her mother, Anna Vasilyevna. After the war – as the two nieces of Lidya's best friend, Katya Budanova, Irina and Lyudmilla, recalled – for many years, Anna dressed in black, mourning and weeping, remembering her only dear daughter, lost in war. But, in the lights of the new testimonies and new data, can be assumed as almost certain that Litvyak did not die on 1ˢᵗ August 1943. Most probably, after she was hit by a *Bf 109*, she flew inside a cloud to parachute more safely. She landed in German occupied territory and was taken to a prisoner camp. Unfortunately the research of the Author in the German *Bundes Archives* and by the association *Deutsche Dienstelle* in Berlin did not lead to the discovery of any proof of Litvyak imprisonment in German *Kamps*, but is well known how the Soviets sequestered all Soviet prisoners files to charge them as traitors. So far, there has been no evidence to show that the Soviet lady seen on a TV broadcast from Switzerland was Litvyak.

NOTE

1 Reina Pennington, *Wings, Women & War*, p. 156

2 Pennington, p. 46

3 Anna Krylova, *Soviet Women in Combat*, p. 284

4 Pennington, p. 133

5 Lois Merry, *Women Military Pilots of World War II*, pp. 168-169

6 Jochen Prien, *Jagdegeschwader 53 – May 1942-January 1944*, p. 431

7 Gordon Williamson, *Aces of the Reich*, pp. 93-94

8 Tomas Polak with Christopher Shores, *Stalin's Falcons – The Aces of the Red Star*, p. 338

9 Pennington, pp. 133-134

10 Noggle, p. 196

11 Pennington, p. 134

12 Noggle, p. 192

13 Hans Seidl, *Stalin's Eagles – An illustrated Study of the Soviet Aces of World War II and Korea*, p. 136

14 George Mellinger, *Yakovlev Aces of World War 2*, Osprey, p. 28

15 Pennintgon, p. 139

16 Pennington, Cottam and Myles

17 Bruce Myles, *Night Witches*, p. 232

18 Noggle, p. 200

19 Merry, p. 169

20 *Devchonki, podruzhki, letchitsy*. Moscow, 2004, p. 146

Yekaterina Vasilyevna Budanova

Name: Yekaterina

Patronimic: Vasilyevna

Surname: Budanova

Born: 6 December 1916

Place of Birth: Konoplyanka, Smolensk Oblast

Rank: Starshy Leytenant (First Lieutenant/Flying Officer)/Kapitan (Captain)

Units: 586 IAP, 437 IAP, 9 GvIAP, 296 IAP (later renamed 73 GvIAP)

Air victories: 6 individual and 5 shared

Day of Death: 19 July 1943

Place of Death: Novokrasnovka (Ukraine)

Awards: Order of the Red Star, Order of the Red Banner, Order of the Great Patriotic War (twice), Gold Star of Hero of the Russian Federation

Yekaterina Vasilyevna Budanova. She is one of only two female fighter "aces" in history, along with her friend Lidya Litvyak. "A boyish forelock of curly, golden hair, cut short; laughing eyes, slightly aquiline nose, and a broad, white-toothed smile," Inna Pasportnikova, one of Budanova's mechanic, recalled this outstanding pilot. "Katya" as she was known, is usually credited with 11 air victories, five individuals and six shared, but according to others, she had shot down more than 20 enemy aircraft. (Archive of Anatoly Plyac)

Surroundings of Konoplyanka (*Коноплянка*), Budanova's native village, located in Smolensk Oblast, in Central Russia. When Katya was still a child in the 1920s, an aircraft landed on the outskirt of Konoplyanka. "For Katya this was a truly memorable day," recalled Pasportnikova. "Finally she was given the opportunity to see a real aircraft and a real live pilot... The emboldened girl climbed onto the wing of his machine and with her eyes soaked in the instrument panel. She was most anxious to know what all the puzzling digits, pointers, and levers meant... it was then that she decided: 'I shall become a pilot!' Henceforward, she could not visualize her future career in any other way"[1].

Children of Konoplyanka. (Archive of Anatoly Plyac)

Vassily Budanov, Yekaterina's father. After graduating from elementary school with a certificate of commendation, Budanova had to abandon her studies due to her father's death, and began working as a nanny. (Archive of Anatoly Plyac)

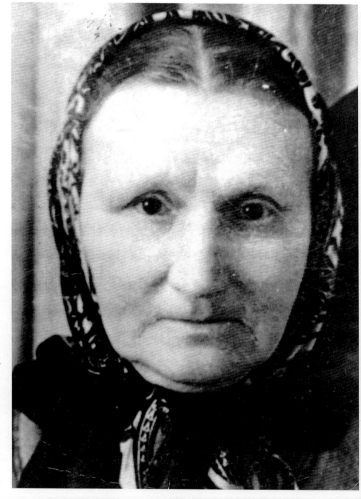

Budanova's mother, a poor peasant of Konoplyanka. At the age of thirteen, Budanova's mother decided to send Katya to Moscow, both to work and study. In the Soviet capital, her older sister was already working in an aircraft manufacturing plant. (Archive of Anatoly Plyac)

Katya Budanova, third from the right, with the Pioneers squad of which she was responsible. When she arrived in Moscow, the "large city simply dazzled her and the letters which she wrote home were full of enthusiasm and delight. Hired by the plant where her sister worked, she saw with her own eyes how aircraft, which she still dreamed to fly, were being constructed"[2]. While in high school, Budanova worked as a carpenter in her sister's aircraft factory. And it was there that she developed an interest in aviation, and she joined an aeroclub's parachute section.

Katya Budanova in civilian clothes, before the war. She obtained her flying license in 1934. When she became a flying instructor, in 1937, she had to part with the plant. Katya was then assigned to Moscow's Kiev District Flying Club. Pasportnikova recalled: "She totally devoted herself to the career, developing the character traits of a fighter pilot: boldness, resourcefulness, and the ability to make correct decisions swiftly"[3].

◀◀ Ekaterina Budanova (extreme left) in front of a *Polikarpov U-2* trainer with her *Aeroklub* cadets in the 1930s. Pilots of *VVS*, in their mails from Khasan and Khalkhyn-Gol, thanked their first flying instructor – Katya Budanova – for her flying lessons. The Soviet Air Force was involved in the Battle of Lake Khasan from 29 July to 11 August 1938. It was an attempted military incursion of Manchukuo (Japanese) into the territory claimed by the Soviet Union. The Battle of Khalkhyn Gol (11 May – 16 September 1939), was, instead, the decisive clash of the border war among USSR, Mongolia, and Japan. "Willingly passing her flying skills and sharing her experience with younger pilots," recalled Pasportnikova, "she trained her subordinates for combat using personal example and wise counsel"[4].

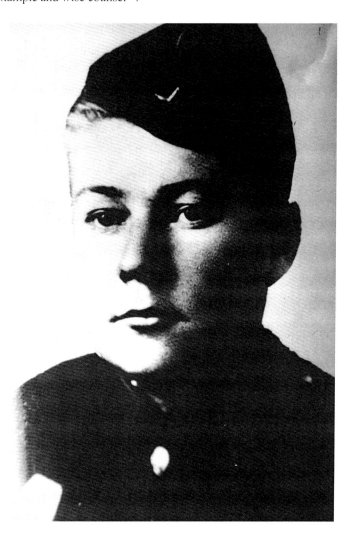

Senior Sergeant Inna Pleshchevtseva-Pasportnikova, aircraft mechanic. She was the unofficial historian of the *586 IAP*. She first met Budanova in October 1941: "I saw her – exuding cheerfulness, decisiveness, and determination – and her image stayed in my memory for ever. At the time I had no idea that I was fated to march alongside her until the very last day of her life... Katya was the life and soul of our group. She was noted for her courage, persistence, and inexhaustible energy, which she successfully combined with plain dealing, sensitivity, and a caring manner of treating others"[6]. Pasportnikova was born in 1920 in the village of Bazarny Karabulak, in Saratov Region, in a family of clerks. She was awarded the Medal "For Courage" (Медаль «За отвагу» Medal «Za otvagu») and the Medal "For the Defence of Stalingrad" (Медаль «За оборону Сталинграда» Medal «Za oboronu Stalingrada»).

◀◀ Katya Budanova with her trainees. She took part in several air parades, flying the single-seater *Yakovlev UT-1*. She was determined to fly fighters even before she was enrolled in Raskova's 122 Air Group. "Soon after the women's regiment began to be formed, Katya convinced us that she ought to become a fighter pilot," recalled Pasportnikova. "When she flew a fighter solo for the first time, everybody was present at the take-off strip and couldn't help but admire Katya's airmanship. The aircraft totally subordinated itself to her capable hands... in recognition of her airmanship and leadership qualities, Katya was appointed flight commander"[5].

Katya Budanova (center) with two other airwomen at the start of her fighter pilot career. They are wearing the Parachute Badge. In veterans' recollections as well as in her archival file, Budanova is presented as an unfearing, instinctive, faultless fighter pilot[7]. "However, success did not always attend her efforts," recalled Pasportnikova. "She had occasion to experience the bitterness of disappointment as well. It took her a long time to learn to deliver aimed fire at towed and ground targets. She ceased to sing and laugh for a while, and increasingly knitted her brows. Finally, the happy day came when the instructor was satisfied with her level of firing proficiency"[8].

Left to right: Lidya Smirnova (left), Katya Budanova (center), and Klavdiya Nechayeva. When her training was finished, Budanova was assigned to the *586 IAP*, created by order of Stalin on 9 December 1941. In April 1942, the Fighter Regiment started its operative service, defending the bridge across the Volga and the *Yak-1's* factory in Saratov, just in front of Engels, where she had been trained as a fighter pilot. Budanova was actually deeply disappointed, as she yearned to be sent to the front, in the thick of events. "Katya was especially intolerant of our situation," recalled Pasportnikova. "By coincidence, around this time she received a letter informing her (erroneously – Edit.) that her mother and sister had been killed . The village of Konoplyanka, where she was born and spent her childhood, lay at some distance behind enemy lines."[10]

Left to right: Katya Budanova, Mariya Kuznetsova, and Lidya Litvyak. Budanova's wish, to be sent to a front line unit, was granted on 10 September when Tamara Kazarinova, her commander in the 586th , sent her to Stalingrad. Budanova was assigned, along with Litvyak, Kuznetsova and Belyaeva, to the *437 IAP*, at Verkhnaya Akhtuba, on the east bank of the Volga River. In Stalingrad, the Soviets were fighting a delaying battle while their new armies were preparing for the counteroffensive of mid-November 1942. The 437th was – like the other air regiments fighting in Stalingrad – badly outnumbered, poorly supplied, and afflicted by severe losses. "We were proud of being sent there," recalled Pasportnikova, "to one of the most important sectors of the front, considering it a great honour and evidence of trust placed in us. And Katya, so it seemed, was the happiest amongst us"[9].

◀◀ Katya Budanova achieved her first air victories in Stalingrad sky. However the sources give different dates. According to American historian Henry Sakaida, Budanova achieved her first air victory (shared) with Litvyak on 14 September 1942, against a German *Messerschmitt Bf 109*[11]. For Yekaterina Polunina[12] on 2 October 1942, under the command of Raisa Belyayeva, Budanova fought an air battle against 12 German *Junkers Ju 88* bombers, escorted by *Messerschmitt Bf 109s*. On that day, Budanova was credited with the destruction of a twin-engine *Junkers Ju 88* (individual kill) and of a German *Bf 109* fighter (in group). For Inna Pasportnikova, instead, Budanova achieved her first victory four days later, on 6 October: "Katya started her engine to confront the thirteen Junkers that flew in the direction of the city... When an enemy bomber appeared in the cross-wires of her sight, she depressed the trigger... her shining tracers grazed the enemy aircraft, and the *Ju 88* became shrouded with a cloud of black smoke. This was her first, long-awaited victory!"[13].

A couple of *Messerschmitt Bf 110*. On 10 December 1942, Katya Budanova spotted two of these German twin-engine fighters and attacked them frontally, shooting down one of the two. In the ensuing air combat she managed to down the second fighter.

Katya Budanova with her sister Valya. About the time of her first double air victory, she wrote to her sister Olya: "I find myself in the midst of the very hell of the war; I am writing from a place in the vicinity of Stalingrad. You know what the conditions are like at the front... I would like to tell you this: though I don't want to die, I am not afraid of it. If and when I must die, my death will cost the enemy dearly. My dear winged "Yak" is a good machine and our fates are indissolubly joined together, if we must perish, we are bound to die like heroes. Keep well... and don't forget me..." At last, on 8 January 1943 she was posted with Litvyak to the *296 IAP* commanded by Major Nikolay Baranov. (Archive of A. Plyac)

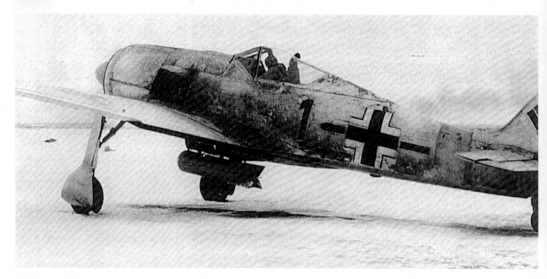

Focke-Wulf Fw 190 – from *JG 51* – in version *Jabo* (*Jagdbomber*, fighter-bomber). Budanova on 10 February 1943 shared a victory against an aircraft of that type. She was protecting Soviet troops with two other pilots (*Starshiy Leytenant* Nikolay Djemkin and *Leytenant* Gorkhiver) of *296 IAP*, when they engaged a *Fw 190* that was attacking the Red Army soldiers, claiming it[14]. Budanova had been credited of another air victory on 9 March 1943 when, along with *Leytenant* Oleg Philipchenko, she claimed a *Bf 109* in the sky of Nikolaevskoe, between 5.30 pm and 6.30 pm. (Archive of A. Plyac)

A *Focke-Fulf Fw 189*. Katya Budanova was credited with the kill of one of this reconnaissance aircraft, on an unspecified date. "This is a highly manoeuvrable and heavily-armored aircraft. I attacked it, and then I saw that it was slipping away from me... I became furious... I rushed at him. He was trying to draw me on – he descended to a lower level and kept going deep into his territory. I went down, too... the Nazi already descended to 20 metres. A furious gunfire came from the ground. I approached the Focke-Wulf to a distance of some 30 metres; then I moved still closer to it and opened fire. Behold, the enemy plunged to the ground... they were firing at me from the ground, but I stayed longer on purpose, to turn a few times above the Germans, then I accelerated and flew home. Suddenly I realized I was running short of fuel. However, I managed to reach my airfield and glided down successfully with my engine switched off"[15].

Katya Budanova (center) with her older sister Valentina (right) and one of her nieces. Katya used to sign the letters to Valya "Your Volodka" (*Tvoi Volodka*). Volodka is a diminutive of Vladimir, a male name. In accord with her Volodka identity, Katya committed herself to a male military appearance and was called by other male pilots by her male nickname[16]. Her nieces Lyudmilla and Irina remembered how she used to fool the girls of the nearby village, letting them believe that she was a boy, but she got scared and flew away when they pretended to be kissed by "him". Still, Soviet author A. Babushkina[17] told how she could turn to a rather opposite, feminine appearance. Actually, when visiting her sister in Moscow while on leave, Budanova exchanged her military uniform for an "English grey coat, light grey hat whose brim hid her forehead" and a huge bouquet of lilacs, adopting a new feminine appearance that made her look "elegant and strict".

One of the last photos of Katya Budanova. She is portrayed in Moscow, in May 1943, during a leave. In the background the concert hall named after Tchaikowsky. She is wearing, on the right, the Order of the Red Star, awarded to her on 9 March 1943. On her epaulets, the three stars show her rank of senior lieutenant of aviation (ста́рший лейтена́нт авиации). On 14 of the same month, "under command of Philipov she flew one of the six *Yak-1* that, while escorting six *Il-2* ground attack aircraft, attacked an enemy train in the station of Uspenskaya. Still, on 30 of May, in an air combat under the command of Sotnikov, she was credited with the group air victory against another *Messerschmitt Bf 109*"[18].

★

Left to right: Katya Budanova, unknown, and Lidya Litvyak. Soviet ace Vladimir Lavrinenkov, colleague of Budanova and Litvyak while in *9 GvIAP*, recalled the two women as quite different. Katya was tall, kept her hair cut short, "and in her flight suit hardly stood out from the fellows." Beside Budanova, Lidya "seemed a little girl." Lavrinenkov described Budanova as a "cheerful, lively character," while Lidya was "thoughtful and quite." Both were excellent pilots[19]. Though her friend Lidya was clearly more attractive to men, that did not affect their close friendship. "Katya was the perfect foil for Lily (Litvyak – Edit.)," reported Pasportnikova. "When her hair was cut really short, she looked more like a young boy than a girl. There was something unfeminine about her and the men in the regiment liked her, but she had never become romantically involved"[20].

The regimental cook (extreme left) brings food to the pilots of *73 GvIAP*. Clouds of fleas made it difficult to the pilots to eat the soup. The caption written on the back of this picture reveals how Budanova's (and Litvyak's) guards fighter regiment was decimated during the summer 1943, while fighting against the *JG 3* and *JG 52*, the two *Luftwaffe* elite fighter-wings, operative in the southern sector of the Eastern Front. Four out of the five pilots portrayed in the photo would be shot down and killed in the following two weeks: "Aerodrome of Berukovo Roseebovskiy, beginning of July 1943. During the dinner on the airfield. Left to right: Odrichiebka Katyusha (the cook – Edit.); Svistunenko (perished); Ugarov (perished 19.7.43); Frolov V.I. (perished 18.7.43); Litovickiy M.N.; Budanova E.V. (perished 19.7.43)".

Katya Budanova, climbing on her *Yakovlev Yak-1* fighter. On 17 July she achieved her 11th air victory (sixth individual), downing a *Junkers Ju 88* on the Mius River Front, in the area of Dyakovo, Dmitryevka, Stepanovka e Yasinovskoy. Two days later, on 19 July, she took off for her last mission. "It was hot and humid, and the fighting was equally hot," recalled Pasportnikova. "A member of a fighter cover group, Katya

was escorting a formation of dive bombers... After fulfilling the mission successfully, our aircraft flew home at various levels, with Katya in the rear. Suddenly, she saw how three *Messerschmitts* were turning to attack a group of our bombers." They were fighters from *JG 3* (or, possibly *JG 52*). Reportedly, Budanova managed to draw the enemy away from the bombers. But a "desperate dogfight was joined. The fighters of the opposing side tried to approach each other tail-on, firing constantly. Katya managed to catch one enemy fighter in the cross-wires of her sight and to pierce it through with a burst. It dropped its nose, lost control, and went down. Katya shot up, rolled over one wing, and rushed at another enemy plane. She let out a long burst, and the second *Messerschmitt* began to fly away in a westerly direction, leaving a black trail of smoke behind it"[21].

Oberleutenant Emil Bitsch, *Staffelkapitän* of *8./JG 3*, one of the best *Luftwaffe* "ace of aces," the so-called *Experten*. He was born on 14 June 1916 at Bad Griesbach in Baden. On 19 July 1943 he shot down a *Yak-1* in the area of Novokrasnovka, over which the last air combat of Budanova was taking place. He claimed his 97th air victory at 12.10 Berlin time, that corresponds to 2.10 pm Soviet time, exactly the time when the witnesses still alive in Novokrasnovka remember that Budanova fell on the outskirt of their village. The page portrayed in the picture is dated 28 August 1943, the day before Bitsch was awarded the Knight's Cross of the Iron Cross (*Ritterkreuz des Eisernen Kreuzes*, often simply *Ritterkreuz*) that recognized extreme battlefield bravery or successful leadership in combat. The drawing shows an Iron Cross 1st Class (*Eisernes Kreuz 1. Klasse*, abbreviated as EK I or E.K.I.) a pin-on medal that Bitsch is wearing on the uniform brest pocket. This photo album is all that Bitsch's wife could save of her husband, while running away from the advancing Soviet troops. (Photo property of Elke-Christiane-Bitsch, via Thijs Hellings)

The *Messerschmitt Bf 109G-2* "Black 1" of *Feldwebel* Georg Schwientek. Schwientek, one of the two pilots who probably shot down Katya Budanova (the other is Emil Bitsch), achieved all of his victories flying the *Messerschmitt*. It was a couple of *Messerschmitt* of this type that Budanova flew against in her last dogfight. "From the ground the inhabitants of the village of Novokrasnovka in Voroshilovgrad Region observed the battle anxiously. They saw how in the end the red-starred fighter turned upside down. Out of control, it began to fall. Then it side-slipped and leveled off. Tongues of fire licked its wings. The plane began to glide onto a field adjacent to the village, all churned up with foxholes, trenches, and craters. After it had touched down, one of its wheels fell into a crater and the fighter nosed over"[22]. In the picture, a "black man" (nickname of the German aircraft mechanics) is checking the cowling of the Daimler-Benz engine. Note the *Jagdeschwader 52* badge on the side of the fuselage. Pitomnik Airfield, Stalingrad, September 1942.

Katya Budanova in one of the last pictures owned by her family. On 19 July 1943, after a short and deadly dogfight with German *Messerschmitts* she fell near the Mius River. "With great difficulty, the collective farm workers (of Novokrasnovka – Edit.) pulled out the mortally wounded pilot from the burning cockpit. An old woman wiped off the blood from Katya's face, loosened the collar of her flying suit, and took off her Communist Party membership card, which read: "Yekaterina Vasilyevna Budanova." The peasants gently picked up the body of the woman pilot and brought it to the nearest cottage. There, on the outskirts of the village, they buried Katya with military honors"[24]. On the back of this picture is written. "To my dearest Lyubushka, as a memory, by her aunt Katyusha – 1 May 1943".

Oberleutnant Emil Bitsch, one of the two pilots who most probably shot down Katya Budanova. Bitsch was – just like Schleef, the probable victor of Lydia Litvyak – serving in *JG 3*. The unit's badge is visible on the cowling of the engine. From July 1941, *Leutnant* Bitsch served with *III./JG 3* based on the Eastern Front. Bitsch recorded his 50th victory on 19 March 1943. On 1 June 1943, Bitsch was appointed *Staffelkapitän* of *8./JG 3*. After shooting down Katya Budanova, in August 1943, Bitsch, with his *III./JG 3*, was relocated to Germany to serve on *Reichsverteidigung* duties. During the Defense of the Reich, Bitsch shot down four USAAF four-engine bombers. At last, on 15 March 1944, Bitsch himself was shot down and killed in his *Bf 109 G-6* (W.Nr. 161 139) in aerial combat with USAAF *P-47* fighters over Schijndel, Holland. Emil Bitsch was credited with 108 victories. In the above picture, he is sitting on the wing of his *Messerschmitt Bf 109 G*. The "Gustav" variant was regarded by Soviet pilots as "a powerful aircraft, fast, and very good in vertical manoeuvre..."[23]. The "Gustav" was equipped with two *MG 151/20* cannons installed in gun pods under each wing. These 20 mm cannons greatly increased the firepower of the *Bf 109*, according to German statistics. Only four hits were enough to shoot down a single-engine fighter like Budanova's *Yak-1*, even if their weight of 298 lbs (135 kg) had a negative effect on handling. It reduced the *Messerschmitt's* performance in air combats against enemy fighters. (Photo Elke Bitsch via Thijs Hellings)

Mariya Kolesnikova, inhabitant of Novokrasnovka, shows the exact place of Budanova's crash: "The plane turned upside down. The soldiers and inhabitants took the pilot out of the plane. They did not let us get too close, but I saw her: she was wearing a green flying coverall and I did not see any blood."

The ruined school on the main street of Novokrasnovka. During the war it had been transformed into a hospital. Here Katya Budanova was carried to when she force landed, few hundred meters away. But when she arrived she was already dead.

The first (presumed) tomb of Budanova, in No-vokrasnovka.

(Below) Right, the sister of Budanova, Olga, and *586 IAP* (the first Budanova's air regiment) commander Tamara Ustinova Pamyatnykh, by the presumed grave of Katya, in 1965. After the war, Pamyatnykh, travelled to Ukraine to locate Budanova's grave and "ensure that it was well maintained," revealed Pasportnikova. "Partly by hitch-hiking and partly on foot, she reached the village of No-vokrasnovka. Here she questioned the villagers, to determine the location of Katya's grave. Two adolescent boys came forward. They led Tamara to the out-skirt of the village and showed her the grave." Actually Budanova had been buried six meters (20 feets) away from the portrayed grave, under a cherry tree. So when, about forty years after Budanova's death, they dug up the grave to exhume her, they found nothing. It was a peasant woman that showed them the exact place. Budanova was identified by a little mirror and a comb that was found on her skeleton. On her flying overall, they only found her earphones and remnants of a belt and buckle, preserved in Bobrikovo Museum.

The earphones worn by Yekaterina Budanova, when she was shot down and killed on 19 July 1943. It has been written that Budanova wore the helmet on her head and that she was still alive when she force-landed in Novokrasnovka. But the melted plastic of the auriculars' part that was in contact with her ears, shows that the poor Bu-danova was already burned to death when her planes crashed at the outskirt of Novokrasnovka. The earphones are preserved in Budanova Mu-seum, inside the school of Bobrikovo, in front of the monument grave where Budanova is buried.

Author (July 2011) pays homage to Ekaterina Katya Budanova at her monument grave, in the village of Bobrikovo, in southeastern Ukraine, near the river Mius. The 12 stars indicate the number of Budanova's air victories credited to her by Soviet authorities. However, Pasportnikova stated that she had only five personal kills at the time of her death[25]. There have been several different versions of Budanova's aerial victory score published, with no official tally. The most common quoted is 11 kills (6 individual and 5 shared). According to some historians she achieved 11 individual air victories. She had been twice awarded Order of the Patriotic War. Although she was recommended for the title of Hero of the Soviet Union during the war she did not receive it officially. In 1 October 1993, Russian president Boris Yeltsin, posthumously awarded her with the title Hero of the Russian Federation.

The author with Budanova's nieces in Moscow, May 2010. Irina (left) and Lyudmilla (right).

NOTE

1   Cottam, *Women in Air War*, p. 263

2   Cottam, *Women in Air War,* pp. 265-266

3   Cottam, *Women in Air War*, p. 266

4   Cottam, *Women in Air War*, p. 265

5   Cottam, *Women in Air War*, pp. 264-265

6   Cottam, *Women in Air War*, pp. 264-265

7   Anna Krylova, *Soviet Women in Combat,* p. 281

8   Cottam. *Women in Air War*, p. 265

9   Cottam. *Women in Air War*, p. 265

10 Cottam, *Women in Air War*, p. 266

11 H. Sakaida, *Heroines of the Soviet Union 1941-1945*, Osprey, p. 14

12 Y. Polunina, *Devchonki, podruzhki, letchitsy,* p. 138

13 Cottam, *Women in Air War*, p. 266

14 Polunina, Idem

15 Cottam, *Women in Air War,* p. 269

16 Krylova, pp. 281-282

17 In *"Devushki-voiny. Ocherki o devushkakh-geroiniakh Velikoi Otechestvennoi voiny",* Moskva: Molodaya gvardiya, 1944

18 Polunina, p. 138

19 Pennington, p. 134

20 B. Myles, *The Night Witches*, p. 221

21 Cottam, *Women in Air War*, p. 269

22 Cottam, *Women in Air War*, p. 269

23 A. Drabkin, *Barbarossa & the retreat to Moscow*, p. 135

24 Cottam, *Women in Air War*, pp. 269-270

25 Pennington, p. 140

SOVIET AIRWOMEN
OF THE GREAT PATRIOTIC WAR

Survivors

Heroines of the Soviet Union going back to civil life. Natalya Meklin (extreme left) and Raisa Aronova (next to last). In fall 1945, Soviet authorities issued a decree that ordered demobilization of all military women, except for a few specialists. Most male combat pilots remained in service, studying in air force academies and upgrading to new equipment. The three female air regiments were deactivated from the fall of 1945 (the *586 IAP* and the "Night Witches") to February 1947 (the *125 GvBAP*). Afterwards, the veterans of the *46 GvNBAP* suffered health problems: stress and illnesses resulting from injuries, wounds, and prolonged lack of sleep during the three years of continuous night sorties. (Archive of A. Plyac)

Знаменитые россияне

ГАШЕВА
Руфина Сергеевна
Герой Советского Союза

A post war portrait of Rufina Gasheva. After the war, she graduated from the Moscow Military Institute of Foreign Languages and taught English for several years at the Military Academy of Armoured troops. She moved to the reserves in 1956 and afterwards became editor of military-technical publications. She lives in Moscow. Soviet journalist Boris Laski, who met her in the spring 1944, wrote a romantic impression of her (*Juliet the Combat Pilot*), in which other airwomen recognized themselves, copying it into their post war recollections: "Try to imagine a Juliet in a flying suit," he wrote. "Let her put on high fur boots, a helmet, and gloves. Let her also put on a belt with a holster. Miraculously here appears a military pilot but Juliet does not disappear either. This is not a paradox. This is how things really are"[1]. (Archive of A. Plyac)

An outstanding "Night Witch" trio of airwomen, symbolically wearing their Gold Star of Hero of the Soviet Union on civilian clothes. Left to right, Natalya Meklin, Polina Gelman, and Rufina Gasheva. None of them were allowed to go on flying after the war. Meklin became a writer and a journalist. Gelman returned to Moscow State University, majoring in history and military interpreting. She received a post graduate degree in economics. Gasheva studied languages and taught English for several years. She still survives her two girlfriends. (Archive of A. Plyac)

One of the first reunions of Soviet airwomen veterans, on the 2nd of May in front of the Bolshoi, Moscow. The ex "Night Witches" look hardly recognizable in civilian clothes. Left to right, sitting: Yevdokiya Pasko (Hero of the Soviet Union, squadron navigator), unknown, Yevdokiya Rachkevich (in uniform, political commissar). Next to last, wearing a hat, Irina Rakobolskaya, former chief of staff. Standing, under Lenin's portrait, another Hero of the Soviet Union: navigator Polina Gelman. "We decided to meet after the war on the second of May in a small park across from the Bolshoi Theater," recalled Nadezhda Popova, Hero of the Soviet Union. "In 1946 we had our first meeting"[2]. The swift demobilization of airwomen from the military was due largely just to pro-natalist policies of the Soviet government and the need of female workers. Actually, most of the 20 millions Soviet casualties of the war were represented by men and there was need to replace their losses. (Archive of A. Plyac)

A study portrait of Natalya Meklin. She was (and still is) regarded as one of the most attractive Soviet airwomen. Reportedly, even high ranking officers like Colonel-General K.A. Vershinin, who publicly praised her, admired her beauty. "She was extremely beautiful," recalled historian Anatoly Plyac, son of "Night Witch" Raisa Aronova, "but very unhappy. Her husband died early and in the last years she did not want see anybody."

Another early meeting of the airwomen veterans, still in front of the Bolshoi. In the center, with the white raincoat, Yevdokiya Pasko. To her right, former "Night Witch" commander, Yevdokiya Bershanksya, and Polina Gelman. Extreme right, with her child, another 46th veteran, Marina Chechneva. "During the years the veterans began to show up with their husbands and children," wrote Popova. "but many of them never married." Instead, Popova married Semen Kharlamov, a fighter pilot. She met him while recovering from her wounds when she was shot down on 2 August 1942. The two had carved their names on the Reichstag together in Berlin, the day after the victory, on 10 May 1945. (Archive of A. Plyac)

Serefima Amosova after the war continued to fly for two years. Then, because of her health, she retired. "After the war we had a lot of headaches, could not relax, and had very severe problems with our sleeping, because for nearly three years we had reversed day and night... for the first year after the war everyone had problems with sleeping"[3]. In 1947 she married a military man and moved from Rostov to Ashkhabad. "There was an earthquake in 1948 when Stalin was in power, and he ordered us not to tell anybody... they announced there was an earthquake and there were no victims... So no help was sent... Ashkhabad was completely destroyed. Only the mosques, the building of the party organization, and some other buildings built before the war survived... My daughter was born in August, and she died in this earthquake"[4].

Five Heroines of the Soviet Union strengthening their friendship in front of Bolshoi Theater. Left to right: "Raya" Aronova, Natalya Meklin, Yevgeniya Zhigulenko, Ira Sebrova, and Dina Nikulina. Zhigulenko, a tall, attractive blonde, amassed 968 combat missions. "By the end of the war I had a greater number of combat hours than most of the air crews," she recalled. "I managed to outstrip them because I have very long legs. There was an order in the regiment that the first pilot to get into the cockpit and start the engine was to be the first to take off; I was always the first because I ran faster! We all volunteered to go to the front and strove to fulfil the most combat mission, even beyond our physical capacity"[5]. She was demobilized in 1947. She moved with her husband to the Soviet Far East. There she worked a few years at a fighter aviation command post, being in charge of young male soldiers. She retired with the rank of guards major. (Archive of A. Plyac)

Ex "Night Witches" at a commemorative ceremony of the 46th Night Bomber Regiment. Right to left: Raisa Aronova, Natalya Meklin, (former standard bearer of the *46 GvN-BAP*) and Ira Sebrova. "After the war I worked as a test pilot," recalled Sebrova, "testing aircraft that had been worked on and put back together. I was still in the military when I had an accident flying, and I was on the brink of death. In 1948, while I was still in the service, my daughter was born in Poland, in Toruń City. This is the city of love. After this we went back to Russia, and it was the end of my flying career - I quit flying"[6].

Photo-group of Soviet airwomen, Heroines of the Soviet Union, in late 1960s. Left to right: Rufa Gasheva, Larissa Razonova-Litvinova, Marina Chechneva, Soviet cosmonaut Valentina Vadimirovna Tereshkova, and Natalya Meklin. Tereshkova (born on 6 March 1937 in Bolshoye Maslennikovo) was the first woman to have flown in space. On 16 June 1963, she piloted the *Vostok 6*. At this time, all the former "Night Witches" portrayed in the picture had been grounded for a long time. Chechneva was the one who was allowed to fly longer. After the war, she served for three years in ground-attack units in the Northern Group of Forces in Poland. She was demobilized in 1948, along with her husband, pilot Konstantin Davydov, and posted to the Central Flying Club in Moscow. She kept on flying as a sport and participated in eight air shows at Tushino Airfield. In these parades she led an all-female acrobatic team. Chechneva established two All-Union records: one of speed on the *Yakovlev Yak-18* (a Soviet tandem two-seat trainer aircraft entered service in 1946), on 10 September 1949, and one of altitude on the *Yak-11* (another trainer aircraft introduced in 1946 also), on 1 June 1953. Still in 1953, she became "Champion of the USSR" for instrument flying. Notwithstanding her successes, she was grounded in 1957 for deteriorating health. She wrote many articles and several books, based on her war memories. Among them: *Samolety Ukhodyat v Noch* (*Aircraft Go Out Into The Night*, Moscow, 1961) and *Nebo Ostaetsia Nashin* (*The Sky Remains Ours*, Moscow 1976). She died suddenly on 12 January 1984.

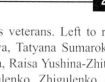

46 GvNBAP's veterans. Left to right: Raisa Aronova, Tatyana Sumarokova, Rufa Gasheva, Raisa Yushina-Zhitova, Yevgh. Zhigulenko. Zhigulenko, after she retired, served in a trade union and subsequently became chief of the Directorate of Culture and councilior in Sichi, a resort on the Black Sea. In 1976 she graduated from the All-Union State Institute of Cinematography and became director of the A.M. Gorky Studio in Moscow. In 1982, with playwright and script writer Vladimir Valutsky, she produced and directed the film "Night Witches in the Sky" about her comrades-in-arms. Yushina, who flew 535 combat sorties, had a longer career in aviation. She worked as a pilot for the Ministry of Geology until 1951. Then a flight crash on a *Yak-12* put an end to her career in aviation.

Photo group of *46 GvNBAP's* female aviators with sailors of Sabastopolis, 1969. Right to left: pilot Klavdiya A. Riskova, Ira Sebrova, commander Yevdokiya Bershanskaya, navigator Larisa Rozanova-Litvinova, pilot Nina Maksimovna Raspopova (died on 2 July 2009), pilot Antoninya Fedorovna Khudyakova, pilot Mariya Smirnova. "After the war our regiment was released," recalled Smirnova, "and we all wanted to fly in civil aviation. I applied to the medical board, but I could not pass the medical examination. I had undermined my physical and mental health at the front; I was completely exhausted by the four years of war and combat. There was a period when we went without a day off for one hundred days"[7]. Smirnova transferred to the reserves and she worked as an instructor of the Kalinin Regional Communist Party and subsequently worked as personnel director for the Worsted Wool Industrial Enterprise in Kalinin. She died on 10 July 2002.

Soviet aviatrixes veterans reunion of 2 May 1982. Right to left: mechanic Aleksandra Akimova, armorer Mariya Fedotova, unknown, armorer Z. V. Vasilyeva, pilot Antonina Fedorovna Khudyakova, mechanic Mariya A. Shchelkanova, regimental commander Yevdokiya Bershanskaya, armorer N. M. Medvyedeva, mechanic Rimma Prudnikova and mechanic Valentina Sheyankina. Thirty-seven years after the end of the war, the friendship that linked the "Witches" was still unwavering. "We are very happy when we come together," remembered deputy commander Serafima Amosova-Taranenko, "and we get together often to celebrate some occasion. We help each other financially and in morale, and we write a lot of letters to each other. We send postcards to each other on VE Day with poems, pictures, or drawings"[8]. Serafima Amosova-Taranenko died in 1992.

Former "Night Witches" commander, Yevdokiya Bershanskaya, holding a model of a *PolikarpovPo-2*. She is recalled as "a capable and innovative commander... Her innovative and unorthodox style enabled the 46th to become one of the top-performing *Po-2* night bomber regiments in the Soviet Military"[9]. This is the last known photo of Y. D. Bershansaya. It was taken on 28 August 1982, 18 days before she passed away.The obituary of Lieutenant-Colonel (retired) Yevdokiya Bershanskaya appeared in *Krasnaya Zvezda* (*Red Star*), on 19 September 1982.

Raisa Aronova (left) and Rufa Gasheva, in civilian clothes, with their husbands, the two Plyac brothers. Aronova flew 960 combat mission during the war, spending 1,148 hours in air. She was glad that the 46th remained an all-female regiment during the whole conflict. This peculiarity allowed its "female spirit to reign supreme". Still, she always believed that military service was inappropriate for women. After the war, Aronova demobilized from the air force. In 1952 she graduated from the Military Institute of Foreign Languages in Moscow and served with the army until 1961, retiring with the rank of guards major. She died on 20 December 1982. Her obituary was published on *Krasnaya Zvezda* (*Red Star*) on 25 December 1982. (Archive of A. Plyac)

Natalya Meklin – She wrote many articles and several books, often based on her war experiences. Among her books: *Na Goryashchom Samolote* (*On Board a Burning Aircraft*), about Rufa Gasheva (Moscow, Moskovskiy Rabochiy, 1968); *Ot Zakata Do Rassveta* (*From Sunset to Dawn*) (Moscow, Voyenizdat, 1968); *Iz-za Party – Na Voynu* (Moscow, 1976); *Vernis'Iz Poleta!* (*Do Return From Mission!*) (Moscow, Voyenizdat, 1979); *Za Oblakami Solntse* (Moscow, 1982); *Povesti. Izbrannoye* (Moscow, 1982). She won the "A.A. Fadeyev Prize". In the late years of her life she did not want to meet anybody, afflicted by dementia. She died on 5 June 2005.

Pilot Olga Nikolaevna Yamshikova, veteran of 586th Fighter Regiment. Yamshikova, after the war, had more than 3,000 hours in 45 types of aircraft and decided to became a test pilot. She "flew for thirty years after the war was over," remembered *586 IAP's* pilot Mariya Kuznetsova[10]. Yamshikova flew more than fifty different types of planes and is credited as the first woman to fly jets (but according to other authors – American Ann Baumgartner was actually first)[11]. She was one of the very few *586 IAP* airwomen who managed to fly after the war. It was a common belief, shared by pilot Klavdiya Pankratova, also, that *Aeroflot* usually rejected former fighter pilots, as civilian aircraft were very different from the fighters.

586 IAP's pilot, Zinaida Fedorovna Salomatina. After the war she was demobilized and hired by civil aviation. At first, she flew ambulance aircraft, transporting patients, drugs, and blood for transfusions. After graduating from Higher Flying School, she became an aircraft captain and could fly twin-engine airliners. In more than 20 years she accumulated 10,000 hours of flight time and then became an air traffic controller. She was awarded the title of Hero of Socialist Labor.

125 GvBAP's veterans reunion. Few of the airwomen of the dive bomber regiment were allowed to fly after the war, even if the *Petlyakov Pe-2* was similar to the aircraft that equipped *Aeroflot*. Three of the airwomen who were hired by *Aeroflot* were pilots Aleksandra Krivonogova and Irina Osadze, and navigator Aleksandra Yeremenko, who already worked for the civil airline before the war. Krivonogova became an aircraft captain of Latvian Civil Aviation and flew more than 4 million kilometres in 25 years. Yeremenko served as a navigator in the Riga Group of Civil Aviation, amassing more than 8,000 flight hours and taking part in rescue missions in the Gulf of Riga, flying the *Ilyushin Il-4*. She was awarded the Order of Lenin for her service.

Mariya Dolina, pilot of *125 GvBAP*, Hero of the Soviet Union, and her husband, Melnikov. After the war, she married her former mechanic and served as deputy commander of a bomber regiment. After five years, she was demobilized and transferred to the reserves in 1950. Subsequently she worked in the Riga City Party Committee until 1975. In 1983 she moved to Kiev, Ukraine. On the 50th anniversary of the end of the Great Patriotic war, Ukrainian President Kuchma promoted her to the rank of major. She passed away on 3 March 2010. Very few other 125th airwomen remained in military service. One of them was Hero of the Soviet Union, Galina Dzhunkovskaya-Markova. She served as chief navigator of an air division until she transferred to the reserves in 1950. A third Heroine of the 125th, Klavdiya Fomicheva (married Levashova), worked first as a flying instructor at the Air Force Academy and subsequently taught air tactics at the Air Force School for pilots in Borisoglebsk, until she was transferred to the reserves in 1956. She died on 5 October 1958 of a mysterious illness.

The Author (extreme right) with veteran Yelena Kulkova-Malyutina, former pilot of *125 GvBAP*. Despite having suffered grievous abdominal injuries during a bombing run, Kulkova went back to military aviation. "I also participated in the victory parade in Red Square," she recalled. "After the war I also flew the Tu-2. I was a lieutenant. We have three lieutenant ranks: junior lieutenant, lieutenant, and senior lieutenant. When the war ended and our regiment was released, I joined a male regiment. While I was in the regiment, I married a pilot, got pregnant, and retired in 1949"[12].

Nadya Popova at the veterans' meeting on 2 May in front of the Bolshoi. Notwithstanding her graceful appearance, she has always been an extremely tough woman, able to endure the weariness and fatigue of post-war years. "We came home to face all the destruction and severe food shortages," she recalled. "We worked eighteen hours a day to reconstruct. Maybe that is why we didn't have much post-combat stress - we didn't have time to reflect on our personal experiences in the war, we were too occupied by the present"[13]. After the war she decided that the career of her husband, Semen Kharlamov, came first, and she saw her main role as that of a supportive wife. Kharlamov became colonel-general, Meritorius Pilot of the Soviet Union. They had a son, Aleksander, who graduated from the Air Force Academy. She joined the Board of the War Veterans' Committee and was named Meritorius Cultural Worker of the Russian Federation. Popova became a widow in early May 1990 after Kharlamov suffered a fatal heart attack.

The Author (extreme left) beside *125 GvBAP*'s navigator, Galina Brok-Beltsova. In the middle, 125th Dive Bomber Regiment Yelena Kulkova-Malyutina. Brok, after working as an *NKVD* agent, became a history lecturer in 20th century history, specializing in the Great Patriotic War. She got a doctor's degree and became the chief of the History Department at the Moscow Engineering Institute. She is one of the very few

airwomen still attending the 2 May's veterans meeting in front of the Bolshoi, along with Nadya Popova, Hero of the Soviet Union. "At these meetings we were crying and laughing," recalled Popova. "And now every year fewer and fewer of our people come." The feeling of pride amongst the surviving women of their heroic role in the war, is even more intense than when they gathered for their first reunion. "We were very young and our friendship very warm, as it is now"[14].

NOTE

1   Anna Krylova, *Soviet women in Combat*, pp. 278-279

2   A. Noggle, *A Dance with Death*, p. 85

3   R. Pennington, *Wings, Women & War*, p. 145

4   Noggle, p. 48

5   Noggle, p. 56

6   Noggle, p. 77

7   Noggle, p. 37

8   Noggle, p. 48

9   Pennington, pp. 165-167

10 Noggle, p. 170

11 Pennington, p. 147

12 Noggle, p. 131

13 Pennington, p.158

14 Noggle, p. 85

ABBREVIATIONS AND TRANSLATIONS

Russian

BAD: *Bombardirovochnaya Aviatsionnaya Diviziya* (Bomber Aviation Division)

BAP: *Bombardirovochnyi Aviatsionnyy Polk* (Bomber Aviation Regiment)

Eskadrilya (Squadron)

Gv: *Gvardeiskiy* (Guards)

IAP: *Istrebitelnyi Aviatsionnyy Polk* (Fighter Aviation Regiment)

Komsomol: *Kommunisticheskiy Soyuz Molodezhi* (Young Communist League)

NBAD: *Nochnoy Bombardirovochnyy Aviatsionnyy Polk* (Night Bomber Aviation Regiment)

NKVD: Narodnyy Kommissariat Vnutrennikh Del (People Commissariat for Internal Affairs)

PVO: *Protivovozdushnaya Oborona* (Air Defense Force)

RS-82: 82 mm airborne rocket projectile

TsAMO: *Tsentralnyy Arkhiv Obedinennykh Vooruzhennykh Sil Soyuza Nezavisimykh Gosudarstv* (Central Archive of the United Armed Forces of the Commonwealth of Independent States – in Podolsk)

VA: *Vozdushnaya Armiya* (Air Army)

VVS: *Voenno-Vozdushnyie Sily* (Military Air Force)

Zveno: Tactical air formation composed of three or four aircraft

German

Experten: German designation for fighter ace

Geschwader: Aviation Wing

Gruppe: Aviation Group, usually three *Staffeln* (see below)

Jagdgeschwader: Fighter Aviation Wing

JG: *Jagdgeschwader* Fighter Aviation Wing

Kampfgeschwader: "Combat Wing" – Bomber Aviation Wing

Mauser: German arms designer

MG: *Maschinengewehr* German machinegun

MG FF: German Oerlikon 20 mm aviation automatic cannon

MG 151/20: German Mauser 20 automatic cannon

Oerlikon: Swiss arms designer

OKL: *Oberkommando der Luftwaffe* (Air Force High Command)

Rotte: Tactical air formation of two aircraft

Schlachtgeschwader: "Assault Wing" - Ground attack aviation wing

Stuka: *Sturzkampfflugzeug* - Dive bomber, referring to the *Junkers Ju 87*

Schwarm: "Flight," tactical air formation of four aircraft

Staffel: Aviation Squadron

RANK EQUIVALENCES

VVS	LUFTWAFFE	USAAF
ENLISTED		
Yefreytor	Gefreiter	Private First Class
NON COMMISSIONED OFFICERS		
Mladshiy Serzhant	Unteroffizier	Staff Sergeant
Serzhant	Unterfeldwebel	Sergeant
Starshiy Serzhant	Feldwebel	Technical Sergeant
Starshina	Oberfeldwebel	Master Sergeant
COMMISSIONED OFFICERS		
Mladshiy Leytenant		Flight Officer
Leytenant	Leutnant	Second Lieutenant
Starshiy Leytenant	Oberleutnant	First Lieutenant
Kapitan	Hauptman	Captain
Mayor	Major	Major
Podpolkovnic	Oberstleutnant	Lieutenant Colonel
Polkovnic	Oberst	Colonel
General-Mayor	Generalmajor	Brigadier General
General-Leytenant	Generalleutnant	Major General
General-Polkovnik	General	Lieutenant General
General Armii	Generaloberst	General (4-Stars)
Marshal Sovetskogo	Soyuza Generalfeldmarschall	General of the Army
	Reichmarshal	

☆

MILITARY AWARDS

SOVIET

Orden Otechestvennoy Voyny 1-y (Pervoy) stepeni – Order of the Patriotic War of the First Grade, established on 20 May 1942. More than 2,627,000 orders were awarded to all soldiers in the Soviet armed forces, security troops, and to partisans for heroic deeds during the Great Patriotic War. During the celebration of the 40th anniversary of the Great Patriotic War, in 1985, Soviet Authorities decided that all surviving veterans of the war would be awarded either 2nd or 1st class of the Order.

Orden Otechestvennoy Voyny 2-y (Vtoroy) stepeni – Order of the Patriotic War of the Second Grade, established on 20 May 1942, more than 6,716,000 awarded.

Orden Krasnogo Zvezdy – The Red Star Order, it was awarded 3,876,740 times to armed forces personnel for exceptional service in the cause of the defense of the Soviet Union. It was also awarded for 15 years of service prior to the creation of the long service awards.

Orden Krasnogo Znameni – The Order of the Red Banner recognized military deeds and was also awarded to *NKVD* personnel. Before the establishment of the Order of Lenin, the Order of the Red Banner was the highest military order of the USSR. Almost all well-known Soviet commanders became Cavaliers of the Order of the Red Banner. Awarded 581,300 times.

Orden Suvorova 1-y (Pervoy) stepeni – Order of Suvorov. The 1st class order was awarded (393 times) to army commanders for exceptional direction of combat operations.

Orden Suvorova 2-y (Vtoroy) stepeni – Order of Suvorov of 2nd class was awarded (2,862) to corps, divisions and brigade commanders, for a decisive victory over a numerically superior enemy.

Orden Suvorova 3-y (Tretyey) stepeni – Order of Suvorov of the 3rd class, awarded 4,012 times to regimental commanders, their chiefs of staff, and battalion and company commanders for outstanding leadership leading to a battle victory.

Orden Lenina – The Order of Lenin was the highest civil decoration. It was awarded 462,184 times, to both civilians and soldiers for outstanding service to the motherland in defense, strengthening peace and strengthening labor. Coined in silver from 1930-1934, it was made of gold between 1934-1936 and from 1936-1991 made of platinum.

Geroy Sovietskogo Soyuza – Hero of the Soviet Union, it was the highest honorary title that could be given in USSR. Created on 6 April 1930, It was awarded 12,755 times (101 twice, 3 thrice and 2 four times).

German

Das Eiserne Kreuz 2. Klasse – The Iron Cross of Second Grade. The most common German awards (about 4,750,000 awarded), it was given for bravery before the enemy or excellence in commanding troops.

Das Eiserne Kreuz 1. Klasse – The Iron Cross of First Grade, it was Awarded (about 730,000 times) for continuous bravery before the enemy or excellence in commanding troops. It was given after being awarded the preceding class of the Iron Cross.

Das Ritterkreuz des Eisernes Kreuzes – The Knight's Cross of the Iron Cross. About 7,500 awards during World War II (about 1,730 to *Luftwaffe* personnel).

Das Ritterkreuz des Eisernes Kreuzes mit Eichenlaub – The Knight's Cross with Oak Leaves. A total of 860 awards during WWII (192 to *Luftwaffe* servicemen).

Das Ritterkreuz des Eisernes Kreuzes mit dem Eichenlaub mit Schwerten – The Knight's Cross with Oak Leaves and Swords. Awarded 154 awarded during the war, including 41 to *Luftwaffe* pilots.

Das Ritterkreuz des Eisernes Kreuzes mit dem Eichenlaub mit Schwerten und Brillanten – The Knight's Cross with Oak Leaves, Swords and Diamonds. Awarded only 27 times (12 to *Luftwaffe* pilots).

Kriegsorden des Deutschen Kreuzes in Silber (in Gold) – Order or the German Cross Silver Class (Gold class). Awarded for significant performances in aiding/supplying the military war effort (in Gold for continuous bravery before the enemy or excellence in command). In silver, awarded 1,115. In Gold, 24,204.

Das Grosskreuz des Eisernes Kreuzes – The Large Cross, Only awarded once, to Reichmarshal Hermann Göring, the C-in-C of the *Luftwaffe*, after his part in the victory over Poland, France, Denmark, Norway and the BeNeLux nations. He was awarded this award on 19 July 1940.

BIBLIOGRAPHY

Angelucci, Enzo and Paolo Matricardi *"World Aircraft: World War II, Volume II"* (Sampson Low Guides). Maidenhead, UK, Sampson Low, 1978

Belyakov, Vladimir *Russia's Women Top Guns* Aviation History, March 2002

Bergström, Christer *Stalingrad – The Air Battle: 1942 through January 1943* Hinckley England, Midland, 2007

Bergström, Christer – Andrey Dikov – Vlad Antipov *Black Cross Red Star – Air War over the Eastern Front Volume 3 – Everything for Stalingrad* Hamilton MA, Eagle Editions, 2006

Boyne, Walter J. *Clash of wings – World War II in the Air* New York, Simon & Schuster, 1997

Braithwaite, Rodric *Moscow 1941* London, Profile Books, 2007

Caygill, Peter *Focke-Wulf Fw 190* Airlife Ramsbury, Marlborough UK, The Crowood Press Ltd, 2002

Clarke, John D. *French Eagles Soviet Heroes The 'Normandie-Niemen' Squadron on Eastern Front* Phoenix Mill thrupp – Stroud – Gloucestershire, 2005

Cottam, Kazimiera J. *Women in War and Resistance – Selected Biographies of Soviet Women Soldiers* Newburyport (MA), Focus Publishing/R. Pullins Co., 1998

Cottam, Kazimiera J. (Edited and translated by) *Women in Air War – The Eastern Front of world war II* Newburyport (MA), Focus Publishing /R. Pullins Company, 1998

de Zeng IV, Henry and Dougles G. Stankey with Eddie J. Creek *Bomber units of the Luftwaffe 1939-1945- A reference source, Volume 1* Hersham, Surrey UK, Ian Allan Publishing, 2009

de Zeng IV, Henry and Dougles G. Stankey with Eddie J. Creek *Bomber units of the Luftwaffe 1939-1945 A reference source, Volume 2* Hersham, Surrey UK Ian Allan Publishing, 2008

Drabkin, Artem *Barbarossa & the retreat to Moscow – The Red Air Force at War – Recollections of Fighter Pilots on the Eastern Front* Barnsley (South Yorkshire), Pen & Sword Military, 2007

Ethell, Jeffrey L. *Aerei della II Guerra Mondiale* Milano, A.Vallardi/Collins Jane's, 1996

Ethell, Jeffrey L. *Aircraft of World War II* Glasgow, Collins Jane's, 1995

Foreman, John – Johannes Matthews – Simon Parry *Luftwaffe Night Fighter Combat Claims 1939-1945* Walton-on-Thames, Red Kite, 2004

Glancey, Jonathan *SPITFIRE The Biography* London, Atlantic Books, 2006

Goodpaster Strebe, Amy *Flying for her country – The American and Soviet women military pilots of world war II* Washington (D.C.), Potomac Books, Inc. 2009

Gordon, Yefim, *Soviet Air Power in World War 2* Hinkley, UK, Midland-Ian Allan Publishing, 2008

Gunston, Bill *Aerei della Seconda Guerra Mondiale* Milano, Alberto Peruzzo Editore, 1984

Hardesty, Von *Red Phoenix: The Rise of the Soviet Air Power 1941-1945* Washington, D.C. Smithsonian, 1982

Heaton, Colin D. and Anne-Marie Lewis *The German Aces Speak* Minneapolis, Zenith Press, 2012

Jackson, Robert *Air Aces of WWII* Ramsbury, Marlborough UK, Vital Guide, Airlife Crowood Press, 2003

Jackson, Robert *Ju 87 Stuka* Airlife – The Crowood Press Ltd, Ramsbury, Marlborough UK, 2004

Khazanov, Dmitry B. *Air War Over Kursk - Turning Point in the East* Bedford UK Sam Publications, 2010

Krylova, Anna *Soviet Women in Combat* New York, Cambridge University Press, 2010

Kurowski, *Franz Major Wilhelm Batz* Flechsig Verlag, 2008

Jackson, Robert *Ju 87 Stuka* Ramsbury, Marlborough UK, The Crowood Press, 2004

Jackson, Robert *The Red Falcons - The Soviet Air Force in action, 1919-1969* Brighton, Clifton Books, 1970

Lepage Jean-Denise *The illustrated Handbook of Flak German Anti-aircraft Defences 1935-1945* Spellmount The History Press, Briscombe Port Stroud, Gloucestershire, UK, 2012

Leonard, Herbert *Encyclopaedia of Soviet Fighters 1939-1951* Paris, Histoire & Collections, 2005

Markwick, Roger D. And Euridice Charon Cardona *Soviet Women on the frontline* New York, Palgrave Macmillan, 2012

Matricardi, Paolo *Aerei Militari: Caccia e Ricognitori Volume 1* Milano, Mondadori Electa S.p.A. 2006

Matricardi, Paolo *Aerei Militari: Bombardieri e da Trasporto Volume 2* Milano, Mondadori Electa S.p.A. 2006

Mellinger, George *Yakovlev Ace of World War 2* Osprey Aviation 2005

Merry, Lois K. Women *Military Pilots of World War II* Jefferson, North Carolina and London, McFarland & Company, 2011

Middlebrook, Martin *The Peenemunde Raid: The Night of 17–18 August 1943* Barnsely, UK, Pen & Sword Aviation, 2004

Milanetti, Gian Piero *Le streghe della notte. La storia non detta delle eroiche ragazze-pilota dell'Unione Sovietica nella Grande Guerra Patriottica* Roma, IBN Editore, 2011

Mondey, David *The Hamlyn Concise Guide to Axis Aircraft of World War II* London, Bounty Books, 1984

Morgan, Hugh *Gli assi Sovietici della Seconda guerra mondiale* Edizioni del Prado/Osprey Aviation, 1999

Morgan, Hugh & Jurgen Seibel *Combat Kill* Somerset/California, Patrick Stephens Limited, 1997

Myles, Bruce *Night Witches: The amazing story of Russia's women pilots in world war II* Chicago, Academy Chicago, 1990

Noggle, Anne *A Dance with Death: Soviet Airwomen in World War II* College Station, Texas, A&M University Press, 1994

Pennington, Reina *Wings, Women, & War – Soviet Airwomen in World War II Combat* Lawrence, University Press of Kansas, 2001

Polak, Tomas with Christopher Shores *Stalin's Falcons – The Aces of the Red Star* London, Grub Street, 1999

Price, Alfred *Focke Wulf Fw 190 in combat* Gloucestershire, Sutton Publishing, 1998

Prien, Jochen *Jagdgeschwader 53 A History of the "Pik As" Geschwader March 1937 - May 1942* Atglen, Pennsylvania, Schiffer Military History, 1997

Prien, Jochen *Jagdgeschwader 53 A History of the "Pik As" Geschwader May 1942 - January 1944* Atglen, Pennsylvania, Schiffer Military History, 1998

Price, Alfred – Spick, Mike *Aerei della II Guerra Mondiale* Santarcangelo di Romagna, Rusconi libri, 2003

Rossi, Marina *Le streghe della notte Storia e testimonianze dell'aviazione femminile in URSS (1941-1945)* MILANO, UNICOPLI, 2003

Scutts, Jerry *JG 54 Jagdgeschwader 54 Grünherz Aces on the Eastern Front* Shrewsbury, Motorbooks International, 1992

Seidl, Hans D. *Stalin's Eagles – An illustrated Study of the Soviet Aces of World War II and Korea* Atglen (PA), Schiffer Military History, 1998

Sharpe, Mike *Aircraft of world War II* Near Rochester UK, Grange Books, 2000

Sheperd, Christopher *German Aircraft of World War II* London, Book Club Associates, 1975

Smith, C. Peter *Petlyakov Pe-2 'Peshka'* Ramsbury, Marlborough UK,The Crowood Press, 2003

Spick, Mike *The complete fighter Ace: all the world's Fighter Aces, 1914-2000* London, Greenhill Books, 1999

Taylor, Michael J *Fighter and Bomber of World War II in colour* London, Bison Books, 1985

Thompson, J. Steve with Peter C. Smith *Air Combat Manoeuvres* Hersham UK, Ian Allan Publishing, 2008

Timofeeva-Egorova, Anna *Red Sky, Black Death – A Soviet woman pilot's memoir of the Eastern Front* Blomington, Indiana, Slavica Publishers Indiana University, 2009

Toliver, Col. Raymond F. & Trevir J. Constable *Fighter Aces of the Luftwaffe* Atglen PA, Schiffer Military History, 1996

Weal, Elke C., John A. Weal and Richard F. Barker *Combat Aircraft of World War Two* New York, MacMillan Publishing Co., Inc. 1977

Williams, Anthony G. & Emmanuel Gustin *Flying Guns World War II – Development of Aircraft Guns, Ammunition and Installations 1933-45* Ramsbury MArlborough, Airlife, 2008

BOOKS IN RUSSIAN

A. Babushkina "Devushki-voiny. Ocherki o devushkakh geroiniakh Velikoi Otechestvennoi voiny" Moskva, Molodaya gvardiya, 1944

Bykov, Michail SOVETSKIE ASY 1941-1945 Moskva, Pobedy Stalinskich Sokolov, Jauza Eksmo, 2008

Golubeva-Teres, Olga *Zvedy na krylyakh* Saratov, 1974

Gorobets I. Ye. et al. *Za muzhestvo I odvagu* Kharkov, 1984

Kanevsky A. *Fifteen victories of Lidya Liltvyak // Motherland's Wings.* (Каневский А. *Пятнадцать побед Лидии Литвяк //* Крылья Родины) – 1997 - № 3 – С.29-30- *1997 - № 3 - pp. 29-30*

Khorobrykh, Colonel A. *Serdtse Gvardeytsa* (A Guardman's Heart) <Aviatsya I Cosmonavtika> Aviation and Cosmonautics – 1979, Nr. 6

Lavrinenkov, Vladimir Dmitrievich *Vozvrashchenie v nebo* Mockba, Voenizdat, 1983

Meklin-Kravtsova, Natalya *Za Oblakami Solntse* Mockba, Russia, Sovetskaya, 1982

Polunina, Yekaterina *Devchonki, podruzhki, letchitsy (Girls, Girlfriends, Pilots)* Mockba, Izdatel'sky Dom "Vestnik Vozdushnogo Flota", 2004

Ul'yanenko, Nina *Nezabyvayemoye. Zapiski letchitsy (Unforgettable: notes of a female pilot)* Izhevsk, Udmurtiya, 1949

BOOKS IN GERMAN

Aders, Gebhard/Held, Werner *Jagdgeschwader 51 <Mölders> - Eine Chronik Berichte – Erlebnisse – Dokumente* Stuttgart, MOTORBUCH VERLUG STUTTGART, 1993

Barbas, Bernd *Die Geschichte del I Gruppe del Jagdeschwader 52 (I./JG 52)* Eigenverlag

Barbas, Bernd *Die Geschichte del I Gruppe del Jagdeschwader 52 (II./JG 52)* Eigenverlag

Barbas, Bernd *Die Geschichte del I Gruppe del Jagdeschwader 52 (III./JG 52)* Eigenverlag

Fast, Niko *Das Jagdgeschwader 52* Bernsberger Buch-Verlag, Bergisch Gladbach, 1990

Prien, Joachim und Gerhard Stemmer *Messerschmitt Bf 109 im Einsatz bei der III./Jagdgeschwader 3* Struve-Druck Eutin, Germany

Schreier, Hans *JG 52* Kurt Vowinkel –Verlag Berg am see, 1990

LINKS

http://www.redarmyonline.org/FI_Article_by_KJ_Cottam.html

http://www.asisbiz.com/Luftwaffe/Luftwaffe-aerial-victories-1943-A.html

http://www.asisbiz.com/Luftwaffe/Luftwaffe-aerial-victories-1944-B.html

http://www.aircrewremembrancesociety.com/Kracker/LuftwaffeGermanPilotsM.html

http://www.jg52.net/traeger-deutsches-kreuz

http://www.acesofww2.com/germany/Germany.htm